Luz Arce and Pinochet's Chile

Previous Publications

Telling Ruins in Latin America (coedited with Vicky Unruh, 2009)

Luz Arce: Después del infierno (2008)

Prismas de la memoria: Narración y trauma en la transición chilena (2007)

Chile in Transition: The Poetics and Politics of Memory (2006)

Los años de silencio: Conversaciones con narradores chilenos que escribieron bajo dictadura (2002)

Luz Arce and Pinochet's Chile

Testimony in the Aftermath of State Violence

Edited by Michael J. Lazzara

Translated by the author with Carl Fischer

Foreword by Jean Franco

LUZ ARCE AND PINOCHET'S CHILE
Copyright © 2011 Michael J. Lazzara

First published in Spanish as *Luz Arce: después del infierno* by Editorial Cuarto Propio, 2008. First PALGRAVE MACMILLAN® edition, with new material, published in 2011. Palgrave Macmillan is a division of St. Martin's Press LLC, 175 Fifth Avenue, New York, NY 10010.

Where this book is distributed in the UK, Europe and the rest of the world, this is by Palgrave Macmillan, a division of Macmillan Publishers Limited, registered in England, company number 785998, of Houndmills, Basingstoke, Hampshire RG21 6XS.

Palgrave Macmillan is the global academic imprint of the above companies and has companies and representatives throughout the world.

Palgrave® and Macmillan® are registered trademarks in the United States, the United Kingdom, Europe and other countries.

ISBN: 978-0-230-62275-3 (hardcover)
ISBN: 978-0-230-62276-0 (paperback)

Library of Congress Cataloging-in-Publication Data

Lazzara, Michael J.
    Luz Arce and Pinochet's Chile : testimony in the aftermath of state violence / edited by Michael J. Lazzara ; translated by the author with Carl Fischer ; foreword by Jean Franco.
        p. cm.
    ISBN 978-0-230-62275-3 (alk. paper)—ISBN 978-0-230-62276-0 (alk. paper)
        1. Arce, Luz. 2. Arce, Luz—Interviews. 3. Chile—Politics and government—1973-1988. 4. Political persecution—Chile—History—20th century. 5. Human rights—Chile—History—20th century. 6. Chile. Dirección de Inteligencia Nacional. 7. Chile. Central Nacional de Informaciones. I. Lazzara, Michael J., 1975- II. Arce, Luz. Depúes del infierno. English.

F3101.A73L89 2010
983.06'4—dc22   2010038677

A catalogue record of the book is available from the British Library.

Design by Scribe Inc.

First edition: March 2011

For Ana and James, the future

[I]n contrast to a certain hagiographic and rhetorical stylization, the harsher the oppression, the more widespread among the oppressed is the willingness, with all its infinite nuances and motivations, to collaborate: terror, ideological seduction, servile imitation of the victor, myopic desire for any power whatsoever, even though ridiculously circumscribed in space and time, cowardice, and, finally, lucid calculation aimed at eluding the imposed orders and order. All these motives, singly or combined, have come into play in the creation of this gray zone.

—*Primo Levi, "The Gray Zone," The Drowned and the Saved*

Such has been my life: trial and error, trial and error. I am responding today in the only way I know how. If I survive and we talk again ten years from now, maybe I'll have found other answers.

—*Luz Arce Sandoval*

Contents

Figures

Foreword

Jean Franco

On resigning the presidency in 1988, after being roundly rejected in a plebiscite, General Pinochet took care to secure amnesty for those who had implemented the torture and murder that sustained his regime. The center-left coalition of parties (*La Concertación*) that succeeded him appointed the National Truth and Reconciliation Commission whose aim was, in the words of lawyer José Zalaquett, to "repair the psychic damage caused by repression and, second, to prevent such repression from occurring in the future."[1] However, the commission had no power to hold the torturers legally accountable. Amnesia became the national remedy for reconstructing the post-Pinochet nation. After Pinochet's 1998 London arrest and the trial of General Manuel Contreras, who presided over national intelligence, including DINA (*Dirección de Inteligencia Nacional,* National Intelligence Directorate), the secret service that ran the detention centers, the past that had been so carefully covered up began to haunt the present. Both "reconciliation" and "truth" became contentious issues as survivors, the families of the thousands of disappeared, and die-hard Pinochet supporters fought over the past. Among the most controversial figures to emerge after the military government was Luz Arce, who appeared before the Truth and Reconciliaton Commission in October 1990. Her deposition, included in the present volume, was a grim account of her capture by the secret service after the Pinochet coup, and of the rapes and torture that led her to capitulate and eventually work for the secret police. *The Inferno,* the book she published in 1993, is a fuller record of her militancy during the last year of the Allende regime, her capture by DINA, her decision to collaborate after extreme torture, her eventual incorporation into the secret service as an officer, and, after the end of the Pinochet regime, the religious conversion that made it possible for her to bear witness and come to some sort of terms with the past.[2] She was not unique. Her cellmate in the secret prisons and fellow collaborator, La Flaca Alejandra (Marcia Alejandra Merino Vega, nicknamed "Skinny Alejandra"), was the subject of a television film and author of the autobiography *Mi verdad. Más allá del horror. Yo acuso.* (My Truth. Beyond Horror. I accuse.) (1993).[3] Both books describe the transformation of their authors from militants—Luz Arce was a socialist and La Flaca Alejandra belonged to MIR (*Movimiento de Izquierda Revolucionaria*, Leftist Revolutionary Movement)—to abject victims, from victims to collaborators, from collaborators to arms-bearing members of the secret service and, in Luz Arce's case, from collaborator to Christian penitent. Through their testimonies, they reconstituted identities that had been buried clandestinely and destroyed by torture. What had made them valuable to DINA was that they had connections to MIR, the party and guerrilla group that Pinochet and his secret service considered the greatest threat. La Flaca Alejandra had been a militant in her hometown of Concepción, and at the time she was captured, Luz Arce's lover, Ricardo Ruz Zañartu, was a member of that party.

Though Luz Arce and La Flaca Alejandra shared the shame of collaboration, their narratives are quite different in style. In contrast to La Flaca Alejandra's dry factual prose, *The Inferno* is a searching account of motives, emotions, and reflections that carefully hedge a story of Christian repentance. Both accounts, in different ways, force readers to weigh personal survival against the deaths of those who were sacrificed. "Distant spectators," like ourselves, can only guess at how we might have reacted under such circumstances.

Lame from a bullet in her foot and damaged by torture, Luz Arce was physically and mentally destroyed in DINA's secret prisons. There were days and nights when she was tortured with an electric prod, raped, and beaten while suspended naked, or when she suffered hunger and verbal and sexual abuse. She gives a graphic description of the prison conditions as "that oppressive combination of filth, panic, the smell of blood being spilled, of raped women, of exhausted panting, of eyes covered by filthy blindfolds and mouths silenced by brutal beatings."[4] When her brother, who had also been brutally tortured, began to capitulate, and when they threatened to take her son, she raised her finger in submission. The decision earned her a lease of life, though always under the threat of death. Though she was still treated as garbage and still abused after collaborating, she not only survived but also eventually became a storehouse of information about the workings of the secret service and the fate of many of the disappeared. What undoubtedly saved her was not only her intelligent evaluation of how to use her power as a source of information but her ability to seek out the patronage and protection of powerful males, most significantly the second in command of the Villa Grimaldi secret prison, Rolf Wenderoth Pozo, without whose help she would likely have been killed. From her point of view, her relationship with Wenderoth was strictly utilitarian. As she points out in the interview contained in this book: "I think it's fair to say that Wenderoth gave me what I needed most in those years: some moments of tenderness—but only moments, short periods of time, false tranquility, but even still, moments that let me breathe and continue." Through Wenderoth, she came into contact with the head of DINA, Manuel Contreras, later charged along with Pedro Espinoza Bravo with masterminding the assassination of Orlando Letelier in Washington, DC.[5] It was Contreras who, while dancing with her, told her she was "the prettiest of the prisoners," and who arranged her move from Villa Grimaldi to an apartment she shared with La Flaca Alejandra and the third but silent collaborator, "Carola" (María Alicia Uribe). She became a valued officer and was consulted as an expert on the Chilean left. Ever an eager student who, when working for Allende, had instructed herself in Marxism and, after her conversion, studied the Bible, in her DINA years, Luz Arce studied at the National Intelligence School (as did Marcia Alejandra Merino), taking courses in counter-intelligence, Marxism, international relations, marksmanship, and cryptography. She later taught there. Arce must have been invaluable to the secret service, for she not only worked for them as an analyst but when the discredited DINA was reorganized as the National Information Center (CNI), she was sent to Uruguay on a spy mission, an episode that she describes in particularly murky fashion, stating that she cannot reveal aspects related to national security. Her unrivalled knowledge of the inside workings of DINA and the fate of the many disappeared made her a valuable, if controversial, source of information. In writing *The Inferno*, she not only gave an account of her collaboration but also explored her state of mind during her detention, her feelings of abjection, her sexuality, and the religious conversion that allowed her to recover and resume her life as a wife and mother. Case closed. Or was it? Michael Lazzara thinks not. He has taken up the loose ends and interviewed Luz Arce more than thirty years after the events.

The discovery of mass graves, the exposure of the Pinochet regime's corruption, the vigilance and persistence of the relatives of the disappeared: all of these happenings revealed to the world the military regime's grim underside and the terrorist tactics of DINA. Abused as a *"traidora,"* (a traitor), Luz Arce did not deny giving names, but claimed that she did not give information about leading militants, only those of minor actors—although this raises more questions than it answers. By what standard does one measure the importance of a life? Are the lives of the rank-and-file of less value than those of the leaders? Are some people dispensable? There is no way of evading these questions. Nor did Luz Arce evade them. Michael Lazzara interweaves his interview with photographs and citations, some of which contradict her. He cites, for example, the deposition of Maria Cecilia Bottai Monreal, who was detained in different torture centers between 1975 and 1976. Her mother and sister Carmen were taken to Villa Grimaldi and, as the deposition states, "they stayed for about 10 days [and] were tortured by ROMO and LUZ ARCE." Osvaldo Romo Mena was one of the most notorious characters of the period. He was a civilian member of the secret police who worked in conjunction with the *Halcón* (Falcon) unit of DINA, under the direction of Miguel Krassnoff Martchenko, for whom Luz Arce was, despite her collaboration, "a Marxist whore." Romo was imprisoned after the return to democracy for his numerous crimes, including some eighty rapes. In 1995 he gave a cynical interview to the Miami television station Univisión, in which he denied having committed rape. "Who would rape these women, who were disgusting, dirty, urine-covered, with blood running down their legs, and covered with grime?"[6] In this oblique self-justification, he defended himself by exposing the brutal conditions to which women prisoners were subjected in DINA prisons.

As a collaborator, there was no escape from the horror that reached a climax when DINA tracked down the head of MIR, Miguel Enríquez, killing him and seriously wounding Carmen Castillo, his girlfriend, who would later confront La Flaca Alejandra in a documentary film called *La Flaca Alejandra: Vidas y muertes de una mujer chilena* (Skinny Alejandra: Lives and deaths of a Chilean woman).[7] The capture of Enríquez was a moment of supreme triumph both for Pinochet and his secret service, which had been obsessed with dismantling MIR. An efficient information machine operating by means of torture led to the capture of most of MIR's leading members, including Lumi Videla Moya and her partner Sergio Pérez. For both La Flaca Alejandra and Luz Arce, the atrocious deaths of Lumi and Sergio would constitute a major crisis. La Flaca Alejandra tried to commit suicide after Enríquez's death, and her encounter with Lumi in prison was a moment of deep personal grief. Luz Arce was with Lumi in a cell from which they could hear Sergio being tortured; he was in such pain that he begged the torturers to kill him. Luz Arce comments in *The Inferno*, "[T]here are no words to describe what happened to Sergio or to alleviate Lumi's pain. I felt powerless because I couldn't even comfort her."[8] One of Lumi's last gestures was to give Luz Arce her leather jacket; Arce evidently sought some kind of absolution from a woman destined for martyrdom. Lumi's naked corpse would later be thrown over the wall of the Italian Embassy as a warning to those who had taken refuge there. Luz Arce only realized that Lumi had been killed when she witnessed guards playing dice for Lumi's clothes.

The destruction of MIR is a crucial moment in Luz Arce's narrative. The militants represented a heroic standard, a willingness to sacrifice themselves for a cause. La Flaca Alejandra and Luz Arce would be forced to judge the weaknesses of MIR and defend its militants' motives.

Hernán Vidal has argued that the childhood abuse Luz Arce suffered at the hands of a neighbor taught her to find space to maneuver even in the direst circumstances.[9] She was somehow able to negotiate a "rationalist distancing from her corporal materiality" that "permitted her to turn her body into a strategic and tactical instrument for resisting torture and penetrating the bureaucratic apparatus of DINA/CNI."[10] He quotes a passage from *The Inferno* in which Arce states, "[For me], sex is just another form of communication, something I can choose to practice or not. Then I made up or adopted a saying as my own, 'I'll give myself to someone, if I want to, but I won't sell myself.'"[11] She demonstrated her capacity for exploiting a situation to her advantage when news of an impending combat with MIR reached Manuel Contreras, the head of DINA, while he was dining with her and the other collaborators. He needed to make a hasty exit and, in the absence of his bodyguard, Luz Arce offered to escort him. As a mark of his gratitude, he gave the women collaborators permission to bear arms. Seeking the protection of powerful males was a strategy that worked for Arce. Francisco Ferrer Lima, the commander in charge of the Ollagüe detention center, almost certainly saved her from death, and with Rolf Wenderoth Pozo, second in command of Terranova (Villa Grimaldi), the most notorious of the DINA detention centers, she had a steady relationship. She herself explained that such relationships had little to do with sex or affection: "I wanted someone to be there who could chase away ghosts and fears."[12] To reiterate a line cited earlier, she convinced herself that "sex is just another form of communication." Thus, despite her abject condition, she preserves an illusion of free choice, an illusion that she defends at all costs.

Vidal underscores Arce's capacity for "long-term rational decisions" by citing an episode that took place during the New Year celebrations of 1975, which turned into an orgy.[13] In the absence of commanding officers, drunken guards began to rape the prisoners. An officer sexually abused Luz Arce in his office, but, because he was drunk, she was able to knock him unconscious. The office was full of guns, and, for a moment, Arce entertained the prospect of using them to escape, but on further reflection realized that without a viable alternative to the military regime, it would be a futile act of individual rebellion. When she reported the breach of discipline to the commanders, she did not tell them that she had been raped because she knew that the standard response to charges of sexual harassment was "you asked for it." It was not until her appearance before the truth commission that she was able to spell it out or, in her words, "*verbalizar.*" As on other occasions, she turned a potential disaster to her advantage.

The officers often addressed Arce as "Lucecita"; the diminutive underscores the masculine hierarchy against which she deployed "feminine" tactics by seeking their approbation. Their protection saved her from the "brutal machismo" of the guards and, for her part, she encouraged the paternalism of officers who felt themselves to be "a kind of father who [had] given [us] life."[14]

The return to democracy did not bring her much relief. She was physically damaged by her confinement and felt herself under threat of reprisal from MIR and from the Catholic Vicariate of Solidarity, which wanted her to clarify the fate of some of the disappeared. As always, her solution was to seek refuge in a relationship. She remarried, abruptly reinventing herself as a housewife with seven children: the son from her first marriage, two children from her marriage to Juan Manuel, and his four children from a previous marriage. The long mental crisis that followed led her to seek help from the church, and with the support of a priest she began to write her autobiography, which was completed while she was living abroad in Austria, possibly protected, strange as it may seem, by the remnants of MIR.[15] Her return to Chile was triggered by reading *Los secretos del comando conjunto* (Secrets of the Joint Command) (1991), a book by a journalist, Mónica González, and a lawyer, Hector Contreras Alday, which documented communist militants who had denounced their comrades.[16] She now found her role as witness, and in addition to testifying to the truth commission, she also took part in several "face to face" encounters (*careos,* legal face-offs) in which accused DINA officials were directly confronted by victims or their families. In one of the confrontations described in *The Inferno,* she faced her former lover Rolf Wenderoth; in another, when forced to listen to the insults of an unapologetic Miguel Krassnoff Martchenko, she found herself adopting the almost fetal position of a torture victim.

Despite its sensational revelations, *The Inferno* did not initially receive much comment in the atmosphere of national amnesia that followed General Pinochet's resignation and the election of the coalition of parties known as *La Concertación.* Chilean writer Diamela Eltit, one of the first to discuss *The Inferno,* situated it within a neoliberal ideology that was indifferent to ethical distinctions. For Eltit, confessions like Arce's circulated "in the amnesiac space of a politics of the marketplace that buried them face down—way down—in order to allow the perpetuation of a simulacrum of abundance that promotes the social death of objects, speech, and the cultural solidity of bodies."[17] Yet, as Michael Lazzara's book suggests, memories have a disturbing tendency to resurface. And although the now sixty-year-old Luz Arce claims that this interview will be her last, it is clear that it by no means exhausts the topic. The figure of the traitor cannot fade away; it is too compelling.

Luz Arce and Pinochet's Chile includes a lengthy summary of Arce's deposition before the National Truth and Reconciliation Commission. For those not familiar with her autobiography, the deposition gives the essentials of the story. In her declaration to the commission, Arce frames her statement with a reference to her religious conversion: "Over the past few years I have experienced a process of encounter with the Lord, and I have a deeply lived commitment to my Christian faith, and therefore, as much as possible, I want to be faithful to the dictates of my conscience." Although a great deal of time has passed since the events of the early 1970s, Luz Arce's memory scarcely falters, though many of her answers to Lazzara's questions are not so much clarifications as a review of her former selves and her ongoing revisions of their meaning. She is committed to a story that, like the Ancient Mariner, she is condemned to repeat. This being said, Lazzara's interviews tease out a host of subplots that may not be apparent from reading *The Inferno.* I found particularly revealing the account of her recruitment to GAP (*Grupo de Amigos Personales,* Group of Personal Friends of Salvador Allende), which acted as a support group for the socialist president. It gives an astonishing picture of the informality of Allende's government—an informality that, in our time of excessive scrutiny and vigilance, seems hardly credible. On her way to a job interview in a clothing store, she takes a bus on which she meets a college friend, Raúl Juvenal Navarrete Hancke (later employed by DINA), who gets her a job as a secretary in La Moneda palace, the seat of Allende's government, even though she hadn't yet learned to use a typewriter. (Imagine wandering into the White House or Buckingham Palace to look for a job!) She then went to work for GAP; this was a semimilitary organization largely run by MIR, which was putting pressure on the moderate Allende to take a hard line against the opposition. As she makes clear, she herself was never a militant, although she was influenced by the confrontational politics of the time and, after leaving GAP, she joined up with GEA (*Grupo Especial de Apoyo,* Special Support Group), a Socialist support group that engaged in armed actions and even planned an attack on the US Embassy.

What emerges from her answers to Lazzara's questions is the benefit of hindsight that allows her to pass judgment on the violent methods she had once endorsed and on the extent of her collaboration. She sticks to her story, that, although she quickly succumbed to torture and collaborated, only a few people "disappeared" as a result of her denunciations, and she was soon able to find tasks within DINA that absolved her from participation in the street patrols (*poroteos*) organized to flush out "subversives" as they walked the streets. Asked why she remained with the secret service even when it might have been safe to leave, she insists that she and the other collaborators "were terrified"; because of this, even when given a taste of freedom, they hesitated to go outside. Like La Flaca Alejandra, Arce asserts that this is *her* truth and that those who have not been in her situation cannot possibly understand. The problem with this defense is immediately apparent when Lazzara confronts her with the words of one of her most important critics, the writer Diamela Eltit. Eltit wrote three essays on Luz Arce, the first of which, *"Vivir,*

¿donde?" (To Live, Where?) appeared in the Chilean academic journal *Revista de crítica cultural* in 1995 and was later reproduced in Eltit's collection of essays *Emergencias: Escritos sobre literatura, arte y política* (Emergencies: Writings on literature, art, and politics) (2000). Eltit wrote that the collaboration of both Arce and La Flaca Alejandra had to do with the seduction of power: "[L]ike chameleons, they kept changing, reformulating their discourses according to the contingent rotation of centralized power."[18] For this reason, these women are "nomadic bodies," prepared to adopt, uncritically, any hegemonic discourses that give them an identity, an identity that is always linked to power. In her interview with Lazzara, Luz Arce complains that Eltit's reading is "always from outside. She can't do a reading from the inside because she didn't live my experience." Arce thus adopts a position of extreme relativism: "[D]iamela and all the rest who are extremely critical of me have *their* histories and *their* suffering and *their* baggage . . . But I have mine." This response erases any attempt to arrive at an understanding of torture that generalizes beyond personal experience. Nor are Eltit's observations on the effects of torture to be set aside so easily. She argues that the aim of the torturer is not to get a confession, but to "break" (*quebrar*) the victim; that is to say, "torture is an atrocious allegory of the body, which is gradually stripped of the reality and validity of all knowledge, of any strategy, to the point of producing the most extreme depoliticization."[19] The DINA officers with power over life and death acted in the name of God and the nation to destroy the "other" physically and mentally through the ritual of pain. It is not the giving up of names of comrades that makes Arce's and Merino's confessions extraordinarily problematic, argues Eltit, but their determination to become officers of DINA and to be part of the military contingent. Thus, terms such as "treachery" and "collaboration" lose their significance when reading these texts, "since the evident problem is much more radical and also simple: it is the absolute seduction of power."[20]

Clearly, there is no way of reconciling such different viewpoints. Lazzara's strategy is to juxtapose Luz Arce's recollections with the testimonies and opinions of relatives of the disappeared, critics, and contemporaries and to add to the long posthistory during which Luz Arce learned to "verbalize" without ever quite clearing up the doubts and controversies around that inglorious past. For her, the personal is not the political because individuals act on the basis of their experience and their time. As she constantly reiterates, "Every person is a product of his or her times." The Catholic religion, the personal confession to God's representative, and the promise of eternal salvation frame her story. When asked about national reconciliation, she speculates vaguely as to its possibility: perhaps it will happen when the present generation has died off.[21]

It is instructive to read *The Inferno* and *Luz Arce and Pinochet's Chile* alongside *Ese inferno* (That inferno) (2001), a collective account of five Argentine women captives who survived the Argentine secret prison called ESMA (*Escuela de Mecánica de la Armada,* Naval School of Mechanics) and collaborated.[22] It took twenty years for the women to record their captivity in the notorious detention center from which so many disappeared. Regarded as "salvageable" by the officers, they were put to work making false identity cards, typing, and translating, and were eventually released into "provisional freedom." But though they were invited to dinner and to dances by the officers, they seemed to have successfully avoided intimate or sexual relations with their captors; they also never became officers in the organization. Perhaps it is fruitless to enquire whether Luz Arce could have adopted different tactics. Her testimonies are what they are: formidable and controversial documents of our time.

Acknowledgments

Writing a book requires the logistical, intellectual, and emotional support of so many people who give us the strength to move forward. I am grateful to those who challenged me to add layers of complexity and depth to this project. Because of their support and suggestions, I know that this book will resonate more deeply and inspire even richer conversations and debates.

Special thanks go to Nadine Retamal for helping me, eight years ago, with the original transcriptions of the Arce interview tapes. I am also grateful to the Vicariate of Solidarity (Santiago, Chile) and to the Human Rights Program, a subsidiary of the Chilean Ministry of the Interior; both of these entities facilitated documents that enriched my investigation.

I am particularly indebted to Marisol Vera, Rosana Espino, and all the staff at Editorial Cuarto Propio whose democratic vision and dedication to fomenting valuable debate have helped to combat forgetting and sustain Chile's intellectual scene throughout the transition to democracy. Marisol took a chance on the original Spanish version of this book, which other publishers undoubtedly would have found too experimental or not "marketable" enough. Likewise, I am proud to publish this updated and expanded English version with Palgrave Macmillan, whose editors were also convinced that it could raise questions worth considering in the US context and for English-speaking readers in general. Robyn Curtis, my editor, provided invaluable guidance along the way.

This publication would not have been possible without the generous support of several grants from the University of California, Davis. I am grateful to Dean Jesse Ann Owens and to my colleagues in the Department of Spanish and Portuguese for their kindness, conversation, and depth of vision. At Davis, Charles Walker and Victoria Langland were important promoters and commentators of my work at a forum on "Collaboration and Dictatorship" that I organized in December 2008. My undergraduate and graduate students, in many seminars and classes, have also illuminated my thinking through our shared readings of texts by Arce and her critics. Moisés Park, Nicholas Sánchez, Manuel Gómez Navarro, Erik Larson, Emily Davidon, and so many others, have challenged me to understand more deeply the dimensions of my work.

In Santiago, Chile, another forum on "Collaboration and Dictatorship" was held on July 21, 2008, to celebrate the original publication of this book and generate polemics around it. Patricia Espinosa, Jorge Arrate, Gloria Elgueta, and Gabriela Zúñiga contributed their wisdom, passions, and reflections. Also in Chile, Juan Camilo Lorca, Olga Ruiz, Margarita Romero, Pedro Alejandro Matta, Nelly

Richard, Diamela Eltit, and so many others were key interlocutors, readers, and resources. And, of course, my experiences in Chile and my reflections on Chile would not have been the same without Ryan Carlin, Mari Spira and Lupe Arenillas, *compañeros de ruta.*

I am perhaps most indebted to Luz Arce Sandoval, who graciously accepted to be interviewed over five years' time. Her sustained commitment to my project taught me much. I hope to have been faithful to her voice, treating her ethically, without sacrificing an intellectual imperative to question, critique, and understand.

This new English version owes an enormous debt to Carl Fisher, whose brilliant translation skills and unparalleled command of Chilean Spanish helped me to render the original poetically. I am also honored to have piqued the interest of Jean Franco, whose "Foreword" orients readers beautifully to Arce and her tumultuous experience.

Finally, without the unflagging, unconditional support my beautiful wife, Julia, and my darling little Ana and James, none of what I do would be.

I hope that this text provides general readers and researchers not only material that can complement a reading of Arce's 1993 book *The Inferno* but also, and more importantly, a testimonial project that can be evaluated and debated on its own terms. I'll feel satisfied if this book can resuscitate the value—in Chile and beyond—of an abject biography that, in my opinion, continues to be emblematic, even though many prefer to forget it.

Introduction

After the Inferno

Michael J. Lazzara

The Chilean postdictatorship period is full of mutilated biographies that have been silenced or have not fit into the Manichean lexicon of official discourse (betrayal and heroism, left and right). Nevertheless, throughout this now eternal transition to democracy (1990–present), few of those voices have dared to speak. Within the human rights community, and more broadly within Chilean society, the official story has tended to reify the martyred militant, rendering him or her untouchable, while the traitor figure has remained stigmatized, hidden from view, muzzled, a taboo subject for former revolutionaries reticent to admit "defeat," as well as for a nation reluctant to face the ethical quagmire of complicity on which the Pinochet dictatorship forged its "economic miracle."[1] Yet, traitorous and complicit subjects—both in the torture chamber and outside of it—are an undeniable part of the Pinochet regime's (1973–90) tumultuous history of state violence. They bring into relief the ethical, moral, and political dilemmas of the "gray zone" and oftentimes encapsulate the breakage of body, voice, and subjectivity that were part and parcel with torture and the denunciation of one's revolutionary comrades.

How can the before, during, and after of torture and betrayal be integrated into an autobiographical narrative that "makes sense" to the speaking subject and permits her a modality for narrating the immense traumas she suffered? How can she invent a place from which to speak after being broken in the torture chamber and turned into a cog in the machinery of state terror? How can she project herself in different times and spaces when she is besieged by flashbacks of torture and collaboration and wracked by shame's many insidious faces? With those questions in mind, returning to the voice of Luz Arce Sandoval—one of the most emblematic collaborator figures to emerge from the dark history of the Pinochet dictatorship—might be a starting point for asking key political and ethical questions, and for reconsidering the "fissures" and "tremors" of representation that official discourse has tended to eclipse.[2]

The texts juxtaposed in this book, which focus on one complex and controversial figure from Chile's postdictatorship period, attempt to place that figure center stage so that she can be critically evaluated and considered by the reader who, undoubtedly, will form his or her own opinions about the multiple discourses constructed here. Ever since her initial testimony to the National Truth and Reconciliation Commission (1990) and the original publication of her gut-wrenching testimonial work *El infierno* (The inferno; 1993), Luz Arce has garnered acceptance by some, rejection by others, and has managed to capture the attention of readers and critics who have responded to her text, offering myriad opinions about her discourse as well as her life trajectory and comportment. Some critique her for having collaborated under torture, others for having become a salaried "functionary" of Pinochet's secret police organizations, others for having developed affective and sexual relationships with military officers, and others for having morphed ideologically—like a chameleon—in sync with the macropolitical power shifts of Chile's recent history.[3] A "revolutionary" during Salvador Allende's Popular Unity government (1970–73), a collaborator during the Pinochet regime, and a repentant Christian in search of personal and national reconciliation during the transition to democracy—Luz Arce's detractors have accused her of accommodating herself at every juncture to the reigning powers of the day. In contrast, certain figures linked to the government, the Catholic Church, and human rights organizations have forgiven Luz Arce's transgressions and validated her repentant discourse. All of this notwithstanding, the question remains, and will continue to linger even after reading this book: Has Luz Arce shared *everything* that she witnessed and remembers from her years as a prisoner and functionary of DINA/CNI (*Dirección de Inteligencia Nacional*, National Intelligence Directorate, and *Central Nacional de Informaciones*, National Information Center, the Pinochet regime's two secret police organizations)? Or, conversely, has her truth had limits?

However, despite the "truth" of the documents presented in this book, the exercise of scrutinizing Luz Arce's discourse—with its merits, lapses, flaws, and obsessions—can be illuminating insofar as it confronts us directly with the terrible abjection to which certain bodies were subjugated under dictatorship, while at the same time it permits a reflection on the protracted process of how a subject remakes herself after radical suffering. Additionally, the texts in this book provide an idea of how Luz Arce has been received, constructed, and read by her fellow Chileans and international commentators. Indeed, her "case" stimulates multiple reflections. First, it sheds light on how certain "unspeakable" experiences like torture, betrayal, and collaboration assume textual form as part of a posttraumatic, postdictatorial history. Second, it raises questions about how the dictatorship unmade revolutionary longings by literally *unmaking* bodies, turning them into abject, depoliticized shells devoid of any sense of futurity. In fact, the unmaking of revolutionary subjectivity that Luz Arce emblematizes speaks volumes about how Pinochet's violently imposed neoliberal endgame left formerly insurrectional subjects repentant, quelled, and confused. Finally, Arce's "case" also inspires meditation on the Chilean left's very ability to generate a cohesive political project and a radical vision for society after being violently dismantled at the hands of Pinochet's henchmen. Sebastián Piñera's current government (2010–14)—comprising direct heirs to the

dictatorship's technocratic and neoliberal legacy—has now taken power, deto-
nating a renewed moment of crisis for the left and a need for rearticulating
visions and alliances for the future.

I first contacted Luz Arce in 2002, while I was researching my book *Chile in
Transition: The Poetics and Politics of Memory* (2006). As part of that project, which
explored the ways in which posttraumatic memory narratives took form during
Chile's transition to democracy, I decided to write a chapter on *The Inferno*, which
had struck me as one of the most intense and disconcerting testimonial narratives
to emerge from the Chilean context or, for that matter, from any Latin American
country that had lived through the defeat of revolution by dictatorship. Each time
I read Luz Arce's book, I found myself asking questions about the complexity of
her voice and about her experiences as a militant, torture victim, collaborator,
and repentant Christian who had engaged in at least two cathartic public expia-
tions of her guilt, first before the truth commission and later in her book. I was
intrigued by the strangely random way in which this lower middle class physical
education teacher wound up working in La Moneda palace, just a stone's throw
from Salvador Allende's office, as part of his inner security circle (GAP, *Grupo de
Amigos Personales,* Group of Personal Friends of Salvador Allende). I was amazed
by the equally happenstance way in which Arce became an arms bearing member
of the Chilean Socialist Party, even attempting to blow up the US consulate with
dynamite. Luz Arce seemed to be a subject trapped by the tidal wave of history, by
the revolutionary imperatives of her time; she seemed confused, to be searching
for her way in life, to be engaged in a constant search for belonging—both affective and ideological—and for identity. Nor did it seem irrelevant that Arce was a
woman navigating the waters of two worlds—the militant and the military—that
were rigidly hierarchical, compartmentalized, and masculine in tenor. In short,
the case of Luz Arce intrigued me *not* simply because she had collaborated with
DINA—in fact, as several Chilean survivors have told me, the stark reality is that
most prisoners collaborated to some extent, even though the topic of collaboration
continues to be taboo, a stain on the martyred memory of the disappeared—but
because she stayed on as a functionary of DINA and CNI for four and a half years.[4]
This *bureaucratization of horror* made it so that Luz Arce, along with two of her
fellow detainees, Marcia Alejandra Merino Vega ("La Flaca Alejandra") and María
Alicia Uribe Gómez ("Carola"), were saddled with—and forced to carry almost
exclusively—the burden of betrayal and collaboration that official leftist militant
discourse refused to accept. It was as if these three women had been pegged as
scapegoats, as Chilean Malinches, Mata Haris, or categorized using similarly flippant cultural commonplaces.

Curiously, every time I asked a former militant about Luz Arce, I was greeted
by odd looks. I got the feeling that a tacit pact of silence surrounded her figure.
No one wanted to tell me anything about her. When I contacted the Villa Grimaldi
Park for Peace Corporation, for example, not one survivor of that detention center agreed to an interview. It was as if, thirty years after the September 11, 1973,
coup, collaborationism—deposited on the bodies of Arce, Merino, and Uribe in
the early 1990s—were a passé topic, a topic that had been sufficiently discussed
and resolved in the transition's early years. What sense would it make to reopen an

old can of worms? Consequently, I had to settle for what Arce herself could tell me about her experience and for what I could glean from reading academic articles, journalistic pieces, and legal documents relevant to her case.[5]

I decided to interview Luz Arce not just because I had access to her; more importantly, I was drawn to her case because, when compared to La Flaca Alejandra and Carola, she had been the most high-profile collaborator figure of the transition. The preexisting discourse that surrounded her offered a chance to do a book that could participate in that established semantic web, dialoging with it and questioning it without, of course, ever ceasing to be mired in the unresolvable battle between illumination and opacity. I wanted to give Arce a chance to respond to critiques levied against her and to revisit certain difficult and murky zones of her experience at further temporal remove from the original events. Even though I agree with Jean Franco's assessment that Arce is like the Ancient Mariner condemned to repeat her story, the nuances and introspection of Arce's retelling open possibilities for understanding how individuals and societies work through and understand a traumatic past.

For better or worse, justified or not, Arce is part of the convulsive imaginary of post-Pinochet Chile. The iconography around her public image portrays her in radically opposite ways. Sometimes she appears as a corrupt, hardened criminal of DINA/CNI; at other times, she appears as a poor, pathetic, abject collaborator figure; still at other times, we see her in the media as a repentant Christian mother struggling to stitch together her life and heal the traumatic wounds leftover from a dark and infirmed era. In contrast, La Flaca Alejandra—with the exception of her short 1993 book *Mi verdad. Más allá del horror. Yo acuso.* (My truth. Beyond horror. I accuse.) and some recent legal testimony—has opted to steer clear of the public eye and live semiclandestinely on the geographically remote Easter Island. Carola, for her part, is the one who has spoken least and who has testified least in court. Even after the transition to democracy, Carola never had the courage to sever her ties with the military. Having carried out several bureaucratic jobs for DINA/CNI, after 1990 she began working for DINE (*Dirección de Inteligencia Nacional del Ejército,* Army National Intelligence Directorate) until she recently retired. Racked with fear, Carola has testified on several occasions that she never witnessed torture and that she knows nothing about the disappeared.

***

The daughter of a lower middle class family, sexually abused by her neighbors as a child, an athlete and physical education teacher, an admirer of her liberal grandfather without actively participating in politics, Luz Arce became a leftist militant by chance during the most tumultuous moments of Salvador Allende's Popular Unity government.[6] As she tells the story, one day in 1972, while traveling home on a bus, she ran into an old childhood friend who offered her a job as a secretary at La Moneda palace. With this dramatic twist of fate, she ended up working right next to the socialist president's office, first in administrative functions and later as a member of GAP (*Grupo de Amigos Personales,* Group of Personal Friends of Salvador Allende), the president's personal security force.

On June 29, 1973, Arce was transferred from GAP to GEA (*Grupos Especiales de Apoyo,* Special Support Groups), an entity within the Socialist Party whose mission was to set up a school that would train construction workers to be militants. As a socialist, Arce devoured books on Marxism and gave herself wholeheartedly to the cause, even going so far as to take up arms to advance the revolution. This was the situation in which she found herself when the September 11, 1973, coup occurred.

After the coup, like many militants, Arce went underground to await orders from her superiors. But on March 17, 1974, before her "cell" could reorganize, she and a fellow comrade were detained while having refreshments at a Santiago soda fountain. From there, she was taken to the Fifth Commissary of *Carabineros* (the Chilean police) and soon thereafter to the 38 Londres Street detention and torture center, one of the very first sites of repression erected by the Pinochet regime. For several months, she was held in different clandestine locations until she was granted a brief period of freedom under surveillance in July 1974. While in military custody, she was raped on several occasions and brutally tortured by DINA agents—a situation that terrified her and left long-lasting psychological damage and a desire to die. On March 27, 1974, she suffered a severe bullet wound in her right foot when a military officer shot her with an AKA rifle. The incident caused her to be interned in the Military Hospital (*Hospital Militar,* HOSMIL) until she was granted temporary freedom. Then, only one week after returning home, DINA operatives appeared at her door, blindfolded her, and took her to the notorious Villa Grimaldi detention center. While there, she resisted torture for more than four months; she gave up the names of comrades for the first time at 38 Londres Street in August 1974. Arce insists that she always tried to be a "good revolutionary" and that her collaboration, in accordance with the manuals that governed leftist militant organizations, only resulted in the capture of "peripheral" people whose detention would not place the overall party structure in jeopardy.

Luz Arce's collaboration was complex and multifaceted. It consisted of (1) giving up the names of comrades under torture (at least four of whom eventually became *desaparecidos*); (2) participating in the so-called *poroteos* (literally "bean counting," raids by DINA agents whose aim was the entrapment of leftist militants); (3) using her knowledge of the power structures of groups like MIR (*Movimiento de Izquierda Revolucionaria,* Leftist Revolutionary Movement) to sketch organizational diagrams for Pinochet's secret police; (4) teaching classes on Marxism to military officials; (5) assuming false identities and carrying out clandestine operations in Uruguay, like *Operación Celeste* (Operation Sky Blue) (1979–80); and (6) engaging in amorous relationships with a number of military officials, particularly with Rolf Wenderoth Pozo, who protected her from the aggression of other military officers.[7]

On May 7, 1975, Arce was officially recruited as a "functionary" of DINA by then-leader of the secret police General Manuel Contreras. Together with La Flaca Alejandra and Carola, she was given a paid apartment and a minimal salary in exchange for her labor. For nearly eight months, she carried out administrative tasks for BIM (*Brigada de Inteligencia Metropolitana,* Metropolitan Intelligence Brigade). Then, on March 2, 1976, she went to work at DINA General Headquarters as a "political analyst" whose job was to assimilate "open-access information that contained references to the military government."[8]

Luz Arce attempted to tender her resignation to CNI three times, but it was never accepted. It was not until March 16, 1980, that her superiors finally allowed her to leave the secret police definitively. Before that, as a kind of exit strategy, Arce was sent to Uruguay on a spy mission—that, according to her, never played out in its entirety—whose ultimate objective was for her to make her way into Argentina, infiltrate the Argentine military hierarchy, and devise a plot against Emilio Massera, a member of the junta and notorious leader of ESMA (*Escuela de Mecánica de la Armada,* Naval School of Mechanics). As Luz Arce tells it, after regaining her "freedom," she found that a "black legend" tainted her public image, a situation that was exacerbated when she practically disappeared from the public eye for several years so that she could confront her shame and trauma privately. She entered a period of silence, profound suffering, and clandestine life in which she not only avoided DINA but also the courts that sought her testimony.

By the late 1980s, Arce's life began to change. She had received psychotherapy and befriended a group of Dominican priests who provided her a support network, helped her to verbalize her memories, and trained her in the study of theology. Thanks to her experience with the Dominicans, Arce's Catholic faith became the belief system (and discursive apparatus) that most facilitated her healing and, later, served as a narrative framework for telling her story. Readers of *The Inferno* will take note of the book's strong religious overtones, which open a space for the "traitorous" subject to expiate her guilt and ask forgiveness publicly before the nation. The inner strength Arce derived from her faith, coupled with the support she received from several members of the Rettig Commission, eventually helped her muster the courage to testify about what she knew of the Pinochet regime's machinery of terror. After spending a year isolated in Europe, she voluntarily decided to return to Chile in 1990. Since then, Arce has testified in hundreds of judicial proceedings, and continues to do so when subpoenaed.

***

My interview with Luz Arce began by email in 2002. Interested in clarifying some details about her book and her experience, I asked a friend, a Chilean human rights activist, to help me locate her. I discovered that Arce was living in Mexico, outside of Taxco, and that she was spending her days running a small business selling handmade jewelry to tourists. As she told me, she and her family had left Chile because job possibilities were scarce and also because some geographical distance would permit a "positive" mental distancing from her painful past. In Mexico, she hoped to find a place where she might no longer be seen as the "traitor and whore"; she longed for a place in which her family could create a better life.

In our initial correspondences, Arce often spoke about the tremendous difficulties she experienced in adapting to life in Mexico. She seemed to feel out of place just about everywhere. At first, we didn't talk about sensitive topics like torture or collaboration; it didn't seem right for two people who hardly knew each other to delve into such complex zones of experience. Above all, it was first necessary to establish mutual confidence, to create, with time, a situation of empathic listening that would make it possible to broach traumatic and difficult topics. I remember that in our initial correspondences, I had to reveal a lot about myself so that Luz would consider me trustworthy and unbiased. Only when I had earned her confidence did she open up and start sharing the more intimate details of her life. I found it interesting that Luz Arce constantly reiterated that her interview with me would be her last. She said she was tired of journalists and academics motivated by personal ideological agendas; she was convinced that I was not like them. So, with a certain mutual trust established, for a period of time I would send her questions and she would respond in writing.

Our treatment of each other, in Spanish, always oscillated between the formal *usted* and the informal *tú*, which served as discursive markers of a relationship that was evolving, but that never settled entirely into a space of familiarity. I read in this pronominal shift a hint of deference to the implicit authority of my position. Even though I was much younger than she, I was an educated, male university professor from the United States, which no doubt had some significance. Curiously, I was usually the one who found myself trying to use the *tú* form, while Arce seemed to feel more comfortable in the more formal realm of *usted*.[9]

Why Luz Arce decided to grant this—her "last"—interview to me continues to be something of a mystery. I can only dare think that it was because she saw me as nonthreatening, or as perhaps more capable of "objectivity" because I was a foreigner, an outsider. By another token, Luz Arce also saw this interview as an opportunity to clear the air, to dispel some misunderstandings that had congealed over time, and to close a very long and painful chapter of her life. At one point, she told me that I reminded her of her son—a comment that made me think that for Luz Arce, in some sense, I symbolized the next generation that needed to be "educated" about the dictatorship's moral degradation. I should confess that I took advantage of that position—which was both advantageous and disadvantageous—to raise the most direct and incisive questions I knew how. I was aware, however, that it would always be necessary to proceed with caution. Asking tough questions without sounding offensive or breaching trust was perhaps my greatest challenge as an interviewer. Yet, because I had never experienced firsthand the dramatic situations Luz Arce lived, it struck me as unethical (and ultimately unproductive) to approach her aggressively, as other interviewers might do. Consequently, as the reader will note, the conversations transcribed in Part II of this book have their own rhythms and progressions, and are oftentimes filled with silences that are difficult, if not impossible to overcome. More than accusing or attacking Luz Arce, then, I interviewed her to understand her, to hear her, to confront her with critiques, to let her explore the moral grays of her case, and to reveal the current state (thirty years after being detained by DINA) of her protracted healing process. I interviewed her to present her as a paradigmatic case of the most noxious aspects of the dictatorship and the darkest secrets of the transition. I respected her request not to revisit her torture in detail, particularly because she had already given that graphic testimony both in court and in *The Inferno*. We limited the scope of our interactions to personal introspection.

After two years of regular email exchanges, I finally had occasion to meet Luz Arce personally in Santiago in November 2004. Around that time, I had traveled to Chile to carry out academic research, and she had traveled from Mexico to testify in human rights trials. Chance brought us together. We made plans to meet in a Bellavista neighborhood apartment that was owned by Dominican priests, right beside San Cristóbal hill. In the hours she had leftover after long, grueling days spent testifying in court, we taped our extensive conversations over four evenings. The interviews began around *onces* time and carried on, without pause, until one or two o'clock in the morning.[10] The scene was austere: a crucifix hanging on the wall, a copy of the Bible on the table. Luz Arce chain-smoked while we talked. She struck me as an affable woman, strongly rooted in her Christian faith, but also as someone who controls and carefully measures her words. Perhaps her personal history has taught her a need for that. She paused frequently and meditated before she spoke. At times, her eyes welled with tears; at other times, when faced with a difficult question, she simply refused to answer or became evasive. In general, though, she always tried to fulfill her commitment to me by responding to whatever I asked.

The centerpiece of *Luz Arce and Pinochet's Chile* is a transcription of our oral and written exchanges that took place between 2002 and 2007. The material is organized thematically and offers a vision of how Luz Arce continues to process her past today, more than a decade and a half after publishing *The Inferno*. To make the interviews legible, I had to edit them significantly and arrange them thematically. The themes I chose—militancy, trauma collaboration, gender, and so on—generally echo the zones of inquiry within which Arce's figure has typically been read. However, despite the need for editing and some minor resequencing of questions and answers, most parts of the interview have been reproduced faithfully, in accordance with how they really took place. I formulated my questions intuitively, based on an informed reading of Arce's book and many of her other public and legal declarations. Follow up questions arose organically, in tandem with the rhythms and needs of my inquiry. In the end, I omitted very little, only digressions that I didn't find relevant or suggestive for general readers. Those digressions, in retrospect, were perhaps necessary for establishing interpersonal confidence or for talking "around" difficult topics before arriving at the heart of the matter. The interviews include a certain amount of repetition, which is not only indicative of how our exchanges actually were but also revealing of how a posttraumatic subject reasons through and rehearses certain memory scripts. The "tics" of our conversation are what readers will ultimately interpret and assess. In short, like any testimonial work, this book is a construction, a *fiction* that seeks to be faithful to the real.

Because I was unable to conduct an exhaustive interview that touched on all the "facts" of Arce's case, I decided to begin (Part I) with an abridged version of her October 1990, declaration to the National Truth and Reconciliation Commission.[11] This document, fascinating in its own right, will allow readers to understand the basic parameters of Arce's experience as she relayed it to the commission. Part I, when considered in juxtaposition with my interview and perhaps with a prior reading of *The Inferno*, will facilitate a more complete picture of Arce's abject experience and of how she integrates and reintegrates that experience into her "life story." The dry, mechanical, factual language of her truth commission testimony contrasts markedly with the emotional, more introspective register of the interviews. This juxtaposition of discursive registers, I think, speaks volumes about how a traumatized subject frames and reframes her experience in different times and spaces and to different ends; moreover, it forms the basis for this book's poetics. Additionally, I have sprinkled the book with epigraphs by Arce and others (without necessarily heeding the factual basis of their words) to give a more complete vision of the verbal webs—opinions, critiques, accusations, characterizations— that have been spun around the traitor figure. These "other" voices, which sometimes appear in the endnotes as well, are meant to generate points of tension or conflict with Arce's discourse. Truth, as we know, is multifaceted, tentacled, constructed from different speaking positions and with differing motivations. This book, I hope, brings that into relief. My wager is that a hybrid approach to creating *testimonial literature*—an approach that does not render discourses relative to one another, but that instead reveals their textures, layers, and complexities—is probably the most "truthful," the most faithful to reality.

For this revised, updated English version of *Luz Arce: Después del infierno,* I have added a third part to the book: a forum section on the topic "Collaboration, Dictatorship, Democracy." Because collaboration, both in the concentration camp context and in civil society, has been a taboo subject in Chile, I took the Spanish-language publication of my book as an opportunity to organize a forum that could air contrasting perspectives and spark critical debate. I describe the details of this forum and my perceptions of it in my own contribution to Part III. Following the July 2008 Santiago forum, I organized a similar forum at the University of California, Davis, in December of the same year; I wanted to give voices from outside the Chilean context a chance to share other viewpoints. Part III of this book, then, contains the contributions of all who participated in the Chilean and US forums, as well as one additional invited contribution, that of Mr. Pedro Alejandro Matta, a survivor of the Villa Grimaldi detention center. The diverse interventions by human rights activists, literary and cultural critics, historians, and politicians offer multiple readings of Luz Arce, the phenomenon of collaboration, and my book. My hope is that these texts will contribute to the pedagogical function that I hope this book can ultimately have.

Luz Arce and Pinochet's Chile obliges us to confront our own human frailty as well as the ethical (and political) gray zones generated by torture, state violence, and neoliberal hegemony. Luz Arce's "case" is exemplary, yes, but it is also symptomatic of a broader, more insidious phenomenon: the repeated acts of barbarism that have been carried out across different times and spaces under the guises of "progress," "civilization," and "modernization." The simple fact is that Pinochet's neoliberal redesign of Chile, which was supported by the United States under Richard Nixon, *required* that bodies morph politically, that they "break" or become complicit with his project to greater or lesser degrees in order for hearts, minds, and souls to be made anew. Pinochet's 17-year reign of terror created not only a noxious dynamic of "winners" and "losers" but also a vast spectrum of grays—of mutated, destroyed, traitorous, or shamed bodies. Today, nearly four decades after the coup, this gray zone continues to be the most intolerable aspect of the nation's collective memory and teaches us that violence goes hand in hand with fostering and upholding the neoliberal world order.

At the same time, for US readers, Luz Arce cannot simply be relegated to Chile, to a different space or time, to a different historical moment that seems to have no bearing on *us,* on our present. Instead, from the US context, we should consider the relevance of what Luz Arce's "case" can tell us about revolutionary dreams torn asunder, about the propagation of violence (in myriad forms) to uphold neo-liberal hegemony, and about the very possibilities for oppositional politics when bodies are unmade through torture or tamed into conformity.[12] Moreover, how do *we,* directly or indirectly, wittingly or unwittingly, create the conditions of possibility for a Luz Arce to exist? Unfortunately, our "enlightened" times do not lack laboratories of power. One need only think of Abu Ghraib or Guantánamo Bay. The list goes on.

Thinking back on my five-year-long experience of interviewing Luz Arce, I found myself asking many times what I should expect of her voice. What could I—what can we—expect her to say? A quotation from Primo Levi comes to mind: "One cannot expect from men who have known such extreme destitution a deposition in the juridical sense, but something that is at once a lament, a curse, an expiation, an attempt to justify and rehabilitate oneself: a liberating outburst rather than a Medusa-faced truth."[13]

Perhaps, even today, Luz Arce's broken biography still holds testimonial value that can prove instructive.

Luz Arce Sandoval presented herself to the Truth and Reconciliation Commission on the morning of September 27, 1990. It is difficult to know what thoughts were going through her mind during the days prior to her decision to tell the truth. What is certain is that, after long hours of painful memories and because of her intimate relationship over 15 years with the repressive apparatus, she reconstructed a nearly complete picture of the largest machinery of terror our history has ever known.

The figure of Luz Arce sums up the tragedy lived by a generation. In her case, there were unimaginable metamorphoses as unique as the singular history of every human being. She was a self-sacrificing leftist militant, full of values, dreams, and utopias. The military coup quickly changed her life. She started living clandestinely. Later came her first arrest and experiences of torture. Shortly thereafter, she was captured again, and there came a moment in which she could no longer keep quiet. She had been trapped by the machinery of collaboration, in a desperate effort to save her life.

What limits does a human being have before breaking with her past, friends, and comrades? When does fear stop dominating and collaboration become voluntary? When does a person assume that she can't change her fate and accept a path that she didn't choose? When does the opposite occur: the decision to make amends? There are no set answers to these questions.

Perhaps there is only one certainty. When a person like Luz Arce makes the journey from victim to victimizer to victim, it's because she has lived, over 17 intense years, one of the most horrific parts of the Chilean nightmare. She is just one of thousands of people whose human rights were violated; it's just that no one has admitted it.

—*Página Abierta, March 18–31, 1991, No author specified*

Part I

Names, Dates, Places

Summary of Luz Arce's Declaration before the National Truth and Reconciliation Commission (Santiago de Chile, October 9, 1990)

DECLARATION[1]

THE FOLLOWING DECLARATION WAS GIVEN BY **LUZ ARCE SANDOVAL**, CHILEAN CITIZEN, IDENTITY CARD NO. X.XXX.XXX-X, LIVING AT XXXX, SANTIAGO, HAVING PROFESSED FULL KNOWLEDGE OF THE REGULATIONS STIPULATED IN SUPREME DECREE NO. 335 OF 1990, WHICH CREATED THE NATIONAL TRUTH AND RECONCILIATION COMMISSION. COMMISSION OFFICES, SANTIAGO, NINTH DAY OF OCTOBER NINETEEN HUNDRED NINETY, 10:52 A.M.

In 1972, I ran into a neighbor of mine on the bus. I told him that I had just recently separated from my husband and that I was looking for work. He asked me if I knew how to type. I told him I did not, but that I could learn.

This person was Raúl Navarrete, a socialist militant and former member of GAP [*Grupo de Amigos Personales,* Group of Personal Friends of Salvador Allende] who would later collaborate with the intelligence services. I learned later that he had collaborated with those organizations because he was married to someone with ties to the armed forces. He was arrested in San Antonio before September 11, 1973, for transporting weapons in a vehicle; this appeared in the news at the time.

In the aforementioned conversation, Navarrete told me that he was working for President Allende's administration and that they needed a secretary starting the next day. That was how I came to be interviewed by Enrique Huerta, a socialist and the *Intendente* of La Moneda, the presidential palace.[2] He had me take a test, which I passed.

My office was next to that of "La Payita" (Miria Contreras). At first I did administrative work, astounded all the while by what was going on around me. I was not associated with any political party at the time, but in terms of casual acquaintances,

I knew more people from MIR [*Movimiento de Izquierda Revolucionaria,* Leftist Revolutionary Movement] than from the Socialist Party.

My brother had ties to MIR through an acquaintance of his, and I ended up identifying more with that movement—even though I was never a militant in it—because of what I was doing in La Moneda. I began to study, and soon I was asked to put together political education worksheets for the people in GAP.

During that time, I met people in GAP. There were members of the group living in the president's house on Tomás Moro Street on an ongoing basis, until a house across the street was set up for them. There were about 18 to 20 members of GAP there, and they served as President Allende's official bodyguards. Meanwhile, there was another garrison of 20 to 30 GAP members living in a different house, known as El Cañaveral. I remember that the name of the youngest one living there was Maximiliano.

No one from GAP was stationed at La Moneda because it was guarded by members of *Carabineros* and the Investigative Police.

When I began working in La Moneda, which was around April 1972, another one of my jobs was to pay the salaries. I was involved in most financial matters, in one way or another.

I was in GAP from May until September or October 1972, but I ended up having to drop out for health reasons. Daniel Bartulín, the doctor at La Moneda, released me from my duties there, and in different conversations with people I was asked where I wanted to work. My father had been telling me for a long time to go work for the national railroad company [*Empresa de Ferrocarriles*], and so in the end I gave in and began working there.

I had a nonpolitical position at the railroad company. I remember that the director there was Alfredo Rojas Castañeda, a militant in the *Cordillera* regional division of the Socialist Party whom I saw detained in Villa Grimaldi years later. Gustavo Saint-Pierre and Delfos López assisted him; I know nothing about them, other than the fact that they were socialist militants. The secretary, a Mr. Silva, was also a socialist.

As I said before, my work there was absolutely unrelated to politics. But just a week into it, I was asked to replace the secretary to the rail company's director general, also a socialist, by the last name of Olguín. I found out that I had been asked to do this following a recommendation from the presidency. I was told that it was a position of trust and that I was to type up the director's dictations and do other tasks that a secretary would do.

Since everyone there was in the Socialist Party at the time, they asked me to join the leadership of the rail company's political directorate, which is how I began to go to the meetings. It really was a scandal, since all we did was get together and talk; I was much more vehement at the time, and I often felt completely opposed to what was being said.

I attended political education courses at the Eighth District of the Socialist Party, which was located at 38 Londres Street in Santiago, and I always had very critical things to say there. At one point, my criticisms must have become particularly harsh, because a Mr. Polanco took me aside and told me that it wasn't right for me to just show up and criticize, and that things were just fine there. So I submitted my resignation to the rail company; this was in January or February of 1973, and I remember because we were in the midst of campaigning for the March congressional elections.

As an aside, and in response to what you've asked me, I should say that one of the members of the Eighth District, a young man named Rodolfo Espejo Gómez—his political alias was Alejandro—disappeared after 1973. He lived on Granado, or Granaderos Street, which is near Carmen Street. I don't know of any other members of that district who disappeared, except for the members of INESAL [*Instituto de Estudios Sociales para América Latina,* Latin American Social Studies Institute], which people said was the military arm of the Socialist Party. INESAL was led by Arnoldo Camú, who always entered its headquarters through a small door so as not to be seen. I know that lots of economists worked there. I remember that Fava, that is, Leonardo Moreau or "Grandpa Moreau," Sergio Muñoz, Gaspar Gómez, and Arnoldo Camú all worked at INESAL, but I don't know anything else about them.

In February 1973, I worked at the Eighth District as a polling representative, and during the congressional elections that year I worked for Altamirano in the Elmo Catalán Brigade (known by its Spanish acronym BEC) [Brigada Elmo Catalán]. The political secretary of the Eighth District was Sergio Letelier, and he was annoyed by the pressure I put on him, because I had been to the places where MIR people worked, and I raised my voice about how their reality was quite different from how they said it was.

As the congressional elections ended, I met Gaspar Gómez, a militant of the Eighth District. He had a glass eye, and he was missing an arm as well. He had lived in Germany for a long time and was something of an extremist; he'd lost his arm while handling some sort of explosive device. He was in charge of the public face of INESAL, located on the first floor of their offices at 12 Bustamante Street.

As I said, Gaspar was quite radicalized, and he invited me to work at INESAL. He said that he was putting together some sort of program in the instruction of political doctrine. We were very aware of the problems that were common at the time, like the long bread lines and the flight of dollars abroad; they were impossible to miss. There were periods of alert, confrontations with *Patria y Libertad* [Fatherland and Freedom in English, an ultra right-wing organization in Chile], and several times we had to stay at the district headquarters and keep watch. It was a difficult, uncertain period. By chance, we began to connect with like-minded people, and we began advocating for some sort of political education in the party's base.

My group advocated for the consolidation of a basis of social support for President [Allende]; we were able to attend the meetings of *Unidad Popular* [Popular Unity, the name of Allende's governing coalition]; we spent hours and hours trying to figure out who was directing the meetings; everything was very disorganized.

My brother joined GAP around 1971, and he stayed on even when I left. Later on, they transferred him to the office of the presidency, though I don't know what he worked on there, and then to COBRESAL [the state-owned copper company], to do some sort of political job. I don't know if this was a formal transfer or if it took place through personal contacts.

Following my transfer to INESAL—this was after the so-called *Tancazo*—I was asked to work for one of the party's security unit, called the Special Support Group [*Grupo Especial de Apoyo,* or GEA]. There were eight of us in the group, doing two kinds of jobs: a public one, which involved training people in different things, and a more undercover one, which involved political education and militancy. The truth is that we never reached the point of teaching classes. The group was led by Wagner Salinas (his political alias was "Silvano"), who died on September 11, 1973, in Talca; he was our link to the political commission. Actually, our real leader was Ariel Ulloa, organization leader of the Socialist Party, even though we never had any direct contact with him.

I remember that on September 11, we called Talca to inquire about Salinas, since we were on high alert and it was unlike him not to be present that day. The young man who made the call was Samuel Antonio Houston, and after he hung up, he said to me, "Comrade, Silvano died last night." He said that he had called a neighbor, who told him that Salinas had been killed at around 4 a.m. on the morning of September 11, right in front of his wife and children. Some time afterward, I ran into "Ignacio," another one of the young men in the group, who told me that they had seen Salinas's body, which was missing its nose. At the time, this was a major revelation because we still didn't realize the magnitude of what was going on.

The members of the so-called GEA were "El Gato," who lived on Italia Avenue and whose real name was Aníbal; Felipe, also known as "Sinbad the Sailor," who lived near Villa Olímpica; Ignacio, who was from Talca; my brother, whose political alias was "David"; and myself.

I know that Ignacio had also been a member of GAP. A woman named Leonor, a secretary who was married to Ricardo Ruz, was also in GEA; they used to say she had infiltrated into MIR. They say Ricardo Ruz died in a shoot-out; I heard that he died while in possession of my ex-husband's ID card, on which I was listed as his wife. In exchange for the information I gave to Ruz, he gave me a false identity, which was the one I had when I was arrested.

On September 11, we called La Moneda and spoke to Carlos Álamos. I told him the names of the people who had gone to the Socialist Party headquarters on San Martín Street: Bernardo, my brother, El Gato, Felipe, and myself. There were also about 25 construction workers there. At the time, we were armed with 4 AKA rifles and 4 smaller guns. Carlos told me to tell them to disband and that the party would be reconstituted later on; the order was to "scatter." The workers didn't want to leave, but we didn't even have sticks for them to defend themselves. Felipe gave it some thought and, since he had a family, he decided to leave; we let him go.

The only people left were Bernardo, my brother, El Gato, and myself, and we decided to head for the Cerrillos Industrial Collective; we had three cars among us, and our plan was to use our weapons if we ran into any trouble. We drove with the AKAs aimed out the windows. Just before we left, another young man from the party showed up. He had an aquiline nose, but I don't know his name. He spoke privately with Toño (Samuel Antonio Houston), who was a party official from the central committee. When he saw that we were preparing the cars, the young man said to us, "everyone go home. Ariel [Ulloa] is going to the Argentine Embassy."

When we saw that there was a communications breakdown between the party and ourselves, we asked Toño whether we should burn the headquarters down. Two people took some gas and they told us what to do, and we were leaving when we realized that they were already burning the Arauco Room of the headquarters on San Martín Street.

Our arrival at the Mademsa [metal workers] factory was very moving, because when the workers there saw us arrive with cars, AKAs, and guns; they let us through right away. Toño had told us that a group was being organized. He also said that [Carlos] Altamirano, [Secretary General of the Socialist Party], was there, which actually wasn't true. The plan had been that Altamirano would be there, but he wasn't when we arrived, and no one had seen him. We made it to Mademsa at about 9:00, and we realized that there was no plan or anything.

So we sat down and listened for a while; someone said that the President was talking. We went outside and listened to his speech, and we decided that we had to do something. We asked to speak to the leaders of the collective. A man who said he was the leader came forward and told us with great pride that they had built wrappings for explosive devices with the people from Cintax, who had built the shrapnel. Since my brother and I had received some instructions on how to use explosives, I asked him about the cones, and he answered that another comrade, whom he didn't know, on account of the practice of compartmentalizing information, had worked on them.

By this time, there were helicopters circulating overhead. The people were ready for action. Professionals from the Christian Left, among others, had shown up. We got together with a group of workers that was going to head to La Moneda. That was when someone came up and said that he knew where the socialist congressman Alejandro Jiliberto was hiding, in Villa Mexico. We went to see him, and he was basically in shock; we asked him some questions . . . we were quite overcome ourselves, although I couldn't say whether it was with anger, powerlessness, or fear. It was a very particular feeling, not being able to do what you wanted to; we wanted instructions, but his main concern was that no one else could fit in the house, and if more came in, people outside would begin to notice. So we said, "See you later, comrade." We decided to take two cars to La Moneda. On the radio they were saying that it had been bombed.

Bernardo began to worry about his wife and children, and he left us. We told him to take one of the cars and then leave it somewhere. The only people left were El Gato, my brother, and me; we made it to the corner of Agustinas Street and the highway, and we saw tanks down Agustinas. We were still armed with the four AKAs and the smaller guns. We got out of the car and walked down Agustinas to La Moneda, where we saw the flames. Everything was absolutely surrounded. No one said anything to us. We returned to the car and El Gato asked what he should do. We told him to go home. Instead, he decided to stay with us.

My brother, El Gato, and I headed for our house, stopping along the way at the homes of all those whom we'd considered friends the day before and who had garages. We wanted to hide the car, but no one wanted to help us, so we had to drop it off in an abandoned lot. We cleaned it up and, from there, walked to our house; we didn't try to hide our entry from anyone.

We stayed in our house for three days straight until the curfew was lifted. I think we were basically zombies for those three days; we were conscious, but all we did was walk around, watch television, and stare off into space.

As soon as they lifted the curfew, we headed for party headquarters. It had been completely burned down.

Since I knew where Toño lived, I went to his house, and El Gato went home. I never heard from him again; I know that El Gato's father owned a jewelry store on the corner of Italia and Irarrázaval Avenues. When the curfew was lifted, my brother didn't want to be involved anymore, and I left, because my father picked up the phone and said, "I'm going to call the Investigative Police to turn you both in."

Once I'd been arrested, I reconciled myself with the world, as well as with the myth that we'd learned in our classes that your political education can sustain you when you're being tortured. Once I was imprisoned, I realized that all thought is impossible; the only thing that can sustain you is not wanting anyone you know to be in the same situation.

When I left my house, I found Toño and I told him about my predicament; he said that since he was in charge of communications, he figured it wouldn't be too difficult to connect with more people, and that I shouldn't worry. I rented a room on España Avenue, and then I moved to Catedral Street. The party paid for all of this through Toño; it was clear to me that the money Toño was giving me was from the party.

I helped Toño out during this period as a go-between in different party-related tasks. We would go out walking in the area near the old party headquarters and La Moneda, because there, we were usually able to contact militants who had come by just for that purpose. Little by little we got a group together.

One day, Toño told me he had made contact with Gustavo Ruz through a different cell. I had seen Ruz at the central committee. He picked us up in a car on Irarrázaval Avenue, and asked us how we were; Toño gave him a brief report on the situation. He told us that things were very precarious.

Toño was very committed, very loyal, but disconnected from the party structure. I was the only one from GEA. My only contact at that time was with Toño. In the end, and unbeknownst to my parents, I began to sleep in the back bedroom of our house; it wasn't a very comfortable situation.

I also was able to get an office, thanks to a friend who sympathized with the left, where Gustavo Ruz could go and receive visitors; some nights he would even sleep there, and then leave the following morning. Before then, though, he had set up his own channels of communication. I probably saw Gustavo Ruz four or five times after we reconnected in March.

On March 17, we hadn't heard from Ruz for 10 to 12 days, because he hadn't been showing up to the established meeting places or even the alternative ones that we had decided on.

That day, we decided to call Leo's house, where we knew that Ruz had stayed for a long period of time, and we went to a place we had arranged for with Leo over the phone. I remember that I called and spoke directly to Leo. I said to him, "My son is sick. Give me the number of your sister-in-law's pediatrician." Leo answered,

"Hold on, let me go find it." I asked where, and he asked me where I was. I said that I could go to wherever he was, and he answered that he preferred to meet somewhere else. We arranged to meet at a soda fountain called "La Ruca," on the corner of Independencia and Nueva de Matte Avenues. It was about five minutes away from where we were.

There, we would meet up with Leo and ask him about Gustavo. Your address was everything back then; you were nothing if you were disconnected. This was particularly true at that moment in time, because the previous week, Gustavo had told us about the possibility of some sort of gathering in Quinta Normal. Also, Ruz had told us that he was the only member of the central committee in the country. Later on, we found out that Ricardo Lagos Salinas, a young man from the political commission, was also there. Even later, we found out about Exequiel Ponce and Carlos Lorca. At one point, I took Gustavo in his MG to meet with someone else, who Ruz said later was Exequiel Ponce.

Anyway, on March 17, Toño and I went to the meeting place we had set up over the phone with Leo. We walked into the soda fountain and asked for an orange drink. I was seated close to the door and Toño was next to me. I looked over and saw Leo walk in. He was dressed very elegantly and his eyes were absolutely red. There were men walking on either side of him. I said to Toño, "They got us. Remember that my name is Isabel Romero Contreras," and they arrested us right then. They made sure that we were unarmed. I was carrying a book in which I'd placed a letter for Gustavo Ruz. I think there had been someone with Leo in his house when I called, lying in wait and using Leo as bait to arrest more people. Leo's last name was Gómez. He was short, a bit overweight, dark brown hair, with light-colored eyes; he was a history teacher. I remember that when I was underground, Leo had asked me if I was afraid; I said I was, and he told me that he wasn't, because he had a number of friends in the Investigative Police.

Later, when I was detained at the Military Hospital [*Hospital Militar,* or HOS-MIL], I found out that Gustavo Ruz had been arrested as well. During my time in the hospital, my brother, who had been a cadet in the Military Academy, had a uniform made, put on boots and a coat, and went into the room where I was being held. He took a look at my foot, and right away I began to ask about our party comrades. It was my brother who told me that Gustavo had been arrested while he was in the AGA [*Academia de Guerra Aérea,* Air Force Academy]—before I was arrested, it seemed. He had obtained that information from a number of people who showed up at my house when they found out I'd been arrested.

When we were arrested they threw us against the wall, confiscated our belongings, used the phone at the soda fountain, and soon thereafter, a truck arrived from the Fifth Police Commissary. The two DINA [*Dirección de Inteligencia Nacional,* National Intelligence Directorate] agents, Leo, Toño, and I all got in. Toño and I were dropped off at the commissary in that truck. It was the last time I ever saw Leo.

I had gotten a look at the two agents as they had walked into the soda fountain, and I think they were members of the Investigative Police. One of them was shorter, a bit overweight, about 168–170 cm tall—although his stockiness may have made him look a bit shorter than he was—with brown hair and green eyes;

the other one was taller, at least 175 cm, black, slicked-back curly hair, and blue eyes. They must have been between 35 and 40; they called the taller one "Brindizzi," and he had some grey hair. They were the same ones who would take me from the Military Hospital to my house, and I saw them much later in 1975 at Villa Grimaldi, as members of the Purén Unit of DINA.

Once inside the commissary, we were separated, and our eyes were taped shut. At the time, I had a very short haircut and I was wearing a wig. They pushed me around a bit, but they didn't figure out I was wearing the wig. I was focused on not being recognized in the neighborhood, since I had been arrested under a false name, so I kept that name until they threatened to fingerprint me. That was when I was taken to 38 Londres Street. Ruz had given me my alias, as I said before.

After a few hours, I was taken to 38 Londres Street (Yucatán), which was known as the "*Venda*" [Blindfold]. I don't know who else went there with me, because I was lying on the floor of the vehicle. I heard them throw Toño into the back, and I didn't hear anything about Leo until I was arrested for the second time. The facility was the same one that had previously been the headquarters of the Eighth District of the Socialist Party, so I was quite familiar with it.

I stayed in the house on Londres Street for three days. There, they took our clothes off, with the excuse that "These whores hide things in their cunts." There weren't female agents searching female prisoners yet; that practice only began after the military parade took place, in the house on José Domingo Cañas Street (known as Ollagüe).

On Londres Street, they took down my information and took me to a place that I now think was the same spot where they left me later on, after I'd been shot. I was dressed, because they'd put my clothes back on after they searched me. I heard that they'd arrested other people as well. They left a guard close to us. I heard that an order had been given to verify where we lived, so we had to create a somewhat credible story on the spot. Toño and I had agreed on one a bit beforehand, to some extent, which was that we were getting to know each other, and that he had invited me out on a date; it wasn't a terribly credible story. During my interrogation I mainly stuck to the story; the false ID card led them to believe that I was someone important and that Toño was protecting me.

They went to see if I actually lived at the place I had said, and right away they came back and knew that it wasn't my real address. When their car arrived, I began to prepare myself. The interrogation began that same night, and the questions they asked me the most were "Where is Miguel?" (referring to Miguel Enríquez) [leader of MIR], and "Who are you?"

Meanwhile, and I don't remember if it was that same day or the next day, they showed me the photo of Leonardo ("Grandpa Moreau"); they showed me an old ID card with his photo and I said that I didn't know him.

This was the procedure: they took you blindfolded up to the second floor, to a bathroom, I think. There was a metal table there, or something like that. There they made you take off your clothes, saying that if you didn't do it, they would do it for you. When I saw that they were serious, I preferred to take my own clothes off. They laid me down on the "grill" [*la parrilla*] and turned on the electricity.

Then, they would ask questions and take the gag out of your mouth so you could answer them.

This was repeated several times, though I couldn't say for how long. Then they took me downstairs, and I think that was when it was Toño's turn. I heard intense screaming.

They always held the interrogations on the second floor, where there was a big bathroom with green tiles. There were other torture devices in other rooms on the second floor. There were times when they would carry me unconscious to the second floor and take me back down later in the same state. I think that another one of the rooms on the second floor was used as an office, because there were often officials walking around nearby.

The first time, I didn't recognize any of my torturers, but now I think it was Osvaldo Romo's group, because they were the ones who suspected that I was in MIR. But at the time, none of the agents were familiar to me.

As I said, they took Toño upstairs and kept him there for what must have been hours. Either the same night or the next morning, they took me back up to the second floor while they were torturing Toño, which was even worse for me. They spoke in very profane terms. I'm sure Toño was on the "grill," because at one point someone said, "Look, the dirty fucker shat himself." And another one said, "Make him eat it; make him eat it." They made Toño eat what he'd defecated, which made him vomit.

Later, they began to interrogate me about my name, my allegiances, and what I was doing with Toño, all peppered with insults and jolts of electric current. They would hit me and say obscene things, like "Let's see if she's a virgin," and then they'd stick objects into my vagina. My wig still hadn't fallen off at that point; I believe it was during that session that it finally did, and it was a big surprise for them. Since my hair was so short, one of them said, "This one must have spent time in jail," and they began to ask me about that as well. They kept beating Toño, pressuring one of us to make the other one talk. It was a long process, and I don't remember how it ended. That day they left early, because usually they left at 5:30 or 6 p.m., unless something was happening.

The next day they did the same things again, and tortured us together. Then someone I didn't know came in and said, "OK, we're fingerprinting you now." As they were putting the ink on my fingers, I told them my real name. Later, I was able to identify this person as Miguel Krassnoff, who was a lieutenant at the time, and my understanding is that he was in charge of one of the groups of DINA.

There was a young man from MIR whose alias was "El Gato," whom they tortured quite a bit at that time. I also remember a "Matías the Parrot," though I'm not sure if he was there at that time or later on, or maybe it was the night I was shot.

The third day, I gave them my real name and they went to my house to search it, but my brother had already gone through and taken any evidence, and they didn't find anything. They told my mother that I had been arrested, that I was OK, and my mother sent me a shawl. I have the impression that the people who went to my house were the same ones who had arrested me. I overheard comments from them along the lines of, "The bitch cleaned the place out [so we won't find anything]."

Something must have happened, because I heard more prisoners arrive and we were taken to Tejas Verdes. I know that Toño went too, because I heard his voice, and he answered me. This was the afternoon of March 19. I knew we were going to Tejas Verdes [one of the military regime's first detention centers located just south of the port city of San Antonio], because another prisoner told me so. Her father had a summer home nearby, so she knew her way around the area.

I wasn't interrogated at Tejas Verdes, and they brought me back to Santiago on March 27, after lunch, about 3 or 4 p.m. There were people at Tejas Verdes who were tortured badly, but things were fairly peaceful in the cabin where I was housed.

The nurses at Tejas Verdes were very moved when they saw us because the torture sessions had left their mark on me. I think that at one point they must have put the gag in my mouth incorrectly and I had bitten my tongue, which was very swollen. When the nurse asked me to open my mouth and she began to cry, I took advantage and asked her for a bunch of Chlordiazepoxide. I left the rest of my belongings in the cabin. Everyone at Tejas Verdes was from the engineering corps.

One day at Tejas Verdes, they pounded on the cabin door and said, "Luz Arce, outside!" Everyone hugged me good-bye. I had eaten very little and I felt sick—which also might have been because of the pills—so I was unconscious for most of the trip.

While at Tejas Verdes, I was able to identify a woman from MIR whose alias was "Patricia" and who was married to "Quila," a member of the MIR central committee; I think her real name was Alicia. There was another young woman from the Communist Party there too, and when she was freed, she let my sister-in-law know where I was. There was also a girl with long black hair, and I gave her my wig. She confided to me that she was the sister of one of the members of the directorate of Arnoldo Camú's apparatus, and that she worked at INESAL. There was a woman who I think was a foreigner, and she was concerned about her husband, who was there as well.

As for the officials in charge of Tejas Verdes, there was one lieutenant with very dark skin and eyes as black as olives. This man joined DINA as an official many years later. His name appeared in a book I read, which might have been one of the ones León Gómez wrote.

When I returned to 38 Londres Street, I was assigned a guard, with whom I talked informally. He asked me what I was in for, about the deaths, and it was the first time I felt like talking. At that point, they had all my personal information, but they knew nothing about my political affiliations; I had no idea what Toño told them. I think that they left Toño at Tejas Verdes.

That night, the guard said to me, "One of your comrades is here." I asked him if this man had said to him that he knew me, and his answer was that we were both socialists, and that this man's name was Giacaman. I think Giacaman was in the Military Hospital at the same time I was, and when I thought about how the rooms were distributed, I realized that he could only have been in the one next to Toño Garland.

I was only on Londres Street for that one day, until about 2 a.m. While they were interrogating me, at about 10:30 p.m., I think, there was an argument among the agents about who should interrogate me, and it ended with someone firing a shot that hit me in the foot. I don't think I even reacted. I just curled up more, and someone said, "If only she had stood up, we would have been able to get her for escaping."

Two people carried me to the basement and left me there. I think I was put in the big room that faced east. I should point out that the place I'm referring to as the basement was near the bathroom, and was about three steps lower than the first floor. The guards must have had a shift change, and a member of the Investigative Police was put in charge; I don't think he knew that I was wounded. He must have thought I was just another prisoner. When he saw me, he asked who I was and what I was doing; then he left and came back in, and said, "I can't take responsibility for this," and asked for them to make a phone call. Two of them put me into a truck, and he said to me, "Don't worry. I'm going to make it my responsibility to take you to the hospital." He saved my life, because I was sure I would bleed to death.

They took me to the Military Hospital, and he told me not to answer any questions. First they began to clean my wound and I asked a woman there to take a closer look at it. Where the bullet had gone in, in my instep, you couldn't see anything really, but the other side of my foot looked like a flower in bloom. I saw it, and I hadn't even managed to lie back down when I heard a voice that said, "Luz Arce, what are you doing here?" It was Peter Dragicevich, an anesthetist whom I knew from my days as an athlete. He looked out for me and treated me very well. I asked him if I would be able to walk again, and he told me, "I promise you'll even run again."

I woke up in a room that wasn't number 303, which was the one they'd taken me to at the beginning, but rather the one next door. I think that was where they put Toño Garland when he got there; he had been arrested and shot. This was close to the end of March. He had been shot something like five times. The only thing I asked him was whether he wanted me to wet his lips, and he told me yes. I asked him if there was anything else I could do for him and he said, "Never forget my name." He must have been in room number 304, which was where I'd been placed initially. I asked the guard why they'd moved me to another room, and he told me that it was so that I would be in the same room as my comrade. They were referring to José Tohá.

[Osvaldo] Puccio and [Julio] Palestro were in the Military Hospital when I got there, and more arrived afterward. They were in the first room. There was another room where they were holding a young man they'd brought from the AGA; he'd had all his fingernails ripped off. I was in the Military Hospital until July 7.

I was treated in the hospital by a traumatologist who helped me in countless ways: Dr. Elgueta, who was young, short, and blue-eyed, had his degree from the Catholic University, and had an office near Bustamante Park in 1981. The other doctors who saw me were Patricio Silva, who was very unpleasant, and the subdirector of the hospital, who was a dentist.

While I was in the hospital, I wasn't physically harmed, but two members of the Navy Infantry interrogated me. They stood out because they were more put-together than most soldiers.

I remember that one Saturday, an older man wearing a white woolen sweater showed up at the hospital and greeted me, and asked me my name. He sat on a couch and asked me if I knew who he was. I told him that I didn't, and so he let me know that he was "in charge of all the prisoners in this country." He asked me if I knew why I was there, and he smiled. I had no reason to think that he had any ulterior motives. He said, "All right, my girl, if you had nothing to do with these things, then you're going to be set free very soon." He seemed like a very kind man at the time. Later on, I found out that it was Manuel Contreras [leader of DINA].

After the Military Hospital, I was set free for a week, and then I was rearrested on the afternoon of July 18, 1974, on Huasco Street, between Venecia and Palermo Streets. One of the people who arrested me, a second corporal in the air force I think, was one of the men who had guarded me at the hospital. They grabbed my arm and made me walk while they had their guns on me; then they made me turn west onto Palermo Street. Halfway down, I saw a beaten-up green truck, and that's where they put me. When we got to the Grecia roundabout, they blindfolded me, but I already knew that they were taking me to Villa Grimaldi (also known as Terranova), which I recognized afterward.

While I was in Villa Grimaldi [one of the regime's most notorious detention centers], sleeping on a sort of army cot, I heard people talking about Rodolfo González. Based on the way they were describing him, I concluded that they were talking about the person who later was arrested under the name Rodolfo Valentín González Pérez. I heard about his case when I got to Villa Grimaldi, because two guards were talking about him in a disrespectful way one night; I think their exact words were, "He's in the clinic because he threw himself out of the Tower." ["The Tower" was a particularly egregious site of torture within Villa Grimaldi. Very few made it out alive.] I picked a photo of him out of a group of photos they showed me. He told me about his brother, and I thought it was a trap; you did these things voluntarily and you knew the risks, but these people . . . When I got depressed, he cheered me up. The same goes for when I was in pain; he arranged things in order to spend more time with me, and he told me about his brother, who had been given political asylum. He didn't know anything about anything; he hadn't received any sort of training, and he couldn't have been in MIR. Plus, he was the one who would carry out letters I wrote to my family when I was in the hospital and deliver me the letters and other things that they sent back. He did the same thing for Toño Garland.

I was with [González] in "the Tower" of Villa Grimaldi. He had a cast on his right foot, which makes me think that he really did try to escape. There, in "the Tower," he asked me to please tell them what they wanted to know. He told me that they "knew everything" anyway. In the hospital, he said to me several times that his brother had received asylum at the Mexican Embassy, and he asked me what I thought he should do, whom he should speak to. I suspected that he was trying to get me to give him information, and I was still denying that I was a militant at the time. During that interrogation at the Villa Grimaldi tower, they asked me what he had said to me, specifically about DINA, and the truth was that he hadn't told me anything.

At one point, Captain Raúl Carevic said to me, "But he told you about his brother." At this point, they had taken off my blindfold and I was tied up and naked, and they had burned my stomach. "Yes," I answered, "but I hope he also told you how I answered him." I constantly heard that they were going to kill [González] and that they referred to him as a traitor and called him other names as well. They asked me several times about what he had said to me about the military, and they took him away. I never saw him again. Years later, the air force officials who were members of DINA blamed me for his death. My impression is that his direct boss was Carevic, Gerardo Urrich or Ulrich, who was later sent as the military attaché to Germany in 1988, as [Rolf] Wenderoth's replacement.

While I was in "the Tower," I was tortured by Ulrich, who at one point left me in the hands of some subofficials. One of them said he knew me, but I didn't recognize him. I think he was married to a woman I had studied with at the University of Chile. I remained tied up, and I didn't eat for 12 days. Every day they came to ask me if I'd talk, and the guards would give me water or a piece of an apple.

After those 12 days, I was taken by truck to 38 Londres Street. I was put in the biggest room there, along with a number of other prisoners. The women were grouped together with our backs to the patio, facing west, while the men faced east. During that time, I was taken back and forth from Londres Street to Villa Grimaldi several times.

On one of those trips, on the way back to 38 Londres Street from Villa Grimaldi, there was another prisoner in the truck whose last name was Chanfreau. I'm not sure whether he was dead or had just fainted, and I don't know whether they carried him out with me or if they took him somewhere else, because his back was to me. One or two guards got in and said, "Get rid of this fucker." I got to Londres Street and I didn't hear anything else about him, but I know his last name was Chanfreau, because one of the guards mentioned it during the trip. Besides, La Flaca Alejandra [Skinny Alejandra] had gone out with Chanfreau, and I think she talked to him in the house on Londres Street. A lot of people were arrested during that time. I also remember that when the guards were getting into the truck, one told the other that they had intentionally run someone over with it.

I should add that my brother was being held in the same facility on Londres Street. My understanding is that he was arrested in early August 1974.

While I was on Londres Street, DINA agent Ricardo Lawrence took my brother and me to an office, and offered us our freedom; we would be sent with our family to another part of the country for a time, in exchange for our collaboration. He said that this would involve us handing over a list of our comrades; if we didn't turn them in, he would have to kill us. He ordered us cups of coffee and handed us some cigarettes, and left us alone for a while.

Actually, my brother had already given up a large amount of information about the structure of the organization, and when Lawrence called me, he really did it in order to say, "If your brother did this, you can too." When he left us alone, my brother told me he thought we should accept and give them all the information they needed. He had been tortured quite a bit.

So we agreed at that moment to collaborate with DINA in exchange for our lives, in exchange for being internally exiled and then freed. I think that my brother believed this would actually happen. They gave us paper and a pen. We made a list of militants on the periphery of the organization, people who had received asylum, people we knew had already been arrested, and lower-level party operatives.

Among the lower-level operatives we named was María Teresa, who worked in the party as a secretary, but I'd seen her in one of the detention facilities I'd been taken to in recent days.

During that period, they took me for a short time to a house that was about 15 minutes away from Londres Street. We went in through an underground entrance, and even though I was blindfolded, I could tell that it was a building with about four floors in downtown Santiago. From the basement, we took an elevator to the first floor, and from there we went up a staircase, which I could tell was made of marble and had a bronze railing, which was typical of those old buildings. María Teresa was there. Because of the list that María Teresa had made, Alejandro (Jano) and Luis Peña were arrested.

In this building, we were given cups of coffee to drink; the coffee must have been drugged, because after a while it made me lose consciousness for an undetermined period of time. While I was in that state, I heard the screams of a child, and I thought it was my son, and I begged them to stop breaking his fingers. He said to me, "Talk to them, Mommy." They tortured us there, too. That was when I realized that it was a very elegant place, with a nice desk, and in front of me there was a person who made me reach out my hands and turn a dial that would give me an electric shock. Every time one of my answers didn't satisfy them, my hands would be shocked. They were asking me questions to make me name more names.

Because of the language the people there used, I'm sure they were civilians. Later, when they came back, I recognized one of them, who told me his name was Javier. Since my name is Luz ["light," in Spanish], his password would be "shadow" [or "sombra"]. I recognized him from his voice, which was familiar to me, as a militant of Patria y Libertad, and he asked me questions about my childhood. He said, "The only thing I can tell you is that your son is OK, and that your parents are as well." They took off my blindfold, and the one whose voice I had recognized was a man named Daniel, who was the accountant at a factory that was on Venecia Street, right by my house. Now, if the other person [Javier] hadn't spoken perfect Spanish, I would have thought he was a German doctor from Colonia Dignidad, because of a photograph I saw in a magazine not too long ago. Later, they took us back to 38 Londres Street. The head of the group that took me was Juan Morales, who was an army captain at the time. I know that he was stationed in Antarctica a few years ago.

The list that my brother and I made included the names of Patricio Álvarez; Carlos Ramsis, a MIR militant who lived in the district of Independencia; and León Gómez. Since [Gómez] had turned me in, my brother said to me, "Let's give them that faggot's name." The other people had already either received asylum or gone into exile. The next morning, the list was longer. Riveros Villavicencio, Álvaro Barrios Duque, and a young man from the Communist Youth named Cañas were all arrested. Heddy Navarro was also arrested that night.

Álvaro Barrios Duque was arrested because of the list that my brother and I handed over, a list that also included Patricio Álvarez. Álvarez, meanwhile, gave them the address of Álvaro Barrios.

One time, in the period when we were already collaborating with DINA, they took my brother, La Flaca Alejandra, and me to Villa Grimaldi and told us that we each would be assigned to work with a group there. Alejandra was to be assigned to the Águila Group, led by Miguel Krassnoff; my brother was to be assigned to the Tucán Group, led by *Carabineros* Police Sublieutenant Gerardo Godoy, who was also known as "Captain Manuel" or "Marcos"; I would work with Osvaldo Romo and a man known as "El Troglo" [The Troglodyte]. But these assignments were never actually made.

Later, "Fat Romo" [El Guatón Romo], as he was known, went to arrest Óscar Castro Videla once or twice. Romo finally found him and arrested him on his third try.

Because of these problems, and also because I wasn't feeling well, the guards removed all the cot mattresses and piled them on top of me. One guard got on top of me, made me open my mouth, and stuck his gun in. He pulled the trigger several times, but no shots were fired. From that night, I remember Patricia Barceló, who volunteered to take care of me. Alejandra said later that I talked about the Chilean landscape and other nonsense for days and days.

In the midst of all this strangeness, I heard my brother protesting loudly and then receiving a beating. That was when all of us prisoners had open wounds inside our mouths from some disease that was going around. One day, a guard, the same one with the gun, gave us all coffee, which we later found out had been brewed with our own urine.

Because of these abuses, people asked [Ricardo] Lawrence to let us speak to his boss, because I guess his own authority was not enough to stop these things from happening. He must have been in a bad mood, because he made a phone call and let me speak to Marcelo Moren. Moren invited us to visit Terranova (Villa Grimaldi), and there he let us spend some time in a room where there was a young man from COBRESAL [the copper miners' association of the Atacama region]—I think his name was Joel Huaiquiñir—who had been implicated for hiding a stockpile of weapons that had been found near a mine in the north. This came out in the news later on, in August.

When I talked to Moren Brito, his attitude was condescending. He told us not to worry, that they were organizing themselves and that the organization was growing. That was when my brother told him that if we were going to collaborate with them, we deserved better treatment. After this, I returned to 38 Londres Street.

In response to your question, I know that Alejandra informed on the woman whose last name was Andreoli, and also on Cecilia Labrín Saso. The Andreoli woman was in the house on Londres Street, and Alejandra figured they were both dead.

Rodolfo Espejo Gómez was arrested around this time. I know that Espejo's name appeared in a list of 119 disappeared Chilean citizens that was published in a Brazilian newspaper. I had met him during the previous congressional elections, and I know that he was a militant member of the Eighth District of the party. But

I never saw him in the facility on Londres Street or anywhere else, except at the moment of his arrest by Osvaldo Romo, "El Troglo," and a man known as "Black Paz," whose alias was "El Pulgar" [The Thumb]. Those three agents were part of one of the teams within the Águila [Eagle] Group that was headed by Krassnoff.

I know that we also turned in a young man during that period whose last name was Cañas. His mother ran after the car that arrested him like a crazy person, all the way down Independencia Avenue.

Around the same time, I ran into Alejandra when I got back to Villa Grimaldi. By coincidence, we ended up sitting together. After a while, I realized who she was and we even tried to stay together. That was around the time that she began to collaborate with them.

A lot of members of MIR were arrested at that time, so they had me sit around and wait a lot. They didn't really notice me much at all.

I remember that during that time, Erika Hennings, a young man named Máximo Gedda, whose alias was "David" and who wore a Star of David around his neck, and Patricia Barceló, who was a doctor, were all prisoners at 38 Londres Street. Patricia Barceló talked a lot about how her father and brother were surely negotiating her release through the French Embassy.

I should also mention Sergio Tormen, who I remember being a prisoner at Londres as well.

I also remember Óscar Castro Videla, who was found alive in what had been the house of Theotonio Dos Santos (a DINA detention center located on José Domingo Cañas Street), after the military parade in September 1974. He and I were interrogated together by Miguel Krassnoff. I think that Óscar Castro must have died, because he was a person who talked a lot about his contacts with the armed forces and things like that. I saw him wearing light-colored khaki pants, a short-sleeved shirt, and his hands were tied behind his back. They took both our blindfolds off and asked if we knew each other. I said yes, and the name of an old man—a very old man, who worked in the Ministry of Education, and whose name I wasn't going to mention, due to his age—came up. I don't remember anymore what his name was, but his last name began with a "P."

Osvaldo Romo, along with "El Troglo" and another member of Romo's team, were the ones who arrested Óscar Castro. I know this because they took my brother and me with them, since we knew him. Castro lived where the Plaza Mulato Gil is now. I didn't know his address, but the DINA team already had it anyway. When he was arrested, we talked to his partner Rosa, and after that I never saw him again until Krassnoff jointly interrogated us.

Miguel Krassnoff and Lawrence, among other DINA agents, were working at 38 Londres Street. I don't know who the boss was. Osvaldo Romo and "El Troglo"— who married another DINA agent, Teresa or María Soledad, I don't remember which was her name and which was her alias—were under Krassnoff's command. There were also some *Carabineros* in the unit. Romo was Krassnoff's right-hand man.

"El Troglo," who I remember had hair like Prince Valiant, must have had the rank of first corporal. The photograph they showed me at the time had to have been of Basclay Humberto Zapata Reyes.

I spent time with another prisoner, Heddy Navarro, in Cuatro Álamos. As far as I know, she was treated well. They took her to Cuatro Álamos the second or third day after her arrest. We shared a room, and then she was quickly freed.

Sergio Alberto Rivas Villavicencio was also arrested because of the list we made; he lived on Los Nidos Street. My understanding was that Raúl Navarrete had given them his address. I think Navarrete was the person who turned me in when I was arrested the second time. Navarrete was the person who got me involved in leftist activities in the first place; he was the person who I ran into on the bus, and who got me the job in La Moneda in 1972; he began to work with DINA afterward.

Some arrests took place in one fell swoop, like when they went and got Patricio Álvarez and Carlos Ramsis, who were members of MIR, and León Gómez. They brought them in as a group and then carried them off one by one. I imagine that they were tortured, which was how all the lists got longer.

As for your question about Jacqueline Binfa, I think La Flaca Alejandra may have mentioned her name to me. I may have heard the last name Andrónicos at Villa Grimaldi. I think they were siblings, and the official version was that they had been taken to their house and that they committed suicide in the bathroom. This came out much later, two or so years later, in Villa Grimaldi.

When I was at Villa Grimaldi toward the end of 1975, I remember that Carmen Bueno, a young woman from MIR, was arrested.

As for Guillermo Roberto Beausaire Alonso, I don't know the circumstances surrounding his arrest, but I know that he was arrested. I know he had a sister, because the agents that raided his house brought us lots of cosmetics as presents, which had the label "Mary Ann" on them. I was in charge of the Villa Grimaldi canteen at this point, which meant that I distributed medications. That's what I was doing when one of the guards came and told me, "There's a problem with one of his ears; he can't hear." I went to see him; I irrigated his ears and asked his name. He said, "I'm Bill Beausaire." I also found out that Edgardo Enríquez had been arrested in Argentina and that "El Trosco" [The Trotskyist] Fuentes had been arrested in Paraguay.

Regarding Edgardo Enríquez, I should add that when I was working at DINA headquarters in 1976, a certain document came across my desk by mistake. It was a "Communiqué Via Cóndor," which was the name of the international intelligence network that DINA worked with; the document was a telex from Argentina saying that the Argentine intelligence service was placing the extremist detainee Edgardo Enríquez at the disposition of DINA.

In August 1974, during my second stint as a prisoner, I was interrogated extensively about a David Silbermann, and about a suitcase full of dollars he supposedly had. I didn't know anything about it.

As for Mónica Llanca Iturra, I can say that she spent time in my room at Cuatro Álamos in September 1974, and she identified herself as a member of the Identification Office, having worked for President Allende's government. She was very scared and was transferred away with the same group Heddy Navarro was. That day, they took a fair number of people from Cuatro Álamos who never returned. At that time, the head of Cuatro Álamos was a member of the prison guard corps whose last name was Manso, but he was known as "Morning Star" [Lucero].

There were three women in Cuatro Álamos at the beginning of September 1974 who had been brought there from the south. I think that one of them was the aunt of the two younger ones. One of the younger ones was the wife of a man who had died of carbon monoxide poisoning in a truck on a highway in the south; the other one was expecting the son of her brother-in-law. I found all this out from the older one. The one who was pregnant had a miscarriage when she was three or four months along.

After that, a very young girl arrived at Cuatro Álamos. I don't think she was a MIR militant, but she could have been a sympathizer. I don't remember if it was she or her mother who was named Vanessa. Within DINA there was a rumor that she was dead. She was 16 or 17 years old. This was September 1974. On the spot, this girl told Osvaldo Romo about a stockpile of weapons underneath a church; I'm not sure whether they were guns or explosives, but they weren't so much under the church as they were inside some offices adjacent to it. Romo and his team found them. I don't know how the girl was arrested. I don't know if it was because she'd seen how they'd tortured her mother, but she insisted that she wanted to turn over that stockpile.

In 1974, they took La Flaca Alejandra to the celebration of September 11, and afterward she went out to do some "bean counting" [*porotear,* to raid the streets]. I don't know how that turned out. I should clarify that they called it "bean counting" when they went out to the streets to find people and arrest them.

After Cuatro Álamos, I was taken to a DINA facility that they were just finishing, located on José Domingo Cañas Street. They took me by myself, and it was there that I met Ciro Torré, who was the head of the facility. Krassnoff, Lawrence, and Godoy had been assigned there as well. I observed disagreements between Torré and Krassnoff, which was the first time that I realized there was friction among the different parts of the armed forces.

To answer your question about the personalities of the agents, I can remember that Lawrence was very hard on the prisoners, until he saw that they were at their breaking point, at which time he'd stop. Krassnoff, on the other hand, was much less measured in his treatment of them. There were other officials, but they followed orders. I remember Laureani, whom they called Pablo; Lawrence, who was known as "Big Cheek" [Cachete Grande]; and Gerardo Godoy, alias "Little Cheek" [Cachete Chico], "Marcos," or "Captain Manuel."

By then I wasn't being tortured anymore, but I still received beatings from time to time. Krassnoff didn't pay much credence to my commitment to collaborate, and he never trusted me.

On October 5, 1974, when I was in the house on José Domingo Cañas Street, Miguel Enríquez [leader of MIR] died. Everyone participated in that operative—Moren Brito and all the agents, and people from other areas too. They said that Lumi Videla turned Enríquez in. The truth is that they found Miguel because of a receipt from a laundromat that was in one of the prisoners' clothing, which tipped them off about the area of the city in which they should set up surveillance.

There was lots of movement that October 5. The first thing they did was tie us all up. I was in a small room with Skinny Alejandra, Lumi, and another prisoner we called Alejandra (whose real name, I found out later, was María Cristina López

Stewart). But that morning they'd taken out the members of MIR and had left me alone in that room. Plus, a large number of reinforcements had been sent in, and the operations center that had been set up in a storage area was in front of me, separated by a swimming pool about 15 meters away, which is how I was able to listen to the radio and figure out what was going on. At the time, they used the group names Águila [Eagle] and Halcón [Falcon], which were led by Krassnoff and Lawrence, respectively.

The woman I mentioned before that we called "Alejandra" was a blond who they said was the girlfriend of Chico Pérez; they called her "Little Alejandra" to distinguish her from "Skinny Alejandra." She was short and had light eyes. La Flaca Alejandra tried to commit suicide around that time, I remember.

The agent that tied me up the day Miguel Enríquez died was known as "El Jote," and he was one of the few guards who were friendly and concerned for the women's general well-being. He had an aquiline nose, blue eyes, and long, thick eyelashes. I remember he tied me up, and I asked him what was going on. He said, "Stay quiet, because all the big bosses are here; if I can, I'll untie you later on."

Another agent I remember was known as "Face of a Saint" [Cara de Santo]. He later left DINA, and the country. I don't know what his real name was.

As for Lumi Videla, I can say that she was in bad physical condition. She thought they were going to kill her, which is why she gave me her leather jacket. After that, her clothes were distributed among the prisoners at the house on José Domingo Cañas Street, and I found out later that her body had been thrown inside the Italian Embassy.

Toward the end of October 1974, Torré was replaced as the head of the facility on José Domingo Cañas Street by Francisco Maximiliano Ferrer Lima, also known as "Max Lenou," or just "Max." He kept the same hierarchy of the groups that were already in place, except for Laureani, who was only in charge of one person. Max Lenou had gotten his alias from a spy novel that I read some years later.

Max Ferrer's trademark was "clean" intelligence. I think Ferrer got there just a few days before Lumi Videla died. Krassnoff, one of the "stars" of DINA, was in charge of her, along with Lawrence and Marcelo Moren Brito.

As for the hierarchy of the José Domingo Cañas facility, I can say that from September until early October 1974, the person in charge was Ciro Torré, a *Carabineros* police captain. His second-in-command was Lieutenant Fernando Laureani Maturana, also known as "Lieutenant Pablito." There were three operative units under them:

1. The Águila Unit, led by Krassnoff: it included Romo, "El Troglo," and "The Thumb," who had that name because he was a smaller man.
2. The Halcón Unit, led by Ricardo Lawrence, alias "Big Cheek" or "Lieutenant Cheek," and under him, the same group that had worked at 38 Londres Street, that is, I think, a man whose last name was Vera, a Mr. Tulio, who was a *Carabinero* (later I found out his name was Tulio Pereira; he's dead now), and a third one whose name was Villanueva, who'd been involved in the Calama case. There was also a woman in the Halcón Unit named Rosa

Humilde, a member of the army, and I know she had a child with Lawrence, who admitted being the father.

3. The Tucán Unit, led by "Marcos," a second lieutenant in *Carabineros* whose real name was Gerardo Godoy. A woman named María Teresa, or Soledad, was also in that group.

There were other people in the organization, but I'm not sure how they fit into the hierarchy, like Urich, who had tortured me at Villa Grimaldi, and Major Carevic, the brother of a lieutenant of the same name who died in an explosion in 1979. Both of them were members of the Purén Unit of the Metropolitan Intelligence Brigade [*Brigada de Inteligencia Metropolitana,* BIM].

Around the same time Lumi Videla was around, I found out from her that a man I knew as "El Tacho," a MIR militant, had been arrested during a shootout and had come to the José Domingo Cañas facility with a bullet wound in his rear end. I don't know what happened to him. His real name might have been Luis Fuentes Riquelme, but I'm not completely sure.

The José Domingo Cañas facility ceased to be used as a detention center about seven to ten days after Lumi Videla's death, meaning around the middle of November 1974. That was when I was taken to Villa Grimaldi along with all the other prisoners there; they had set up a large barracks for us. The José Domingo Cañas facility was then used to house single DINA men, apparently.

As for the facility located at the corner of Irán and Los Plátanos Streets, I was never there, and I only know that it was also used as a residence for single male members of DINA around 1977. The residency for women in DINA was at 214–218 Rafael Cañas Street, a house owned by Pablo Rodríguez Grez and used previously by Patria y Libertad; Rodríguez gave it to DINA as a gift, even though a formal deed was drawn up for legal purposes.

I remember Carmen Bueno among the detainees at Villa Grimaldi. They were asking La Flaca Alejandra and Carola for information about her. By this time, I was only with Alejandra and Carola; we were separated from the other prisoners. Rolf Wenderoth was stationed at Villa Grimaldi toward the end of 1974.

Villa Grimaldi functioned in the following way: Commander Pedro Espinoza Bravo, alias "Don Rodrigo," was at the head, and there were two brigades, or units, under his command: Purén, led by Major Iturriaga Neumann, and Caupolicán, commanded by Marcelo Moren Brito.

I should clarify that within the organization of DINA, when they talked about the "Brigade," they were talking about the Metropolitan Intelligence Brigade, but the term was also used sometimes as a synonym for "unit."

Beyond the structures of the aforementioned brigades, there was a subarea known as the Staff Officer Leadership Division [*Jefatura de Plana Mayor*], commanded by Major Rolf Wenderoth, who reported directly to Pedro Espinoza. The main function of this area was to handle the administrative aspects of the operation, such as sending daily reports and lists of prisoners to DINA General Headquarters [*Cuartel General*]. These lists were very detailed, with space to detail the prisoner's name, his or her charge, the number of days he or she had been detained, and any militancy.

Three people worked with Wenderoth: the first was an official from the Investigative Police, whose last name was Fieldhouse and whom I later identified as implicated in the murder of Alice Meyer, because he was the one who gave the official version of Delfín Díaz's death; he was the subprefect of the Investigations Police at the time. The second was a subofficial from *Carabineros,* a clerk. The third was Sergeant Iván Cofré, from the army, who worked as the secretary. The man from the Investigative Police was Wenderoth's right-hand man.

There were four operative units or groups within the Caupolicán Brigade: Águila (Krassnoff), Halcón (Lawrence), Tucán (Godoy), and Vampiro (Laureani).

Miguel Krassnoff commanded the first unit, Águila. Lieutenant Andrade (his real name) was assigned to the group around that time as Krassnoff's second-in-command. There were two groups within that unit: Águila One and Águila Two. I'm not sure whether Osvaldo Romo continued to be part of the Águila groups, but El Troglo and The Thumb did. Águila's main focus continued to be MIR, and it worked in coordination with Halcón—led by Lawrence—which intervened in "important" situations. When that happened, Tucán was put in charge of dealing with the other political parties.

The second group, Halcón, was led by Ricardo Lawrence, and was divided into two operative groups, known as Halcón One and Halcón Two. Lawrence was in charge of Halcón One, with Rosa Humilde as his second-in-command. Halcón Two was known as the "Fat Guys' Group" [El Grupo de los Gordos], and I think all the people in it were *Carabineros* police subofficials. I remember one was named "El Gino."

The third group, Tucán, was under the command of *Carabineros* Second Lieutenant Gerardo Godoy, and was also divided into two groups. Tucán One was headed by Godoy, and included the female agent María Teresa or Soledad. (Also known as Marisol, she was the same woman who married "El Troglo" in 1978 or 1979). I don't know the names of any of the agents in Tucán Two.

The Vampiro Group was headed by Fernando Laureani Maturana, alias "Lieutenant Pablo" or "Pablito." This group had been formed thanks to the initiative of Marcelo Moren, to give Laureani, who had lost prestige following a series of foibles, a chance to redeem himself. Agent Nibaldo Jiménez, also known as "The Bird" [El Pájaro], who worked in the Investigative Police, worked as his driver. A *Carabineros* subofficial named Jara was in the group too, as was an Investigative policeman—I don't remember his name, but he was blond, tall, and thin.

I don't know too much about Purén, the other unit, which was under the command of Iturriaga Neumann (I don't remember his alias). I do know the names of some of the officials that were in it, even though I don't know how they were divided up within the unit. At that time, there was Major Raúl Carevic, Captain Manuel Vásquez Chahuan, Lieutenant Marco Antonio Sáez, Lieutenant Rolando Mosqueira (he was implicated in the Letelier case since he was the official that replaced Fernández Larios), the *Carabineros* official Ingrid Olderock, and the army official Germán Barriga.

All the units worked together in exceptional situations, sometimes even with the support of the Purén Brigade, like when they attempted to arrest Dagoberto Pérez in his house on Venecia Street.

Wenderoth's group wasn't directly involved in any arrests, but I do know that he kept his ear to the ground and knew what was happening.

When Wenderoth arrived, the treatment we were receiving was still constantly in flux, because Krassnoff's people never accepted me, and they beat me whenever they could. Wenderoth got along well with Alejandra; Tulio got along with both Alejandra and Carola; and Pablito and Wenderoth got along with me, which is how I ended up working in Wenderoth's office.

There was a period when it was common to find lots of boxes of large-format photographic paper in the MIR safe houses that got raided. But when the boxes were opened, all the paper inside them was exposed, so it couldn't be developed or reused. So they began to suspect that MIR was storing information and documents by partially developing photographs of the information and then leaving them for others to use the chemicals needed to finish the developing process later, in more secure conditions. DINA, which was unfamiliar with this system at first, proceeded to open the boxes, which exposed the paper to light and made it impossible to develop. They found so much of this material that they decided to set up a darkroom in the lower part of "the Tower" at Villa Grimaldi, with high-quality equipment that had been stolen from MIR over a period of time.

Once they began to develop these documents, they discovered, among other things, a personal letter from each one of the four MIR leaders who appeared holding a press conference in the Diego Portales Building. In these letters, written to Pascal Allende and the Chilean Political Directorate abroad, they took responsibility for the press conference and other acts of collaboration with the military government and placed themselves at the mercy of the MIR leadership. I found out that the discovery of these letters led to two of these four leaders being rearrested; I personally saw them arrive at Villa Grimaldi in chains and handcuffs.

The guard known as "El Jote" [The Womanizer] was always nice to me and brought me cigarettes and things like that. I think I saw Liliana Walker around that time, and I don't think she looked at all like the Liliana Walker who has appeared in the press so much lately.

At Villa Grimaldi, I heard from an in-the-know agent that Liliana Walker was there, and I saw her once as well, which is why I don't think it's the same person who was in the papers not too long ago.

By the way, I'd like to take a moment to say that last year, when I was working with Wenderoth at a school in Maipú, I asked him what had happened with the Letelier situation. He was calm about it and told me that he hadn't had anything to do with it, and that it had been a pansy act on the part of Pedro Espinoza to mention him in an affidavit about the case while he was in custody at the Military Hospital. Wenderoth never told me that Letelier's assassination had been planned right there inside DINA. All I remember is that at one point, when we were at DINA General Headquarters, he left, came back red in the face about two hours later, and locked himself in his office. Later, he had me come in and asked me to close the door behind me; he then took a complete dossier of information about the [Orlando] Letelier assassination—which still hadn't been revealed in the newspapers—out of his briefcase, which was on his desk. But "Mamo" [Manuel Contreras] had seen it already. The briefcase contained photos, declarations, and other information about the crime. [Eugene] Propper's upcoming visit to Chile had already been published in the papers by then. [Propper was one of the lead attorneys on the Letelier case.]

I think that Wenderoth knew about a lot of what was happening in the country, and even though he didn't tell me what he had spoken about to Contreras, in the conversation we had following those two hours he spent outside the office, he gave me the impression that DINA was involved in Letleier's death. He said, "What are we going to do now?" and pounded the desk. He was in a terrible state.

As is well known by now, four detained MIR leaders appeared in the media in early 1975, giving a press conference at the Diego Portales Building. This press conference was planned by DINA. To this day, I'm convinced that Pedro Espinoza Bravo was the one who orchestrated this conference, because he bragged that he had begun to do intelligence work.

There was lots of activity before the press conference. In the two weeks leading up to it, the four members of MIR who were collaborating, plus two men known as "Coño Alberto" and "Chico Santiago"—the latter's real name was Lautaro Videla Moya—and another, lower-level MIR member who was short, curly haired, and had shifty eyes, were all moving around a lot. This last young man received protection from "La Pepa," a *Carabineros* second lieutenant whose real name was Julia. In all, there were seven members of MIR collaborating with DINA, and they were all living in the room next to ours.

These seven young people, plus Krassnoff and Pedro Espinoza, and sometimes Max, worked on the press conference for at least two weeks. Since our door was always open, we could see that they were preparing extensively. They spent many hours together, particularly Krassnoff. The point of the conference was to demoralize MIR.

The press conference was held in February, but those young people were imprisoned for quite a while after that. All that photographic material wasn't found until after the press conference, and by then they had been set free. But when they found all the documents that were to be sent abroad, at least two of them were rearrested, and I saw them when they arrived at Villa Grimaldi. I know that at one point Carola stopped and read what she was developing, and she saw the signature of one of them, and went right away to let her bosses know. Marco Antonio (Hernán Carrasco) and Lucas (Humberto Menanteaux) arrived in chains the very next day. Less than a week later, the clerk from the Staff Officer Leadership Division (a *Carabineros* subofficial who I mentioned earlier) told me that they had killed them and then disposed of different parts of their bodies all around one area of the Andes. But rumors like this spread among the prisoners all the time.

I do remember that they took Marco Antonio out of the truck in a very showy fashion, and it was clear that they had beaten him up quite a bit. Marco Antonio and Lucas arrived together. Carola had found the information about them late the night before, and by midmorning the next day they'd been arrested. I saw them come in, because the Investigative Police official, the second-in-command at the Staff Officer Leadership Division, came in and said to me, "Come with me, I want you to see something." So I went and looked out from the balcony of the office at Villa Grimaldi, and the truck was parked right in front of me. There was a green canvas cover on the back of it. I thought it was strange that Purén brought them in, rather than Caupolicán. Two or three days later—that same week—the clerk told me that they'd been killed and thrown off a cliff. I never saw the other two. I should add that DINA handpicked the four who showed up on television.

Now that a video of this press conference has been shown to me, I can say that one of the people on the screen is Miguel Krassnoff; he can be seen for just a few seconds, but he was there in the room. I also think I saw the face of Marcelo Moren, but I can't be sure.

I know that after the photographic material was developed, an operation took place that intercepted MIR's line of communication with its allies abroad; DINA would take these documents, develop them, copy them, and then replace them, sending the material abroad as if nothing had happened.

There was one moment when Pedro Espinoza called us in one by one and asked me, "Even though you're a socialist, how would you communicate with MIR?" His second question was, "What do you think you could do to demoralize the militants in your party?" These questions took me by surprise, because he knew that I'd been detained too long to be able to answer them. I told him that I would put information I wanted them to have in some foreign publication. Espinoza took note of this; my impression is that the intellectual of the group in intelligence matters was Krassnoff.

In December 1974, there wasn't an archive at Villa Grimaldi yet, so all declarations were sent to DINA General Headquarters. By 1976, however, the declarations were placed on microfilm and stored in the subdirectorate. You couldn't get to them if you didn't have access to the subdirectorate. I know that these microfilms were incinerated later on, because in 1978 a computer center was set up in an apartment on the corner of Vicuña Mackenna and Belgrado Streets. Once this unit—which was called L-5—was created, all the declarations were entered into computer databases.

They contracted with a company called COMDAT, a representative of Basic Four, to buy the mainframe computer. Starting in 1978, the contents of the microfilms were digitized thanks to four or five data entry personnel, and I worked on this project as well.

I entered data into two systems: one database was of detainees, and I erased my brother's and my names from this list with the authorization of Ítalo Seccatore, who calls me once a month to this day; another database was called LIDES [*Listado de Desaparecidos*], which was short for List of the Disappeared. By this point I had a bundle of photocopies of press declarations from the Vicariate of Solidarity—or at least I was told that that's where they were from.

When I arrived at my new assignment at the General Headquarters in February 1976, I also had material that had been stolen from the Pro-Peace Committee [*Comité Pro Paz*, an entity of the Catholic Church that advocated for human rights during the dictatorship]. I know that this material was stolen by DINA, specifically by the Caupolicán Unit. All of it had been in storage somewhere, and it only came out when DINA was restructured.

The subdirector of DINA at that time was Jerónimo Pantoja, whose nickname was "Black Plum." He was the uncle of Cecilia Pantoja, also known as

"Cecilia the Singer" [La Cantante Cecilia]. I know that Jerónimo Pantoja was in CNI until 1980.

In response to your question, I did meet Michael Townley [an American who worked closely with DINA and who plotted various international assassinations] following Contreras's resignation from DINA. Contreras introduced me to Townley so that he could make me an alias that I'd be ready to use when the time was right.

As for Manuel Contreras Sepúlveda, the former director of DINA, I know that in addition to coordinating and planning the work of the service, he was a very close personal collaborator with General Pinochet. He also oversaw a number of ongoing operations, in which I would imagine that he worked with a series of special ops groups.

I found out from Wenderoth that "Mamo," as Manuel Contreras was called, had written out a confession while he was under arrest in the Military Hospital for the Letelier case. I know that Wenderoth has a copy of it, and that Contreras talks about everything in it, starting with the day they began to plan the military coup. Wenderoth told me that he hadn't read it or even taken it out of the envelope it came in.

Wenderoth also told me that Mamo had told him that there were five copies of the confession, three of which were outside the country. I think that everyone in the army knows about those five copies.

Contreras wrote out this confession because he felt betrayed by General Pinochet, who had taken advice from a number of people that Contreras had told him over and over were not acting in his best interest, like Jaime Guzmán [one of Pinochet's closest economic and ideological advisors].

Wenderoth also told me that Mamo had given him the "DINA Seal," which was apparently made of steel, and that he had hidden it near the river by Tejas Verdes in a place where only he knew where to find it. Wenderoth didn't usually tell me things, but last year when we were working together at the school in Maipú, he told me all of this, and I think he has the copies of Contreras's confession under lock and key. I think he has a perfectly clear idea of whom he wants to give them to.

As for the photos you've shown me of the people who disappeared in December 1974, I can say that I know about María Teresa Eltit. Krassnoff and other members of his team asked the girls (Carola and Alejandra) about her. I can add that she was imprisoned in the room with the other women; from something La Flaca Alejandra told me, I got the idea that she was in very bad shape.

At Villa Grimaldi, the most common torture technique was the use of electricity, and in the area known as "the Tower," their specialty was to string people up and then burn their skin.

"Fat Romo" specialized in raping the female detainees, and he preferred the heavier ones. "El Troglo" never forced himself on anyone; his technique was to pressure and pressure women to say "yes," and they always did.

There were mass arrests at that time, and they would ask La Flaca Alejandra and Carola for information about the detainees; they participated quite a bit in those arrests. I didn't participate in the arrests at that time, which is why I don't have much information about it.

I do remember the name of one detainee, Sergio Lagos Marín, but just his name and nothing more.

I also remember Claudio Thauby, whom they called "El Gato" [The Cat], a socialist militant from the Cordillera regional organization of the party. I know that he was a classmate of my brother and Fernando Laureani in the Military Academy. He was tortured extensively, because he was considered a traitor to the armed forces and the army. They showed him to me at one point to see whether I knew anything about him. He was first interrogated by Krassnoff, and since he was a socialist, he was probably passed over to Lawrence.

They made a number of cuts in Thauby's chest using a bayonet; they cut a circle with a cross inside it. Laureani told him "that he was going to learn how traitors died." Laureani would hold the bayonet in his hands and make him lift up his head with the point of the blade on his chin.

Thauby was alone in one room, sitting on the floor with his hands tied behind his back; his head was down, but he was alive.

As for the detainee whose last name was Robothan, I'm sure I saw his name in the reports of the Staff Officer Leadership Division that I made for DINA head-quarters, but I never saw him personally.

The name of another detainee, Anselmo Osvaldo Radrigán Plaza, was definitely on one of those lists as a DINA detainee around that time, but I never saw him either.

I also remember someone I knew as "El Coño Alberto," who had both Chilean and Spanish citizenship. He was a dentist who was imprisoned at Villa Grimaldi since before the press conference, and because he was the smartest one of the group, he was the one who went the deepest into political detail at the conference. This satisfied Krassnoff, who wanted the conference to be believable to the militants of MIR.

As for Carmen Bueno Cifuentes, I know that she was imprisoned in Villa Grimaldi around that time too, because members of the Águila group were constantly asking Carola and Alejandra about her. But I know she was arrested with a man, or maybe he'd been arrested just before or just after she had, but they were together. The Águila group was concerned about some sort of international link they may have had. It is established that in accordance with the information that this commission possesses, it was Jorge Müller Silva who was arrested with Carmen Bueno Cifuentes.

I also remember a man known as "Joel," whose real name was Emilio Iribarren and who made an agreement with Krassnoff around that time to collaborate with the DINA in exchange for the release of his girlfriend. They had both been arrested, along with their baby, who suffered from Down's Syndrome; she and the child were released. Later, I worked with Joel and I remember that since we were both good at drawing, we created a series of false documents that could serve as credentials from different public administration offices, and be used to gain entry into private homes in order to search them. At one point, we created a signed warrant from *Carabineros.* Joel and I spent time together in Villa Grimaldi until about the end of July 1975, at which time I was sent to Marcoleta Street. I received some vacation time for Christmas of that year; but since my salary was so low, I asked a cousin of mine for a job during the month of December. While I was working there, I saw Joel pass by outside the window. So I suppose he was freed, and I never heard from him again.

Another person I remember was a MIR militant I met in early 1974, whose real name was Hugo Martínez González, alias "Tano." He was introduced to me by Ricardo Ruz Zañartu, alias "Alexis." I saw Tano with a bullet wound in his right hand at Villa Grimaldi, in what they called the "Corvi Houses" [Casas Corvi]. I pushed for them to let me give him antibiotics, because the condition and temperature of his wound indicated that it was seriously infected. I received authorization after using the argument that he needed to be kept alive for a few more days so he could continue offering information.

A few days later, I found one of his sandals on the ground on the patio, an artisanal type of sandal that I hadn't seen before, so I checked the report from the Staff Officer Leadership Division. He didn't appear as a detainee at Villa Grimaldi, so I think that he died. I also know that he had family members in the navy, and that he was a militant of MIR.

As far as I can remember, the night of December 31, 1974, we were given dinner at about 21:00 hours, and a few minutes later, the official on duty (named Pedro), who was a member of the Investigative Police, came into the room. This official talked to me informally, telling me that he wanted me to go to his office, because there were some matters related to some of the detainees that he wanted to talk to me about. I told him that I had expressed orders from then-Captain Ferrer and Major Wenderoth that any requests related to my personal activities in the barracks had to go through them. Despite that, he had the guards take me to his office at about 22:30.

When I got to his office, he said to me that it was New Year's, a holiday, and that he thought it needed to be celebrated in a special way. He had a tray ready with a bottle of whiskey and two glasses. That was when he called one of the guards on duty, whose name or alias was "Samuel," and told him the same thing, giving him his authorization to hand out bottles of wine and liquor to the staff on duty.

It was a difficult experience for me personally, because by about 3:30 a.m., this individual began trying to take advantage of me. At one point, the whiskey ran out and he took out a bottle of pisco. I told him that I didn't like liquor, and that he should drink more of it himself; I said that the truly "macho" officials drank until, in their words, they "downed the whole thing."

From what I heard outside the office in the following hours (machine gun fire, women and guards screaming and yelling), I think some of the people working there had taken the women out of their cells. I could tell from the women's screams that they were being raped.

Meanwhile, I asked the guard whose office I was in for permission to go to the bathroom right next door, and when I got back, he was pouring himself more pisco with his back to me. On an impulse—it wasn't my intention—I took one of the metal DINA seals on the desk and I hit him with it on the back of the neck. I don't know if it was a very strong blow, or if it was all the liquor he'd drunk, but he fell to the ground. At that point, I took advantage and took some handcuffs out of a drawer where I knew there were some, and I cuffed his hands behind his back.

When I realized what kind of situation I'd gotten myself into—any guard who came in could have easily shot me—I locked the door from the inside, grabbed the telephone book, and I called a number that I found out later belonged to the government switchboard. Luckily, then-Captain Ferrer was at home celebrating New Years, and was shocked to hear what I quickly told him. I expressed to him my fears, and then he handed the phone over to a friend of his, an official who spoke to me for about 15 to 20 minutes until Max, Wenderoth, Moren Brito and Pedro Espinoza arrived with some military personnel to take charge of the situation.

I remember that when I was speaking to that other official on the phone—I don't know what his name was, because he wasn't in DINA—I asked him what to do if a guard came into the office where I was. First he asked me if I knew how to handle a gun, and then he said to try to get the guard to talk to him via intercom, but that if he got violent, I should shoot, and the official would take responsibility. Luckily, this didn't come to pass.

A doctor arrived with the rest of the military personnel, and he examined me right there in the office, gave me a sedative, and then went off to examine the other female detainees.

When I woke up the next day, I was taken to the offices of Colonel Espinoza, who had me give a detailed declaration. He told me that all the personnel implicated in the incident would be let go, and made some comments about "the honor of the men in the armed forces." He was the one who told me that one of the women, who was in an advanced stage of pregnancy, had been raped and had subsequently had a miscarriage and had to be taken to the DINA clinic.

A few hours later, Pedro Espinoza, Max, and Wenderoth came to my room and asked me to step out for a moment. They took me to the official who'd been on duty the previous night, and he was handcuffed, blindfolded, and chained. They took him to the "Corvi Houses" [Casas Corvi] after that. That man, whose name was Pedro, was discharged from DINA, but then he was welcomed back into the Investigative Police with a great deal of fanfare. I heard a few years back that he was a prefect in Maipú.

I also heard that they fired from DINA a number of guards who had been in Villa Grimaldi that night. Later, I found out that the woman who had lost her baby had recovered—at least physically—and had returned to her cell or wherever it was that she was being held.

As for me, the treatment I received from the Investigative Police changed, because they blamed me for that official's discharge from the DINA. That was when I realized that the sexual exploitation of detainees was a frequent phenomenon, and even considered normal.

In about January or February 1975, the Caupolicán and Purén Groups participated in a massive operation, with aerial support from army helicopters; the goal was to arrest Dagoberto Pérez Vargas, who lived on Venecia Street along with Nelson Gutiérrez—both were leaders in MIR. Their house was on the southern side of the 1700 block of that street, between Freirina and Quezada Acharán Streets; it was the first house that could be directly accessed from Venecia Street. I think that some leftist militants had lived in that house before they did; my understanding was that the mother was a communist and her youngest son was a member of one of the more tangential sectors of MIR. This woman and her son sought asylum and put the house up for rent.

The operation definitely failed, but DINA took possession of the house, and no one ever tried to get it back from them. The oldest son of that family was involved in drug trafficking. I know that the house was used as a detention center in January or February 1977. Since the house was given to the Halcón Group, the person in charge there was Ricardo Lawrence. I know this, because at one point I was asked to go to the facility to take a look at some documents they'd found on some detainees from MAPU [*Movimiento de Acción Popular Unitario*, Popular Unitary Action Movement]—actually some division of it called PPR [*Partido Popular Revolucionario*, People's Revolutionary Party]. These detainees were being held at that facility.

I can also say that there was an incident at that facility at one point during 1977—I don't remember which month—where it came to light that a young man from the neighborhood who was mentally ill had been raped repeatedly by a DINA agent. This, of course, created a huge scandal in the neighborhood, and the facility ceased to be used as a detention center. It remained vacant for a time, and then it was handed over to a DINA agent named Mirta Espinoza Carrasco (her real name); her formal job was as a secretary, but I know that she travelled abroad several times on DINA official missions—one time in particular to the United States. She went to live in the house along with her family. It was common for houses to be "laundered" by having an agent live there with his or her family. The people who would definitely be able to offer more information about this, with exact dates, are the family of a young man whose last name was Cañas, because they live in that area. Cañas, a member of the Communist Youth, was arrested in August 1974, by Osvaldo Romo and held at 38 Londres Street.

As for the documents they confiscated, I should say that a member of Patria y Libertad was working in the Halcón Group as an analyst of leftist political parties. I don't remember his name, but I do know that there's a plaza with his name in front of the Industrial School as you're coming east into Santiago from Cerrillos. This young man was later killed (in 1977) by Eduardo Garea, who was also a civilian DINA employee. In the internal report of the incident, it was established that Garea accidentally shot him.

In January 1975, a group of MIR leaders from Valparaíso was arrested and taken to Villa Grimaldi. Among them, I remember Carabantes, Eric Zott, and a man they called "In Parentheses" [Entre Paréntesis]. Just a few days after his arrest, Eric Zott was taken to Colonia Dignidad [a secret colony in Chile's Maule region that was used as detention center and founded by ex-Nazi Paul Schäfer]; I think several officials travelled there with him, including Ferrer ("Max"), who asked me at that point if I wanted to go there with him, almost as if it were a vacation. He talked to me about the area, near Parral, as if it were paradise, and said that they were taking some "MIRachos" there. I didn't want to go, so La Flaca Alejandra went; she later told me that she'd been to the place where they'd interrogated the detainees. She said they had taken Eric Zott, who I guess stayed there; she also told me that they'd held her in a cell and asked her for information about Zott, which, she thought, they interrogated him about later. They didn't take "In Parentheses" on that trip; he stayed at Villa Grimaldi.

I think I saw the name "Carabantes" on one of the daily reports.

I think there must have been some sort of arrangement with Colonia Dignidad in those days to take people down there. I think Max joined the group that did that, in order to practice so-called clean intelligence. He seemed enthusiastic when he talked about taking the "MIRachos" down there, and said that interesting things were happening at the Colonia, which is why I think that he was talking about this clean intelligence phenomenon.

I do know that the Colonia was where the officials closest to Manuel Contreras, like Wenderoth and Moren Brito, used to go for their summer holidays, as recently as last year. I've even heard that there's a copy of Manuel Contreras's confession at Colonia Dignidad.

Alejandra also told me that there was a barracks of rooms in the Colonia, painted white on the outside, with small windows at the top, and that she had eaten and slept there. In response to your question, she never said anything about strange noises and didn't mention anyone else.

At one point, I asked Wenderoth if there was any kind of relationship between the Colonia and DINA. He just laughed and didn't say anything to me about it, because his practice was to never talk about those things with anyone.

In response to your question about Nelson Haase, I think I recognize that name from 1976 or 1977 as the commander of the DINA barracks on Bilbao Street, the outside of which had a sign advertising a false business called Implacate.

As for Alan Bruce Catalán, I remember him as a detainee at Villa Grimaldi. I saw his name on the reports I've mentioned. I saw Alan Bruce one time when they were taking him to one of the offices, and I remember that Marcelo Moren Brito was angry because Bruce was his nephew, so this arrest was personal. I don't remember Moren saying to me what he was going to do with him.

When we moved to a better location inside Villa Grimaldi, to a little cottage there, we lost sight of the detainees. I think we moved there around February 1975, and stayed until July of that year. Wenderoth was still at Villa Grimaldi at that time.

In early 1975, one detainee was taken to Villa Grimaldi in his car, which was a very nice car, like a Mustang, big and green, with curvy lines and four doors; the car was painted a bright orange color and Moren Brito wanted to affix some machine guns to it. In the end, they let him keep it.

Looking at photos [you are showing me] of people arrested around February 1975, I recognize Alfredo Rojas Castañeda, whom I knew from when I worked at the rail company. Since DINA knew that I had worked with him as his secretary, I was taken along on his arrest, which took place early in the morning before he was to leave for work. Romo went, which meant that Krassnoff's unit was in charge of the arrest. We arrived at a two-story house at the end of a street. His mother opened the door and Romo asked for Alfredo; she let him in. When Alfredo came down, Romo asked him to come with him. Alfredo didn't resist at all, and Romo even added, "Go in your own car, just so you can see that you won't have any problems." So a DINA agent drove Rojas's car, with Rojas in the passenger's seat.

Two or three days later, someone from Krassnoff's group asked me to go with him, and he took me to Alfredo. Alfredo was in the bathroom of Villa Grimaldi, which at that time was fairly bare-bones. He was sitting down, with his hands and feet bound, and it was clear that he had been beaten or tortured. He looked ill and worn out. The agent told him, "All right, you're going to begin to collaborate now," and Rojas shook his head no. He looked at me and didn't say anything. That was the only time I saw him, other than when he was arrested.

When I left Villa Grimaldi in July 1975, Alfredo Rojas's car was still there. It must have been used by one of the lower-level groups, run by Marcos or Pablito. The person who had taken me to see Rojas Castañeda was a subofficial in Krassnoff's unit.

Looking at the list of people who witnessed Rojas Castañeda's arrest, I recognize Gladys Díaz Armijo, who was in "the Tower" then, although I never saw her. If you were there, it meant you were being intensely tortured. I also remember Alfonso Guerra, whose name I saw in the reports to General Headquarters. The same goes for Juan Patricio Negrón Larré.

Germán Barriga, an army captain, arrived around March 1975, and took charge of the Purén Brigade's repression of the Socialist Party.

Around the same time, Moren Brito, the commander of the Caupolicán Unit, channeled all the efforts and resources available to him into the persecution of MIR. Repression of the other leftist parties, the Socialist Party in particular, would be up to Purén from then on.

That was about the time I remember that the Purén Brigade carried out a raid against some Christian Democrats; one of them was of Yugoslavian descent and was trying to go into business with a gold mine.

I remember a man named "Mauro" from the period around March 1975, but nothing else.

Another piece of information I heard around then was that they executed a detainee by injecting him with the rabies virus. I think that was about the time I went to work in Wenderoth's office. I don't know if "El Trosco" Fuentes was the one who did it, but he might have been.

In terms of cars that were being used at the time, I can remember three gray Fiat 125s, which were used by Max, Krassnoff, and Lawrence. Each one of them had his own driver.

Each group had a car, and they all had access to other vehicles as well. Some of the C-10 trucks from the previous period were still in use; there were red ones, green ones, and light blue ones, and a green canvas could be placed over the back of them. These C-10s were used often to move prisoners around from one center to another, and less to make actual arrests.

The Purén Brigade had three gray Fiat 125s, which belonged to Germán Barriga, Marco Antonio Sáez and Rolando Mosqueira. Barriga had the rank of captain then, and the other two were lieutenants. I also remember a red Fiat 125 in the Purén Brigade, which was assigned to Raúl Carevic; it was the only red Fiat in Terranova. Romo used a truck at first, and then later on he used Krassnoff's gray Fiat 125 when Krassnoff received a white Fiat 125.

That was around the time when the Purén Brigade began to work on a project that Mamo Contreras had given them, which consisted in carrying out a study to lay the groundwork to garner more popular support for the government. At least some of the points of the Chacarillas speech [a 1978 speech that was one of the military regime's founding documents] were taken from this project. Contreras's idea was to create a massive groundswell of support for Pinochet's leadership. I didn't participate in the project, but I know that Alejandra and Carola did.

I can remember that one night in January or February 1975, before the night guard finished its shift, Lieutenant Laureani told me that he could take me to see my son, on the pretext that we would be going out to make some arrests. On the way there, our car was hit on the corner of Bellavista and Pío Nono Streets by a bus that was heading west. "Pablito," his driver, was mostly concerned with hiding the weapons in the car. He locked the automobile and we then went in a *Carabineros* vehicle to a station on the corner of Dávila and La Paz Avenues. He, Pablito, and I, went in that vehicle. I was worried they would find out that I'd been detained, because I didn't want to go to jail, and so I stayed with Pablito.

There was a kitchen inside the main house of Villa Grimaldi that was run by Corporal Rojas, or "Rojitas"; I'm not sure what part of the armed forces he was enlisted in.

There were also some trucks at Villa Grimaldi, for refrigeration, but they weren't part of the facility's fleet of vehicles. Some of them were unmarked, and others had a blue logo on them. I don't remember how often they appeared.

Every guard at Villa Grimaldi had an AKA rifle with two clips and an unlimited supply of loose ammunition. Plus, each agent had a smaller gun for personal use. There weren't any standard issue weapons; most of them had been confiscated from members of MIR. The officials had AKAs, and each unit had a certain number of them, but no more than four or five, I think. There was also a cabinet with five additional AKAs in the office of the on-duty official. In 1976, all personnel received a standard handgun after DINA purchased a large quantity of 7.65 mm Llama brand guns, made in Brazil. Contreras, being the director, had his own arsenal.

In March 1975, I was still detained at Villa Grimaldi, but I was separated from the other prisoners by then, because I was in a position of some trust with some of the DINA agents.

The same hierarchy in Terranova (or Villa Grimaldi) stayed in place throughout 1975, and only at the end of that year did changes begin to take place: Pedro Espinoza went to Brazil, and was replaced by Marcelo Moren Brito as head of the facility. I think he remained in that job definitively—or, at least, I never heard about him being replaced later on.

Espinoza must have left in March of the following year. When he returned to Chile the next December, he was stationed at the General Headquarters as head of the Department of Operations.

As for your question about the detainee Adolfo Ariel Mancilla, I should say that I never saw him, but I remember his name on the list of detainees at Villa Grimaldi.

I also remember that they arrested a MIR militant in Concepción toward the end of 1974, a doctor who was dark-skinned and relatively short—he couldn't have been any taller than 170 cm. He had an ulcer, and I think he must have died, because he was in very bad shape.

Some of the detainees at Terranova or Villa Grimaldi were housed in some small barracks that had been constructed for prisoners; they were known as the "Corvi Houses." They remained locked inside them and never came out.

There was also a larger room with several beds from the army, and people were tied up and kept there.

As for the prisoner known as "Trosko" Fuentes, whom they also called "El Pichicho" [The Little Guy], I can say that they shaved his head and that he contracted a number of diseases that left him in terrible physical condition. He was arrested in Paraguay and brought to Chile. Marcelo Moren Brito, as chief of barracks, was responsible for him at Villa Grimaldi.

I spent the days in Wenderoth's office sitting at a desk all day and typing out memos, letters, and other documents like that, including the list of detainees that Wenderoth personally wrote out and sent to the General Headquarters. The other women who enjoyed privileges similar to my own, Alejandra and Carola, spent their days in the photo lab.

In response to your question about how decisions were made about what to do with each detainee, including whether to execute them, I should say that I don't know anything beyond what I heard from the guards, like "We have to kill him," or "We're going to kill you." They did the same thing with us, and the possibility of our being killed was never far off; in the José Domingo Cañas facility, we knew people died when their clothes got distributed among the prisoners, and at Cuatro Álamos, we knew because the people who were killed had names assigned to them that corresponded to places in Chile. For example, I heard that they called Mónica Llanca, who disappeared in 1974, "Puerto Montt," which was some sort of code to signal where she'd ended up.

The procedure for arresting people was fairly arbitrary at the beginning of 1975. People would be arrested without any charges. By the end of the year, though, orders came down to charge the detainees formally. Moren Brito wasn't very happy about this, because his technique was to carry out raids, arrest people, and make up charges against them later on.

There were times when people were arrested and didn't appear in the reports, so that the director of DINA didn't even know who had been detained. I remember one time when I said to Manuel Contreras, "I saw Ricardo Lagos arrested," and he answered that I was wrong, but added right away that he would check to make sure. At that time, I thought that people weren't telling him everything. Today, though, I think that the leadership of DINA had to have known when a detainee disappeared. Moren Brito was constantly asked to go to DINA General Headquarters, for example.

At one point, I saw Ricardo Lagos Salinas and spoke to him; he told me that Exequiel Ponce and Carlos Lorca had been arrested. I remember that I asked to speak to Lagos and received authorization to do so, as long as I asked him to collaborate with DINA. He asked me for candy, and I brought him some from the

Villa Grimaldi kitchen. This conversation took place on the patio, and I remember it perfectly because I knew him from before; he was wearing a blue suit then. I never saw him again, though. I think Lagos knew that they were going to kill him. In any case, he didn't look that bad off when I spoke to him, despite the fact that he was a little bit disheveled, dirty, and not wearing a tie. It didn't look like he had been tortured, but then again, the electricity doesn't leave any marks unless something unexpected happens. I asked Contreras about Lagos, Lorca, and Ponce in 1976, and he told me that they'd been set free.

I did hear something about a pregnant woman whom they kicked until she had a miscarriage, but I couldn't say when that was.

As for your question about the Zamora case of May 1975, I should say that I knew him, and he was a militant based in the Central Santiago regional headquarters of the Socialist Party. He was close to Sergio Muñoz. At one point, Barriga came to Wenderoth's office at Villa Grimaldi when I was there, and asked me what I knew about Zamora. I told him what I knew, and later, Wenderoth told me that he'd escaped while in DINA custody, and had run to the Pro-Peace Committee to seek refuge.

As for the detainees known as the Group of 119, I can say that I read the list of prisoners while I was at DINA General Headquarters, and at one point I asked Manuel Contreras about it. He told us the official version that had come out in the papers.

One of the 119 was a man whose last name was Espejo, a militant of the Eighth District of the Socialist Party headquartered at 38 Londres Street. In general, though, none of those names were familiar to me when I read them in the daily reports. I talked to Alejandra about what had happened to those 119 around July 1975, and we agreed that they had likely died while in DINA custody.

As for your question about Operation Colombo, my understanding of it was that it was a foreign DINA espionage operation.

There was a time when Wenderoth was out of the country and [Eugenio] Fieldhouse [Chávez] replaced him. During that time we were mistreated and beaten, to the point where my health was affected. After that, we managed to receive authorization to lock the door to our cottage from the inside, and from then on we had more control over who came in and out. In any case, DINA agents often kicked the door and threw stones and things like that at it. Wenderoth really offered us quite a bit of protection, actually.

Wenderoth traveled abroad with the 1974 graduating class of the War Academy [Academia de Guerra], where he was an alumnus. They took a group tour of Paraguay, Buenos Aires, Rio de Janeiro, and the United States. When he got back, we told him about the problems we'd had, like the damage to our house and the fact that we were occasionally denied lunch. I think he must have talked to someone in DINA, because on May 7 he sent me home, telling me to tell the other girls to get dressed up, because we were going to go out. We thought that we were going to be killed.

Wenderoth, along with an official and then-Captain Manuel Vásquez Chahuan—a member of the Purén Group—took us to DINA General Headquarters on 11 Belgrado Street. Cavalry captain Alejandro Burgos, the director's assistant, received us there.

I should add here that later on I found out that there was a second assistant under Burgos, a man named Hugo known as "El Cacho" [Worthless] Acevedo, and two secretaries.

They had the three of us go in one by one. I went first because I'd been detained the longest of the three, and we were received by the director, Manuel Contreras. He told me that he'd decided to set me free, and made reference to a paper that Wenderoth had shown me previously, saying that MIR had condemned the three of us to death. Then he said that he had decided to hire us as functionaries of DINA and that we were to live in Tower 12 of the development known as San Borja, and that we'd have access to telephones. As a joke, he said that he was putting us there in order to "launder" the apartment. I'm not sure, but I think that apartment used to belong to someone from GAP, or someone from the Letelier family.

When Contreras said he would hire us as agents, I asked him if there were any other options; he said no. Later, he told me that Wenderoth would be my direct supervisor, and that the same would go for the other two. He concluded by saying that he had allocated some money for us to go out to dinner with Wenderoth and Vásquez, and we went to Caledonia restaurant in the district of La Reina.

At the end of May, Wenderoth showed me a copy of the official government newspaper, in which a decree had been published giving me my freedom as of May 5 of that year.

In June, we moved to the apartment in San Borja; we had to wait a while for them to fix it up, because the officials that had lived in it before us left it in very bad shape. I lived in that apartment from June 1975, until Contreras left DINA, because when Odlanier Mena took over as director, the apartment was taken away from us.

From the time I became a functionary of DINA until December 1975, I worked as Wenderoth's secretary, mostly doing clerical work. He had greater responsibilities, since he was in charge of the entire section.

To answer your question, I can say that the Arauco Fish Company belonged to either Mamo or some friend of his, because I heard that they used trucks from the company around that time to transport prisoners.

A subofficial who was a major in *Carabineros* was in charge of logistics for DINA. He bought the food for the workers there.

DINA's vehicles were maintained at special garages that they kept for that purpose.

At one point, MIR shot Urich and a young woman who worked with him, a *Carabineros* police officer who worked in the Caupolicán Group. In response to your question, I never heard of MIR liberating any prisoners. When DINA would use one prisoner to lure another into captivity, they would send him off alone to do so, but they would attach explosives to his testicles, which they could set off by remote control if he tried to escape. So they never had to worry about him trying to get away while he was alone out in the open.

Among the DINA guards, there was utmost respect for the intellectual and military capabilities of MIR, but Krassnoff always said that even though they were strong, when push came to shove, "We'd still fuck them over."

In 1974, at least around the time that Rodolfo González was arrested, there was a facility in the Rinconada de Maipú (where the University of Chile's Agronomy School used to be) that was used as a DINA training center.

When I lived in the San Borja apartment, my daily routine began when Wenderoth would pick us up at about 7:30 a.m. We got to Villa Grimaldi around 8, and we stayed there until about 5:30 p.m. He would then take us back to the apartment. At that time, we didn't even dare open the door, much less run away, especially when I brought my son to live with me. We were afraid to go to the Vicariate of Solidarity because we knew that if we went to them, we'd have to testify at the military court [*fiscalía militar*].

As for your question about the detainee José Santos Rocha Álvarez, I remember that he was a prisoner at Terranova because I saw his name in the reports.

I worked at Terranova until December 23 or 24, 1975. For a number of personal reasons, I'd brought my son to live with me at the San Borja apartment, which led to problems with Carola, who didn't want any children living there. She talked to Pedro Espinoza about this, and in the end they moved her to an apartment owned by DINA on the corner of Estado and Huérfanos streets, above the Astor movie theater.

In March 1976, I was moved from Terranova to General Headquarters; Alejandra and Carola were moved there at the end of March. Carola was to work as Pedro Espinoza's secretary, and La Flaca Alejandra was to remain for a short time in the same section as me, before switching over to work with Iturriaga Neumann.

In response to your question, I don't know when Iturriaga began working in what we knew as the Economic Department. I think that he had a degree in economics from the Catholic University and thus he worked with different businesses. I think that Iturriaga was Carevic's boss.

Roberto Lailhacar Chávez was the CNI psychiatrist; I think he also worked at the psychiatric clinic at the University of Chile. He was the psychiatrist who all the DINA workers saw, and I know that he was concerned because the rate of alcoholism among DINA agents was very high.

The Santa Lucía Clinic, which was located on the street of the same name, was owned by DINA and offered medical and dental services to all agency workers. There was a nurse there named María Elena, who I heard married "El Cacho" Acevedo, the assistant to Contreras's assistant.

There was a doctor at that clinic with red hair whose last name was Sangellini. Most of the personnel there were in the military. I also remember Rodrigo Vélez, a surgeon who works at the Santa María Clinic. There were medical specialists of every kind. This facility was mostly for DINA functionaries, but some detainees also received treatment there, like the young woman who had a miscarriage as a result of what happened at Villa Grimaldi on New Year's.

After 1978, I met someone at the CNI headquarters on Borgoño Street who said he was a psychologist, a man by the last name of Basaure who interrogated people by injecting them with some kind of substance. But this was later on.

I remember a strange sort of man at Villa Grimaldi who interrogated people using hypnosis. We knew him as "The Talk" [El Charla]. I think that he'd been a tarot card reader somewhere up north—in Coquimbo, maybe. He worked with Moren.

The London Clinic was established later on, in 1976, on Almirante Barroso Street between the Alameda and Moneda Street. This facility was for DINA personnel as well, and the same doctors from the Santa Lucía Clinic worked there. The Santa Lucía Clinic closed when the London Clinic opened.

To summarize, I remember the following DINA facilities: the house at 38 Londres Street, Tejas Verdes, Tres Álamos, the house on José Domingo Cañas Street, the facility on Venecia Street, the one on the corner of Irán and Los Plátanos Streets, Implacate, and Cuatro Álamos. Later, there was one on Perú Avenue, and another on Borgoño Street. There was also a facility, which exists to this day, on Lastarria Street, right near the Alameda, next to the facility that belonged to the *Concertación* [center-left coalition of political parties].

In early 1978, I found out that there was a CNI facility on Alférez Real Street that functioned as a technical unit and worked on disguises, false documents, and other things. In general, they took care of everything related to the agents' aliases. The facility had a metal gate that led to the street, and it was located right in front of a restaurant called "El Rey del Lomito."

I went to work at DINA General Headquarters on Belgrado Street in early 1976, at a time when the organization was growing quickly.

The director and the subdirector of the organization worked in this facility, along with their respective staff members. I remember one member of the staff in particular, Colonel Vianel Valdivieso; a man named Saldías was in charge of General Logistics. Commander Arturo Ureta, who later was named a military attaché in El Salvador, was in the Foreign Affairs Department. He joined CNI when he returned to Chile.

Rolf Wenderoth was named chief of the subdirectorate of domestic intelligence. Vianel Valdivieso was in charge of telecommunications. Captain Cerda was head of the General Barracks Company, which was in charge of the guards and security. There was also a group of bodyguards, which reported directly to Contreras. Major Juan Morales was in charge of this group.

I met Orozco the day after Contreras resigned, because Odlanier Mena had asked him to take charge, and he went asking for files, section by section; we didn't have anything to give him. As a result, an internal investigation was ordered, and it turned out that the day before, a huge number of documents had been burned, shredded, or removed.

As for the organization of the DINA leadership, I know that Contreras was at the head, with Army Cavalry Major Alejandro Burgos as his assistant. Army Lieutenant Acevedo, alias "El Cacho," was there too, along with a secretarial staff that included an older woman named Norma—the widow of a military official— who later moved to the subdirectorate. Norma left in 1978, and was replaced by a secretary named Maribel Maringue, who was the daughter of an army subofficial.

Mireya and Ody were the other secretaries. During the last few months that Manuel Contreras was director, a woman named Gabriela came to join them, and she stayed on after Odlanier Mena replaced him.

A woman named Nélida served as Contreras's private secretary, and she had a separate office.

Jerónimo Pantoja worked in the subdirectorate. Norma and Mireya went to work there later on. Mamo was directly in charge of some things, while others he delegated to Pantoja.

Pantoja was the public face of DINA; he answered all the letters and signed the reports that different courts requested.

In 1976, around June, the Directorate of Operations [Dirección de Operaciones] was created. Pedro Espinoza Bravo was named head of this section, which had been a subdirectorate until then, and he transferred Carola over there to work with him. This organization coordinated all the operative groups within DINA, and was also in charge of analyzing the daily situation within the country and any other matters the different units deemed necessary.

The domestic intelligence subdirectorate (known as "C") was headed by Rolf Wenderoth and had a pool of secretaries; Ketty was the name of one of the secretaries. This subdirectorate was made up of different sections: there was C-1, headed by Augusto Deichler, whose secretary was Pilar, and I don't remember what specialty it had. Then there was C-2, which dealt with subversive activities; Rolf Wenderoth was in charge of this section, and that's where I worked too. C-3 focused on unions and workers' organizations. It was headed by Major Lopresti. His secretary was Mirta Espinoza Carrasco. Section C-4 was in charge of the Christian Democratic Party and MIR; I think it was headed by Deichler, and that was where Alejandra worked.

When Deichler went to Argentina, Lieutenant Colonel Guillermo Pávez replaced him as head of C-1. Pávez has a twin brother who is also an army official.

There was also a subdirectorate of foreign intelligence, headed by Commander Arturo Ureta. His secretary was named Carmen, and he married her later on. The structure of this subdirectorate was fairly similar to that of the previous one, but I don't remember the names of the people who worked there because the different areas were very compartmentalized. I do remember that Captain Willike—who later on, in 1977, went to head up the DINA branch in Argentina—worked there. Willike was also in charge of intelligence in Uruguay.

Three departments reported directly to Manuel Contreras, because he didn't delegate the functions that he considered important. The first of these three was Telecommunications, which I think was also the counterintelligence operation that Vianel Valdivieso headed up. Jorge Aros, the son of an army general, worked just under him, and then there was his main secretary, Sonia, although there was a large pool of secretaries. The second was the Legal Department, with a number of lawyers: Víctor Manuel Áviles Mejías, who currently works in the Central Bank; Miguel Ángel Poblete; a short, blue-eyed and red-haired man whose last name was Alfaro; and a military lawyer named Blanchet, who I think was the department head. Guido Polli, who had been arrested for the [General René] Schneider assassination when Frei was president, worked there too. There was another lawyer, a short, dark-skinned man named Miguel Ángel Parra, who hadn't actually received his degree yet; I remember that he took the exam in 1981, and did poorly. He was the lawyer who got Alejandra free after she was arrested a few years ago. I also remember a lawyer (170 cm tall, black hair slicked back, thin, with a round face and blue eyes) named Gálvez. The third department that reported directly to Manuel Contreras was the Economic Department, headed up by Iturriaga Neumann.

It's hard to describe in an exact way the relationships among the different companies linked to DINA, but I do remember that the Villar and Reyes Corporation operated as a shell company for DINA, hiring its civilian personnel as if they were its employees. It was a formally established company, and I would imagine that it had a government ID number and everything; in fact, it paid taxes and functioned as a normal company would. Its offices were located on the corner of Vicuña Mackenna Avenue and Belgrado Street, in a residential apartment building that was the property of DINA.

One of the partners in the company, whose last name was Villar, was an army official whom I saw several times. He was a shorter man, about forty years old. I never met the other partner, a woman whose last name was Reyes, but I know she exists.

DINA's link with the Arauco Fish Company, which was owned either by Mamo himself or by one of his family members, was channeled through the Villar and Reyes Corporation.

A review was carried out of all the properties that DINA had confiscated from political parties, people in exile, or the disappeared. I even heard about an employee who received an apartment as a gift; he was a civilian, a cosmetologist who was a personal friend of Contreras; he was over sixty years old and he was from the port city of San Antonio. This man had been in Cuba before 1973, and had gone to work for DINA as a makeup instructor; he taught at the National Intelligence Academy [Escuela de Inteligencia Nacional, ENI] at the Rinconada de Maipú, and was in charge of disguising the agents. His name was Santiago Mangiola Marchessi or Marketti—I'm not sure about his second last name. He had a son who was named after him, but the son was not involved in any of this. Mangiola received an apartment on the second floor of San Borja that faced south and east, number 24 I think it was, as a gift. I think he still lives there because I ran into him on the street nearby not too long ago. He's an old man now.

Another one of the shell corporations was called Diet and Lobos. I know that Pedro Diet was a personal friend of Contreras and was one of the civilians that organized fundraising dinners and luncheons for DINA.

There was also a Personnel Department, headed up by an old retired colonel, which had the résumés of the entire staff on file. That was where the DINA ID cards (known as TIDs) [tarjetas de identificación], and later the CNI ID cards, were made up, in conjunction with the identification office.

All DINA agents had two ID cards: one with our real name, and one with our alias. My alias was Ana María Vergara, a name given to me by "El Cacho" Acevedo. Alejandra's alias was Marta Vergara, and Carola's was Gloria Vilches. Apparently the names were chosen for them because there were three women by those names who participated in the Battle of La Concepción.

There was a member of the Investigative Police working in the identification office. His wife, whose name was Elsa, worked in the DINA Personnel Department making the ID cards.

The Personnel Department was also in charge of benefits, which included packages of groceries, subsidies for dependents, sick leave, substitutions, and other things like that.

A number of professional social workers worked there, including one whose real name was Sara Águila.

There was also a Department of Agitation and Propaganda, where a number of professional journalists worked. They analyzed domestic publications and publicized the government's policies via propaganda. Sometimes they would work with the operative units, spreading around likenesses of Miguel Enríquez [miguelitos] and fake pamphlets signed by MIR. This was the office in charge of whitewashing the government's role in the Letelier case, for example.

And then there was the so-called General Headquarters Company, a group of soldiers and subofficials led by Captain Julio Cerda, charged with standing guard 24 hours a day. They had vehicles, radios, and whatever else they needed. They drove Peugeot 504s in 1976, and before that, they had Fiat 125s and trucks.

DINA functionaries had quite a few benefits; I never had to pay anything for medical attention, for example. We could also take whatever we wanted from the Arauco Fish Company without paying a cent. We were given a monthly box of groceries, which was smaller or larger depending on how many family members we had.

I remember that Armando Fernández Larios used to go to the General Headquarters, but he didn't work there.

Marcelo "The Rabbit" [Conejo] Escobar was another official at the General Headquarters, along with Major Carlos Parera Silva. I never knew what the latter's job was, but he was in charge of a special group. One member of that group was Captain Patricio Ureta, but I don't know what he did there.

I don't remember exactly when Moren left, but Manuel Provis Carrasco was put in charge of the Caupolicán Group in late 1977, or early 1978. I remember that when Contreras left DINA, Moren left too, along with the other officials known as "Contreristas." The only one of those who stayed was Pantoja, which was why no one spoke very highly of him.

La Flaca Alejandra became seriously depressed in 1978, because of a number of issues that came one after another. First of all, the Vicariate was putting pressure on her mother. Alejandra had wanted to get plastic surgery so that she wouldn't be recognizable, and Manolo told me that he'd ordered pamphlets to be spread around saying that MIR had condemned her to death. This helped her, because that way DINA was obligated to pick up the cost of her surgery.

After her operation, she was transferred to the DINA unit in the city of Arica, where she was to live under an assumed name. While she was there, she had an affair with Gabriel Hernández Anderson, which brought her new problems that caused her to be sent back to Santiago.

I tendered my resignation from DINA in October 1978, when a group of family members of detained-and-disappeared people held a protest in front of the

Congress building and a radio station mentioned my name in connection to them. My resignation wasn't accepted, but I was suspended at work.

Following my attempt to resign, I went to my mother's house to await new orders. After a while, Ítalo called me and told me that Odlanier Mena was offering me my freedom in exchange for three years of work abroad. He said that I could also go live in a cottage behind the facility on Borgoño Street, where I would be able to enter directly into the facility and receive the instructions I would need to travel abroad.

There was a CNI detention center in that facility by then, with Manolo Provis Carrasco as chief. The Caupolicán Unit was headquartered there, and I think there were other offices too that had nothing to do with Manolo.

One day in the facility on Borgoño Street, I ran into an official named Patricio del Piano.

I went to Borgoño because I had to see a detainee there who had epilepsy. I was also going to see a young man from Argentina, a supposed spy, who had been arrested in southern Chile. Captain Patricio del Piano was in charge of the unit where they were being held.

I'm certain that Manolo was still working at the Terranova facility when [Michael] Townley turned himself in, but that's all I can say about the period in which Terranova was closed.

I think there was a facility on Perú Avenue during the time that I lived on Borgoño Street, but I never went there.

I think that Major Juan Zanzani, who was in charge of DINA's operation in Valdivia, told Wenderoth that he'd had a radio station known as the "Voice of the Coast" [La Voz de la Costa] burned down, because it was agitating too much. I think that the radio belonged to the Catholic Church. Around the same time, Wenderoth told me that DINA had burned a theater tent that belonged to Jaime Vadell and Nicanor Parra, but I don't know the circumstances surround this.

A bag arrived every day from the postal service, full of letters that were thought to contain important information. These letters were processed daily by DINA; some were shredded, while others were returned to the postal service for normal delivery.

In early 1976, I was working in the DINA archive along with Ketty, who was very familiar with it, and she gave us whatever papers she felt were pertinent to domestic intelligence; other personnel processed the rest, because there was always an enormous number of documents.

Contreras sent Max, who had been at Terranova, to Brazil for a course on intelligence, and when I got to the General Headquarters, I found him working on the cases of the disappeared. Max later went to Geneva to represent the Chilean Government regarding this matter.

I received a file from the Pro-Peace Committee in May 1976; I found out from Max that the documents in it had been robbed by DINA.

In response to your question, I can say that I found out about the Joint Command [Comando Conjunto] because there were some meetings about it at DINA General Headquarters. People from Carabineros, the air force, the navy, and the army were all present at the meetings, which took place around the time that

[Carlos] Contreras Maluje was arrested. Pedro Espinoza represented DINA at the meetings, as its the head of operations. When I found out about them, I was told that there had been pressure from the government for DINA to carry out the repression, an idea that was met with resistance from the other branches of the armed forces.

I remember that Espinoza Bravo received heavy criticism for a mistake either he or his people made. I think it was related to the Contreras Maluje case.

I know for sure about the meetings of the Joint Command; members of the Navy attended them as well, because Alberto Padilla, who had an affair with La Flaca Alejandra around then (1979), attended them.

Another case I remember is that of Carmelo Soria. I know that Ricardo Lawrence came to see Wenderoth one day, bragging, "We got rid of that guy." He said that they'd made someone drink an entire bottle of pisco, and then, "we got him into the car and got rid of him." Lawrence added that someone got into the car with the detainee, and when the car reached a certain speed, this person jumped out of it and the car ended up crashing or falling off a cliff. Later, I read about the Carmelo Soria case in the newspaper, and the story Lawrence had told was just like the one I read.

I worked as an analyst until 1977, when I went to the ENI [National Intelligence Academy] for an intelligence course from February to August of that year. There were 22 students: two from *Carabineros* and the rest from DINA.

I met Manuel Provis Carrasco, Patricio Ureta, Patricio del Pino, Roberto Guiza, a lieutenant known as "Little Maldonado" [El Chico Maldonado], an Army Captain named Canobbio, and a detective named Bustamante in that ENI course.

The director of the ENI at the time was army major Díaz, who had set up a sort of cooperative to buy houses for DINA officials. Later on, the houses and the land never materialized, and everyone lost their money.

Díaz was replaced as ENI director by Francisco Maximiliano Ferrer, who was known as "Max."

The classes offered at the ENI included secret service and observation, taught by Max Ferrer; Marxism, taught by Wenderoth; makeup, taught by Santiago Manggiola; Shooting, taught by army lieutenant Pérez, or Catalán (I'm not sure which was his real name and which was his alias); explosives, with the same teacher; raids and searching, taught by a detective; and karate, taught by some Korean karate teachers. All of this was supplemented by exercise regimens.

A graduation ceremony took place at the end of the session, with Sergio de Castro and Mónica Madariaga handing out awards. Manuel Contreras was in attendance as well.

Manuel Contreras went to our house at least once a month. I remember that Juan Morales and Burgos would come first to do reconnaissance and then Mamo would show up. At one point, he asked us about the possibility of the United States ambassador interviewing us, so that we could show him that there were leftists in the country that were still alive and in good shape. This idea never came to pass, though.

When I came back from the ENI, I went back to my old job, but Contreras was fired soon after. When most of the "Contreristas" left, I made the best of the moment and took some vacation time and traveled to Arica to visit my son.

I went to Arica in the private car of Commander Del Canto, who was in charge of DINA there.

Meanwhile, Odlanier Mena had spoken to the other two girls (Carola and La Flaca), who continued working in the same jobs as before. As for me, when I got back from Arica, I was promoted within the same section, from analyst to section chief.

Daniel Concha, a retired army colonel and former head of the mail service, came to work in the subdirectorate of domestic intelligence. Daniel Concha was a trusted professional acquaintance of Mena and Jerónimo Pantoja.

Around the same time, a colonel whose last name was Suau replaced Pedro Espinoza. He was really dense, and wouldn't approve any reports unless they were at least one hundred pages long. I had a poor relationship with him.

On account of the fact that Concha and I got along poorly on a personal level, I spoke to Ítalo Seccatore and he had me moved to the computer unit (known as L-5) so I wouldn't have to work with Concha anymore.

There was a civilian engineer working in the computer unit by the name of Andrés Terrisse Castro, who was considered to be a computer genius. I received authorization to study computers, and I enrolled in the Institute of Computing and Methods [*Instituto de Computación y Método,* ICM].

The computer unit was established in about 1976 in a facility on Condell Street, which also housed administrative and human resource personnel.

When Ítalo arrived in March 1978, his job was to digitize all the data, and work began to be done to broaden the system, which was technically very rudimentary at the time. A manual was put together with instructions in data analysis, and some templates were created, such as the HT1, the HT2, and the auxiliary sheet, in order to offer instructions to any agent who wanted to analyze a certain text and then write a report about it in a uniform way. Since the idea was to put together a database, they wanted a standardized method for gathering the data.

A number of subpoenas requiring my testimony were sent to my mother's house starting in early 1976; they were related to legal cases sponsored by the Vicariate of Solidarity, cases inquiring about disappeared persons. When I asked some people in the Legal Department about this matter, I was told that the service did not authorize its personnel to testify before any court.

And then there was the matter of my attempt to resign; that happened right before I was offered the chance to carry out a three-year CNI mission in Argentina, after which I would be given my freedom.

Before I went to go live in Argentina, I was first to spend a year in Uruguay to sever my connections with Chile and elude the legal actions coming from the Vicariate. In Uruguay, I would be charged with establishing a home base and an identity for myself, which would later allow me to carry out my mission; this mission was known as "Operation Sky Blue" [*Operación Celeste*].

Before leaving for Uruguay, Manolo and I went to the cemetery to look around for a name I could use as an alias. But in the end, Manolo gave me the name of a real live person, a housekeeper from Osorno named Mariana del Carmen Burgos Jiménez. So I received an ID card and a passport with that name, which became my official alias. The practice of using real names for aliases was common when you traveled abroad, although they didn't always use the names of people who were still living.

They gave me US$3,000, with which I traveled to Montevideo as a tourist. Once I got there, I requested and received temporary residency. I traveled there via Lan Chile airlines on February 11, 1979. When I arrived in Montevideo, I opened a bank account in dollars, connected to another account in Uruguayan currency, and I received a monthly deposit of US$350 in an account at the Sudamericano Bank in Santiago, as well as a monthly sum of US$50 for my mother in Chile.

I was to sever my ties with Chile that first year and take on a Uruguayan identity; I was to "become" a citizen of that country and then enter Argentina a year later.

I read newspapers, history books, and other things in order to learn more about the country, and I tried to meet people as well. I never managed to take on a Uruguayan identity. Actually, I didn't even work much on it, because I got there in February, during Carnaval, and then came the harvest festival, and after that I studied computers at two institutes. So it just wasn't possible.

Ítalo was the one sending me my orders from Chile. I remember that when I was still living on Borgoño Street, Odlanier Mena came and gave me instructions with different suggestions, like to try to become [Emilio] Massera's girlfriend in Argentina, which was a big joke for Manolo and I. [Massera was head of the notorious ESMA (*Escuela de Mecánica de la Armada*, Naval School of Mechanics) and an original member of the Argentine junta.]

I had a post office box in Uruguay where I received my mail, and Manolo came to visit me about halfway through the year. A different official came in September, however, which made me think that Manolo and Ítalo weren't in charge of the operation anymore. There had been some problems with the money transfers too, and I began to suspect that there were problems with the plan. So I decided to go back to Chile on October 12.

Ítalo and Manolo went to pick me up at the airport, and that was when I found out that Ítalo wasn't working for CNI anymore. Manolo was still working there in a facility on the corner of República and Gay Streets, but he wasn't in charge of Operation Sky Blue.

So my first contacts when I went back to Chile were with Ítalo and Manolo, but they were informal and unofficial.

One day, Arturo Ureta came by and picked me up, and spoke to me about an espionage operation that seemed to me to be ill-conceived and that showed a lack of understanding of the elementary aspects of espionage. Again I tendered a letter of resignation, and Ítalo told me that he agreed that it was time for me to leave.

A month later, Ureta let me know that he had accepted my resignation and that he was sorry about it. In the letter, I had cited personal problems as my reason for resigning.

After my resignation, I met the person who is my current partner. He had recently separated, so we were both single. I worked for a time at the Indumotora

Company, and later at a computer school that my partner owns. Later, we became business associates there. Little by little, I began to live a normal life again.

This went on until May 1982, when an order for my arrest was issued in a judicial trial sponsored by the Vicariate of Solidarity. Mireya, Colonel Rivera's secretary, called me and told me that I was to report to the CNI facility on República Street, and I found out about it when I went there.

I felt that I was falling into the clutches of CNI once again, which was something I didn't want under any circumstances.

To avoid this, my partner and I went to live at a house on Rondizzoni Street, near O'Higgins Park. We got there at night, and I stayed inside and didn't go out, not even to buy things or take out the trash, until about February or March 1983. After that, we moved to Antonia López de Bello Street, and only then did I begin to go out for errands that were absolutely necessary, like doctor's appointments related to my pregnancy. My second son was born on June 16, 1983.

I found it strange that La Flaca Alejandra didn't come to visit me when my son was born, but later I found out that she had been arrested that very same day in connection with a trial that ended up taking place in a Military Court.

Alejandra came and visited me sometime after my son was born. I received a call from Alberto, a young man from the navy whom she was seeing at the time, who said she wanted to see me. So she came and stayed with me for a week, but we began to have problems, because she drank a lot. I think that she's better off now, but at the time I had to tell her that she had to stop drinking, or she would have to go. So she left, and I haven't seen her since.

In early 1984, we lost our lease on our apartment, and we moved to Víctor Manuel Street, where we lived for a year or so. During that time, I broke all my ties with everyone I'd known over the previous years.

By then, my son started going to daycare, and I only left the house to pick him up and drop him off. After that, I moved to the place where I live now, on Perú Avenue. During those years, I had no contact with CNI at all.

In mid-1987, Rolf Wenderoth was transferred from Antofagasta to Santiago, before leaving to become a military attaché at the Chilean Embassy in Germany. I had some contact with Wenderoth then because he called me and came to my house to visit my children and me when he arrived in Santiago. He sent me about three or four letters a year from Germany.

When Wenderoth got back from Germany, around February 1989, he was eligible for retirement from the military, and he began to work as the principal of a SOFOFA [*Federación Gremial de la Industria,* Chilean Federation of Industry] trade school in Maipú. In late February, he called me and offered me a job there. I worked at that school until October 1989, at which time I quit for health reasons.

At that time, I still didn't have any identification documents, so I called Ítalo in late October and asked him to help me obtain some. Ítalo got in touch with Harold Reyes, an army major who currently works in the Army Intelligence Brigade [*Brigada de Inteligencia del Ejército,* BIE]. Reyes put me in touch with Rodrigo Salas, alias "Aníbal," who was working as a CNI adjunct at the Civil Registry office in the old office on General Mackenna Street. About a month later, I was given an ID card.

During the time I was working on getting that ID card, I remember a conversation with Aníbal about the outcome of the elections, and he told me that they'd wasted their opportunity. He also told me about something I hadn't heard of before: selective terrorism. In a rude tone, Harold said to him, "What kind, theirs or yours?" "It doesn't matter," Aníbal answered; the conversation shifted to a confrontation that had taken place on Pedro Donoso Street. When Harold asked Aníbal for more details about this, Aníbal avoided the question.

As part of this official testimony, I am handing over a business card with a phone number corresponding to "Aníbal," on which his name appears as Rodrigo Vidal. I don't know whether it's his real name or his alias, but I know him as Aníbal.

On the subject of Aníbal, I remember that there was a CNI agent named Antivil who worked with him; he lived in the Independencia district, on Maruri Street or very nearby. This man Antivil must be about 170 or 175 cm tall, and he's a bald man, somewhat stocky.

A few days after I received my ID card, I got a call from Manuel Provis Carrasco, Manolo, who told me that he had just gotten back from Israel and that he had been transferred to the Ministry of Defense. He said that one of the first papers he'd come across in his office was a report from Harold, detailing how I had received my ID card. That was when I found out that Harold was in the BIE, and from then on, Manolo called me periodically to check in with me.

One time, he called me to offer me a job at the BIE, where Andrés Terrisse would be in charge of the computer unit. I told him that I wouldn't take the job no matter how much money it paid, because I just wanted to live a normal life with my children.

Ítalo called me in May or June of this year and asked me if I had all my papers in order. I told him that I didn't have everything I needed, like my driver's license, for example. He asked if we could get together, so my partner and I met him at a café in Plaza Italia. Ítalo told me that he'd moved up to the rank of general, so he'd be able to help me. He also offered me legal assistance, since my name had appeared in the newspapers in connection with Wenderoth and the school in Maipú.

He then asked me what I would do if summoned by the Truth and Reconciliation Commission, which had just recently been created. I told him that I could offer my testimony if the commission asked me for it. His response was, "Well, since you don't know anything, there's nothing you can say to them." He added that DINA would offer no acknowledgment of my time working there unless there was no possible way they could deny it.

When we said good-bye, he told me that he would give me a list of lawyers to choose from, and that he would find a way to pay for it. That was the last time I heard from him, because even though he said he would call me, he never did.

In a phone conversation later on with Manolo, he expressed similar concerns about the commission.

The person to whom I've referred a number of times in this declaration as "Carola" was a MIR militant who was arrested some time after me, when a number of members of that organization were arrested. She was considered important to DINA because she had worked in MIR's Information Unit [*Unidad de Informaciones*]. The person in charge of her interrogation and torture was Ricardo

Lawrence, in conjunction with the "Fat Guys' Group." As a result of the torture, she began a process of forced collaboration with DINA. Her real name is María Alicia Uribe Gómez, although at the time she was arrested her name was María Alicia Gómez Gómez because her father had not yet acknowledged paternity. She took his last name when he did so, which was in June 1979.

The person mentioned in this declaration as "Alejandra" or "La Flaca Alejandra" is actually named Marcia Alejandra Merino Vega; she was also a MIR militant, and her experience after that was similar to Carola's.

I should add that thanks to a CNI functionary, I got access a few years ago to a file with personal information about me from the period of 1976 to 1980. Among other things, I found my résumés from 1976 to 1978, photos of me and of my older son when he was smaller, and a series of photos that I turned over when I came back from Uruguay. I also found all the fake ID cards and passports that I'd used back then.

There was also a document there that described Operation Sky Blue in detail, my letter of resignation, and a written evaluation discussing what to do with me. It broached the possibility of killing me, either in Chile or abroad, but in the end it scrapped this idea for a number of reasons that are outlined there.

As for where those who disappeared ended up, I do remember one thing that made quite an impression on me: in about 1976, at about one in the afternoon, a Major Jara came into Wenderoth's office at the General Headquarters when I was working there. He was in charge of the DINA unit in Rocas de Santo Domingo. He was invited to stay for lunch, but he turned down the invitation, because some commission that he didn't name was going to be inspecting the campground that DINA had in his area for its personnel to take summer vacations, and he had to have "some stiffs" buried there dug up and moved somewhere else. Wenderoth responded with a somewhat awkward gesture, and the two left the office together.

I wish to make it clear that I am testifying before this commission because I feel that I have the duty to try to make reparations however I can for my actions, having collaborated with DINA and having worked for the organization. It's also important to me to contribute to clarifying the truth and carrying out justice, in the context of reconciliation. Over the past few years I have experienced a process of encounter with the Lord, and I have a deeply lived commitment to my Christian faith, and therefore, as much as possible, I want to be faithful to the dictates of my conscience.

I authorize the National Truth and Reconciliation Commission to send this declaration to the courts if it deems necessary, particularly in connection with case numbers 361–80 and 653–81 of the Santiago Military Court. I tried to testify in those cases, but I was unable to, because they had been sealed indefinitely in accordance with the Amnesty Law of 1978.

This declaration has been read, ratified, and signed by the person who appeared before the commission, which will retain custody of the one, single copy of it.

Part II

Interview with Luz Arce
(Mexico, Chile, 2002–7)

My goal was to dedicate all my time to the party because I wanted to train myself politically . . . I was young, ignorant, and full of energy that I didn't know how to channel . . .

**

The Popular Unity coalition was weakened by the wide spectrum of positions at its core. Violence began to take center stage. Right-wing groups frequently attacked the headquarters of the left's political parties. For this reason, in addition to working all day, we had to spend our nights guarding the party's headquarters and some public administration buildings near the Moneda Palace [La Moneda, the presidential palace]. We held off the attacks with stones that we threw from the terraces and the upper floors in the buildings . . .

**

It is true that I did participate in armed confrontations. I am not trying to defend this, but I do want to clarify that the GEA [*Grupos Especiales de Apoyo,* Special Support Groups] never tried to kill anyone . . .

**

It took me months to realize the real dimensions of our actions. I became aware of this once I was undercover and had a conversation with Gustavo Ruz Zañartu, who was my superior then and a member of the Central Committee. I realized that he didn't know anything about these activities and that he didn't agree with them.

**

I remember today the naïveté of our dreams.

—*Luz Arce, The Inferno (1993)*

I

The Militant, the Sympathizer

In the first part of *The Inferno*, you refer to your militancy in the Socialist Party. Reflecting from the present, why and for what were you fighting as a militant?

I always try to be precise, so I want to begin by saying that I love my party very much: that is, the party as I knew it back then. I don't identify 100 percent, as I did years ago, with today's Socialist Party. Today I would define myself as a supporter of the *Concertación*.

I think it's fair to add that, strictly speaking, I was never a militant. I only managed to obtain a "sympathizer's" ID card. In truth, when the coup occurred, my association with the Socialist Party was very recent. It's just that daily dynamics and the speed with which we lived back then forced me to take on certain roles. I know that if today I claim that I wasn't a militant, it might seem like I am shirking responsibilities. But no! I assume personal responsibility and don't want to saddle the Socialist Party with my actions from during the dictatorship. Quite honestly, I entered political life accidentally in 1972. And between May 1972 and September 1973 time flew. Consequently, the training I received in such a short period was precarious. Also, the time I could dedicate to my formation as a militant was minimal.

Nevertheless, according to what you write in your book, you managed to assume roles in very formalized and privileged groups like GAP (*Grupo de Amigos Personales*, Group of Personal Friends of Salvador Allende) and GEA (*Grupos Especiales de Apoyo*, Special Support Groups).

Sure, but that was all circumstantial. One of life's paradoxes, Michael, is that, curiously, the same person who led me to GAP in 1972—I'm talking about the era in which GAP depended organically on the Socialist Party—"led" me to DINA (*Dirección de Inteligencia Nacional*, National Intelligence Directorate). The boy's name was Raúl Juvenal Navarrete Hancke (well, he was a boy in 1972), and very soon he will retire from the army's National Intelligence Directorate (*Dirección de Inteligencia Nacional del Ejército*, DINE). Raúl was one of those people who, like Carola, took a strong turn—a *very strong* turn. Anyway, this young man was a neighbor of mine since the time we were kids. I would say that we learned to walk together in the same plaza where our mothers knitted. (I'm just giving you a sense of our relationship, an image. Raúl is a year younger than I am.) We were in the same classes together at school. So what happened? One day after I had recently separated from my husband, jobless and bearing sole responsibility for feeding my son and for our financial needs, I ran into Raúl on a public bus. At that time, I was a physical fitness trainer and was working in the same place as my ex-husband. Being the rather rigid young woman that I was, I irresponsibly decided to quit my job. At least, today it seems irresponsible to have done that, though at the time, because I wanted to avoid my ex-husband, it was what I had to do. So, unemployed and needing to provide for my son, I was riding along in the bus, headed toward a store where I heard they needed sales clerks, when I happened to run into this guy whom I hadn't seen forever. He asked me what I was doing. "Looking for work," I said. "Why?" he asked. "I just got separated," I told him. "Oh, look, I'll get you a job. Let's go." And instead of getting off the bus at the store where I thought I'd find work, I got off with Raúl and we headed for La Moneda, the presidential palace.

At that time I had a genuine social conscience, much more developed than that of my family. My father was an administrative employee who worked for the National Railroad Company. He could barely make ends meet. Nevertheless, my parents had many dreams that they wanted us kids to realize. From the time I was very small, for example, they sent me to an expensive young ladies' school run by nuns. Oh, how I fought with those nuns! In class, I always asked why the sign outside said "a school for *young ladies*" (*colegio de señoritas*). I told the sisters that there were other girls who were also "ladies," even if they didn't know how to set a table or use silverware properly. I looked up the word *señorita* in the dictionary and told the nuns what it meant. But the nuns said "no," that girls who do not come from well-heeled homes and who have no resources are not *señoritas*. I was always fighting. But that's to be expected because I had a Spanish grandfather who was left unemployed at a very young age despite the fact that he was never a communist. In the years when the repression against the Communist Party was intense, my grandfather had unionist ideals. He was aware of the workers' need to organize, and he was exonerated. When I was a little girl, I was very attached to my grandfather. When I was six years old, I remember he gave me a book by Victor Hugo. By age ten, thanks to him, I had already read all the classics, or at least the most important ones. Really, I think it was my grandfather who programmed my soul. In short, I was very feisty, a fighter, ever since I was really young. Because of that, I had a social conscience.

So it was your fighting spirit and social conscience that led you to "sympathize" with the Socialist Party?

Generally speaking, up until that time, I lived in a way that I thought was normal. I studied at the university, married a classmate, had a child, worked, and managed to build a home. The situation seemed rosy from the outside. Simply wonderful! We were a happy young couple and the world was our oyster! But I felt that things weren't perfect and that the marriage was failing. So I decided to get separated. And there I was, riding on the bus, when Raúl Navarrete, after only a brief conversation, took me to La Moneda and got me a secretarial job. It seemed that for the first time in my life everything was right with the world. All my fighting with the nuns, my struggles with my family . . . (I have family members who, to this very day, for example, speak to the maids pejoratively. And the irony is that they can't even afford a maid! It's a strange attitude that I really can't understand.)

"My family is a bunch of decadent snobs," I used to tell myself in those days when I was working at La Moneda and starting to read Marxist texts. It took me a long time to understand my parents, to realize that with all their idiosyncrasies I love them just the same, so much. It took time to reconcile them to my social conscience, to love them without feeling conflicted, as I do now.

That daily existence, that closeness to Salvador Allende was very special. Looking back objectively, I think I had an academic advantage over my comrades in GAP. I'm not talking about their abilities as people, but rather about their ability to have access to schooling, to higher education. Because my parents and I thought it was important, I went to school. GAP, in its Socialist Party phase, was made up of people who came from shantytowns, from poorer areas.[1] Not all of them were poor, but most were. I'm sure that none of them had the opportunity to finish primary school. But thanks to my grandfather and to the fact that I loved learning, I was always an avid reader. I read a book a day, every day! I didn't have money, so I borrowed books from friends who had personal libraries just so I could read. That characteristic, my insatiable hunger to learn, which benefits me to this day, was very useful when I was in GAP. The leaders of GAP observed my drive to learn and started giving me books: Che's [Ernesto (Che) Guevara de la Serna] book, Lenin's *What Is to Be Done?*, and so on. I read and read every night. Soon they discovered that I had a knack for summarizing my readings. Speaking and writing have always come easily to me. So I studied the books they gave me quickly, and I typed up summaries that could be photocopied and distributed among my comrades. At that time, we didn't have computers like we do now. We had to use typewriters. Since I had been a teacher, they also asked me to teach classes because it came easily to me and I liked it. I still like teaching classes.

Because you were so physically proximate to Salvador Allende, did you have any kind of personal relationship with him?

Personal? No. It was the same kind of relationship that every member of GAP had with him, although there were certainly some members of GAP who were closer to him than others. He and I would greet each other when we met in the hallway or whenever we were together somewhere . . .

What impression did he make on you?

Ah, for me he was . . . well, the guy was truly wise. And charismatic too! And I was young. We looked at him as our leader, as our president, with great respect. The silence was deafening when he entered a room.

So, anyway, when Raúl and I got off the bus that day, he took me to see Enrique Huerta, one of GAP's three main leaders (who to this day is disappeared), and Raúl said to Enrique, "Look, she's a friend. We grew up together." And Huerta says to him, "OK, but is she a militant?" "No," Raúl tells him, "but she can learn. She's really intelligent, college educated." "And you, what do you do?" Huerta asked me directly. So I told him my whole story. He stood there starting at me and said, "Do you know how to type?" "No, but I can learn," I replied. And that very night I memorized all the keys on the typewriter, and that's how I learned to type.

My first assignments in GAP were basic and easy: mainly administrative tasks, keeping track of petty cash. But soon things started happening. For example, one day the president had to attend an event, so the chief of security said to me, "Hey, you know what? I have a problem. We've swept the whole place, but the security people won't let us into the women's bathroom." And everyone automatically looked at me. They said, "OK, then you go today." And that was how I became a guard—out of simple, everyday need.

At that time, I didn't know the differences among the Socialist Party, the Communist Party, and MIR (*Movimiento de Izquierda Revolucionaria,* Leftist Revolutionary Movement). I was clueless! Sure, I knew that there were some communist countries, but I didn't know any specific details. None! Not a one! My life had played our rather simply, though I always had a strong social conscience. And that conscience manifested, as I'm telling you, in personal fights, in my squabbles with the nuns, with my family, and with those who were close to me. That was all. But suddenly I started to observe the world of GAP and to read many doctrinal books that seemed like the Bible itself. It was as if my life had changed from one day to the next.

So reading those books politicized your worldview?

Absolutely! I was still ignorant of what the Socialist Party, the Communist Party, or MIR were, but I was studying Marxism. My comrades would ask me at meetings, for example, "Comrade, are you sure about what you're saying?" Oftentimes we would have meetings and I would give opinions according to my Marxist-Leninist readings. They would tell me, "Comrade, what you're saying is not something the Socialist Party believes, but rather one of MIR's ideas." And I would tell them, "Fine, I have no idea what MIR thinks, but I believe what I'm saying is correct because Marx, Lenin, et cetera, et cetera." From there I'd launch into a big speech. By late June or early July 1972, I was already living in the president's residence and later in the GAP house, Payita's house, located in the foothills of the Andes.[2] It all happened so fast. I still knew nothing about the different Chilean political parties, but I was learning about security. I entered the Socialist Party's training school. I took a course on explosives, another on ballistics, and a basic course on politics. But all of this was on the fly.

Given what we know, GAP was a hypermilitarized group whose members customarily received rigorous training in weaponry and military tactics. The vast majority of GAP was even sent to Cuba for training. Given what you've told me, I'm having a hard time understanding how someone like you could have become a member of GAP. In other words, how could someone who claims not to have been a "militant" and who landed at La Moneda so circumstantially be allowed so near to Salvador Allende?

GAP passed through various stages. The brief time I was a member is exactly as I narrate it in *The Inferno.* Don't forget that GAP was originally made up of MIR militants, and it's my understanding that that was the stage in which training was most rigorous. Later, when I was a member, there were cells that received political and military training, but at the micro level. I don't know details about how those people were trained.

So you had military training. When and how were you trained?

My training was subpar. In such a short time and given the nature of the moment, I was never able to get more extensive training.

What, specifically, was the nature of the military training you did receive?

I took a few classes on ballistics and explosives, mainly theoretical. I never bore arms as a member of GAP, except for when I had to do guard duty at the barracks. Every day before breakfast we had to do some physical activity: normally jogging, cross-country running, and general fitness. In GEA, I learned how to assemble and disassemble a pistol, load it, clean it, and maintain it.

What was your cell like? Who was in it?

I was never in a cell. In democratic times, the Socialist Party called its small-scale organic structures "nuclei." I only managed to attend a couple of meetings of a nucleus that was forming in the railroad sector. Very quickly I joined the Eighth Comuna, and shortly thereafter the *Tancazo* happened.[3] I never got to be part of a Socialist Party nucleus.

If you had to sum up in a few words what you were fighting for, what would you say?

My assumption was that the Popular Unity process had to lead the pueblo to a greater state of justice, equality, and solidarity. In other words, my social conscience is what governed and continues to govern my actions.

So, when I was in GAP, one day I found out that my organization was part of the Socialist Party. And since I was already part of the group, I guess that by association I became a socialist. Do you understand? It was that accidental. I entered GAP in May 1972, and by May 1973 we had already suffered one coup attempt, which was abated by the army's commander-in-chief, Carlos Prats. After that first coup attempt, everyone said that a definitive coup was inevitable. It was coming!

On the day of the *Tancazo,* I was in one of the local militant training schools. I was trying to get better training so that I could later enter the militarized part of the Socialist Party. And barely ten days after my arrival, the *Tancazo* came, and my chief said, "Luz, it gives me both joy and sadness to tell you that you have to leave. I recommended you to the central committee because they need people for GEA, an organization that will be made up of eight political-military units. We will not see each other again, nor will you see any of your comrades from this training school. Your new assignment is highly compartmentalized." That very day, June 29, 1973, I was taken to the central committee. When I arrived, I could see who my comrades would be. The eight of us looked at each other, and I recognized them because several had been GAP members. They gave us the whole spiel. They said, "You are now all part of GEA and your mission will be highly clandestine, highly compartmentalized. From this moment forward you have no homes, you have no names, and you have no families." Typical stuff. Our public mission as members of GEA was to set up a militant training school for the "old timer" construction workers, as we affectionately called them, who were meant to be the backbone of downtown Santiago in the "Santiago Defense Plan." The "Star Plan" or "Santiago Defense Plan" was a defense plan that Allende and his government had developed in case of a coup. It was assumed that we would react militarily, with armed force. Our "soldiers" would be the most militant "old timers" from the unions and construction workers' organizations. The eight of us GEA (two of whom were women and the rest men) had to set up the school and find teachers to give classes for the unionists and corporatists so that they'd be ready if a coup came.

In your book, you talk about weapons hidden in your house.

Oh, but those were something else entirely. In GEA, we never received weapons for our people. We couldn't even arm ourselves on September 11. We never received weapons. I had my pistol, and that was it.

Regarding the weapons at my house, it turns out that the coup came and then the clandestine phase began. During that phase, many of us assumed that we would remain active clandestinely. Before the coup, we had been a leftist party in times of democracy. When we wanted to speak with a comrade, we simply called him or her on the phone. Or when we wanted to keep our activities secret, we sent messages encoded in the commercials that played on the party's radio stations. But then September 11 came and the party radio stations disappeared. We were left with nothing! Zero! No infrastructure! No resources! So, after the coup, I went out into the street hoping to find some of my comrades. That's how we started reconnecting with one another. Eventually, thanks to Gustavo Ruz Zañartu, we managed to connect with the Socialist Party's central committee. Gustavo said that we had to reorganize the party. We moved forward and started bringing people together to form the foundations of the party's new compartmentalized structures. We started disseminating directives from the party leadership among the militants and helping them with their needs "insofar as it was possible" (as President Aylwin's famous phrase said).[4] The first thing we did was help those who were being persecuted. We did what was necessary: we carried messages and created infrastructure. But it was all so precarious. Then, one day Gustavo said to me, "You know what? There are a bunch of militants who have weapons in their homes. They're scared and want to know what to do." They didn't want to hide arms because they were afraid. We figured that if the weapons were in working order they might come in handy someday. We thought that the weapons were a resource that we had to preserve. The issue was where to hide them. Suddenly, I found myself making rounds to gather up the weapons of those comrades who didn't want to hide them. Then we found out that some of those weapons weren't functional. Consequently, our idea was to get rid of the bad ones. But it's certainly not easy to discard weapons in times of dictatorship. Toño (Samuel Antonio Houston Dreckmann) and I had the idea of going out one day well before curfew, posing as a couple, with the goal of tossing the bad weapons into the Mapocho River. We never managed to do it. That's why the weapons were in my house.

On September 11, the party alerted me about what was happening. A comrade called me at home at five o'clock in the morning and cried, "Red alert!" I left my house. All public transportation was on strike and Chile was paralyzed. The political right already had the country paralyzed with the black market and all of that—but you already know that part. I went out to the street and walked to the party headquarters. My comrades started arriving one by one. It was there that Toño (with whom I was later detained because the same person turned us both in) told me that they couldn't find our leader, the person in charge of the party organization, from the political commission. They couldn't find Carlos Altamirano either.[5] In other words, they couldn't find anyone! That's what they told all of us

GEA folks. The central committee never was able to locate Altamirano, at least not during the time we were there. Never! Then our construction worker comrades started asking, "Where are our weapons?" And we didn't have any! It was then that I asked Toño if he knew anything about Ariel Ulloa, and Toño said that he did. He told me that Ariel, GEA's leader, sought refuge at seven o'clock in the morning in the Argentine embassy. (Everyone knows that. At least all the socialists do. That's why Ariel Ulloa is alive today and is now the mayor of Concepción, or at least that's what I heard a few years ago.)

In short, that was my history with the Socialist Party.

Let's start with the idea that you were a "militant" for a very short time.

If you put it that way, I guess that in practice I was. I guess I was a militant in practice, even though by the strictest of definitions I was only a "sympathizer" with the Socialist Party.

OK. Then if it's true that you spent such a short time as a Socialist Party militant, a logical question arises: How and when did you decide to take up arms for the cause?

Today I feel that armed struggle was part of a moment that the country and the world were living. In those years, I was very young. In my political education, the first thing that they taught us was that revolutionary change meant a change at the state level. The teacher would tell us, "When water turns from liquid to vapor, such radical change requires a certain amount of violence for it to occur." That's what they told us. When a chicken is born, it has to hatch out of the eggshell, because if it doesn't, it can't change states of being. So for us it was logical. Like it or not, if we were going to change our state of being, violence was one possible method. At least that's how I saw it. Don't get me wrong; I never liked violence. In fact, we aborted some missions we were ordered to carry out and took responsibility for our actions with the party leadership. This was so we wouldn't have to kill a police officer, for example. In reality, when I was in GEA, we dedicated ourselves from the very start to what I already mentioned, to setting up a militant training school. We had to teach people. The school operated between the Monday following the *Tancazo* and September 10, 1973. Occasionally, when our leader required it, we participated in operations, in armed military actions.

So you accepted armed struggle *de facto*, without questioning it much.

What I'm saying is that I landed in the Socialist Party totally ignorant. Everybody was talking, and I just stared at them. Everyone surprised me. They spoke a language I had never heard in my life. And everything sounded logical. Later, when I started reading, I began spouting off Trotsky's ideas, and they would ask, "Is our comrade a Trotskyite?" "No," I'd tell them. "I'm a socialist." I read voraciously. I could recite "The International" [*"L'internationale,"* the socialist anthem] from memory, and everything Marx said, and the *What Is to Be Done?* and the whole ball of wax. But I could only do that because I read and studied. My intellectual formation was never adequate, nor did I have enough time to process the knowledge I was acquiring—or to question it. That's the truth. That was my formation.

You've said on several occasions (in the media, in your book) that you haven't divulged everything you know about the period of militancy. Why the silence?

First of all, regarding my comrades from the era in which I was connected to my country's Socialist Party, it's not my place to say anything. Second, I've already testified to everything that judges, actuaries, lawyers, journalists, and those linked to human rights or legal organizations thought necessary to ask me over the course of more than a decade—both about me and my comrades, both about the facts in question and the personnel of DINA/CNI (CNI, *Central Nacional de Informaciones*, National Information Center).

Because I don't want to leave gaps in my answer, I want to clarify that despite my good memory, I don't remember every day of the period in which I was connected to the Socialist Party, nor of my time in prison.

Ever since I left Chile, I made a decision that I honor to this day: I am only willing to make myself available for questions and consultations that come directly from the courts or their auxiliary organizations, or from people deserving of my trust.

The only exception to my rule has been you, Michael. I want you to know that this is the only interview I've granted in more than five years. And this will also be the last one.

How real was the threat that revolutionary groups like yours represented in Chilean society in the early 1970s? In other words, what concrete impact could you have had as radical militants?

We were all followers of Carlos Altamirano. GEA's structure was aligned with Altamirano, and Altamirano had formed an alliance with the left's most radical sectors: MIR; the Christian Left, MAPU (*Movimiento de Acción Popular Unitario*, Popular Unitary Action Movement). I already told you that our public function was to establish a militant training school. But, as I also pointed out before, GEA was an operative group that functioned clandestinely just before the coup. To be frank, I planted a bomb outside the Chilean-American Cultural Institute. What shame! We didn't even have real explosives, so we just used sticks of dynamite. What did we achieve by doing that? We blew up part of the door and that was it! We didn't do any more damage than that. But we were ordered to do that by the party.

Listen, when you publish this, the Socialist Party is going to hate me even more. Oh well, I'm going to say it anyway because it's the truth . . . What day was it? Oh yeah, I guess it was late August 1973. Our orders were to take the US Embassy—the new one. Have you seen it? They call it "the bunker" because it's an indestructible fortress. We drove by the embassy in a car to scope it out from the outside. We saw a bunch of marines guarding the place. I was really skinny then, and I looked at those marines and said, "How am I ever going to get past them? I'll never manage it!" I swear this is true! I was doing exactly what they suggested we do: seize the US Embassy and blow it up. I'm not talking about the Consulate that's over there by the park, but about the *Embassy*: the new one, the one they just built! Do you get it? Not even a divine miracle—provided that there's a God—would have helped us manage to blow up the embassy. To do it, we would have needed other resources that we just didn't have.

So after we scoped out the embassy visually, we went back to the central committee and told them that the mission they were proposing was suicidal. I think it would have been more effective had we each worn a bomb on our person and killed ourselves right there. We weren't even going to manage to blow up the grass! So we said, "This is impossible." With the minimal resources we had, it was just impossible. What's more, there were already some dissenting voices in the group that were asking, "Are we really helping Salvador Allende by doing this, or are we just pressuring him to make decisions?" It was supposed to be the political right that was boycotting Allende, not us. But we were always told the same thing, "You only have partial information. Only the political commission has full information, and they make the decisions. You just follow orders. Amen." We felt unsettled. But what did our voices matter? We went back to the central committee and said, "Sir, if it's your will, we'll each wear a few sticks of dynamite and kill ourselves on the doorstep of the US Embassy . . . because we're not going to be able to blow up . . . maybe we'll manage to scuff the door if we all stand there together, that is, if we manage to light the fuses before the guards get us." And they told us, "OK, then find something else to blow up, as long as it belongs to the United States." So we decided to blow up the door of the Chilean-American Cultural Institute, because, well, it was right around the corner. That's how things were back then!

I've asked myself many times, how much, as a party, as socialists, were we contributing to Allende's fall? The reality is that the Socialist Party's most radical faction, Altamirano's group, together with MIR and MAPU-Garretón (because the other MAPU was more moderate), were all pressuring Allende to make more radical decisions. Allende wanted to move more slowly, using the tools of democracy and operating within its framework.

And looking back, if you had to offer a critique of Allende, what would it be?

I guess my critique wouldn't be of Allende. There was a joke back then that people told inside La Moneda. It went like this: There was a government minister, Minister Vergara, who hardly knew how to write his name. Vergara summons his secretary and says, "*Señora*, call a meeting for this Thursday." And the secretary says, "How do you spell Thursday?" So Minister Vergara stopped to think, and then he said, "You know what? You'd better make it Wednesday."

I think that don Salvador (Allende) had well-intentioned people working for him, but they just weren't skilled enough to do their jobs. I think he was elected prematurely. I think that the left, in general, wasn't ready to take power. His best advisors did all they could, but the rest of the jobs were filled by incapable people, people who lacked experience or didn't have enough training. For my part, I was absolutely ignorant. I tell you this in all honesty. It was as if I could sense that things weren't going to go well, but I wasn't able to articulate the reason, to say, "Comrade, we can't go on like this." In the end, everything was so Stalinist, but I had to keep quiet, because if I didn't, I'd be perceived as the difficult one. They told me I was a drag, that I was ignorant, that I had no clue. And the more I read, the more complicated things got for me, because the truth is that what I was reading wasn't playing out in reality.

Additionally, the Communist Party and the Socialist Party were always embroiled in a visceral and cannibalistic fight. Sometimes when we'd have Popular Unity demonstrations—where it was assumed that we should all be marching together—suddenly some factory workers would pass by (either from the Communist Party or from MIR, with their head coverings, sticks, and stuff) and they'd act aggressively toward us. They even shot at us! Or sometimes they'd nab us and hit us with chains during the demonstrations. Sometimes we socialists would be on the Alameda, Santiago's main thoroughfare, and the cops would spray us with tear gas from one side while the communists waited behind us to beat us. We were like trapped rats. So you see, the conditions just weren't right for alliances to form.

Do you think that today, thirty years after the coup, our vision of Salvador Allende is adequate?

Look, I sincerely believe that Allende was much more lucid than many militants from the parties or movements. I think that the man truly knew that radical change would destroy the country. I think that Allende knew that Marxism-Leninism wouldn't take root here, that Chile wouldn't become another Cuba. I think he knew all that. (Sure, if any of today's party militants heard me say this, they'd undeniably call me a "traitor." You know?) On the other hand, Allende was very much a bourgeois guy. But don Salvador was a lot more lucid than the rest of his people. I sincerely believe that. But, then again, maybe I don't have all the necessary tools to pass judgment.

Wherever you looked, there were cracks in Allende's government. Despite his efforts, despite the fact that he included military people in his cabinet, despite that he eventually started dialogues with the Christian Democrats, despite all that, foreign and domestic interests that vehemently wanted to avoid a "second Cuba" won the day.

When I talk to people today who maintain radical views, they tell me stuff like, "Well, in Mexico, Subcomandante Marcos is alive and well." "Yes," I say. "So what?" Don't get me wrong; I like Subcomandante Marcos, first of all because he's intelligent, second of all because he's gotten things done, and so on. But in today's world I would never send a young person to the sierra to be killed like a carnival duck. I'm not saying that we were irresponsible, because I believe that all things must be understood in their context. But I do think that we contributed (and when I say "we," I mean "I") to the climate of violence. Violence existed! We lived it! The right attacked our party headquarters. We had to work all day and then stand guard at our headquarters all night. And it wasn't the kind of guard duty where you drink coffee, stare at the moon, or dream about Che Guevara. No! It was a vigilant type of guard duty where you had to watch for enemy fire. They never attacked the central committee, but there were neighborhoods that got attacked. On the roofs of all our barracks we had heaps of stones, piled high, but we had little else to defend ourselves.

Getting back to Allende, do you think he is an icon? What does Salvador Allende signify today?

Boy, you really want me to put a noose around my neck and . . .

No, not at all.

Sometimes I feel like I'm being discriminated against so heavily because something has been gained from my testifying in court. Sure, they call me a "traitor," an "informant"—everything in the book. But then they say, fine, leave her alone so that *she* can face all those people. Do you understand? That's how I feel. And now you're asking me to give opinions that will make everyone hate me even more.

Look, I seriously think that Allende was a very lucid man. I believe that he knew that he would not be able to sustain his government using violent methods. If you think about the fact that he incorporated military people into his cabinet, it's clear that he was trying to maintain governability in the country—because the country was really destroying itself! The right strategically tried to provoke food shortages in the major cities. And that created much discontent and a black market. It exacerbated differences among people because the homes of the wealthy were like supermarkets. To give you an example, there's a part of my family that has money, and I remember going to visit them just so I could have something to eat. Their dining room tables were covered with nonperishable goods that they were hoarding. Do you get it? And you'd go back to your barrio (which wasn't poor, just lower middle class, a regular barrio) and you'd see the bread lines, people trying to get basic foodstuffs and supplies that were being sold at prices no one could afford. There were no supermarkets in those years. Things were so bad that—shamefully—I remember times when my comrades and I would go to a restaurant and steal sugar off the tables and take it home. Soon restaurants stopped putting sugar on the tables; they'd give you just enough for your coffee. Things were that extreme! So, honestly, Allende couldn't govern. Had he been able to govern, had he really had *control* of the government, with good ministers, with good infrastructure, with the parties behind him, then things might have been different. But Allende never had that support. He didn't have it because he lashed out against civilian power and against the greatest power of all: economic power.

I understand that Allende was a visionary. Maybe if instead of being Chilean he were Swiss, Norwegian, or Danish, he would have been a good governor. Maybe none of what happened in Chile would have happened. But that wasn't the situation.

I think that Allende must have often dreamed of change—of a major future change. But he clearly knew that his government would have to be "reformist," as we pejoratively called it. Allende wanted to stress social issues, but his hands were tied on many fronts. Curiously, that kind of self critique, that kind of debate, hasn't existed in my country—neither within the parties nor from individuals.

Today I look back on those years and I know that I wouldn't wish anyone to relive that experience—not under any circumstances! Not under any circumstances! What's more, I spent the rest of my life trying to make sure that my children were pacifists, to have them grow up distanced from politics, to be good people, with values, but isolated from political life. But in those years there wasn't even time to think. I didn't have the capacity to think, to question—although I'm not sure that having any more clarity would have mattered. There was no time to lollygag.

Personally speaking, I never had the training or knowledge to object. It never occurred to me to escape. It just never occurred to me. The dynamic was such that I was always running, running, running, like when I used to train as an athlete.

But I saw what happened next. I saw the army in action. I saw 38 Londres Street. I saw Krasnoff (Miguel), Lawrence (Ricardo), Godoy (Gerardo), Moren (Marcelo), and his henchmen. And they made minced meat of us!

So, to use an exaggerated metaphor, as a young person I was pretty naïve. With a couple of books in our heads and with a deep desire to make the world a better place, we did what we thought we had to do. That was all.

What values do you hold dear from that period of militancy?

Some time ago, a leftist friend in Mexico who was reacting to a very specific social problem asked me a question, "And us? What can we do?" I looked at her and said, "Nothing—not you, not me, not anybody."

That friend remains chained to the old discourses of the 1960s and 1970s. So I told her, "All our generation has left, since we're all almost 60 years old (I just turned 59 in March 2007), is to try to live in greater solidarity with one another." I try to nourish myself with every value I have conserved, but not so my children will run off to the sierra and become *guerrilleros* (No! No! No! Because they'll get massacred!). I do it so they'll raise even better children. Hopefully someday we'll all be able to refashion ourselves as human beings.

I still believe in certain things, and some of them stem from those utopian, Marxist dreams—those crazy dreams, lived irrationally, with youthful energy. And if it's true that I don't believe in *everything* from that time, there are values I cherish and that are also part of my Christian faith. At bottom, the search for the "New Man" has been going on for two thousand years. I'm not necessarily talking about the new descendents of Che; I'm talking about the Bible's call for us to be Christians, about the gospels' call to be a "new man." The gospels tell us, "No one puts new wine in old wineskins," because the new wine is effervescent and will break the wineskin. We have to remake ourselves. That's what a "new man" is: a nonviolent man, an understanding man, a man who can put himself in another's shoes, a man of solidarity. In the face of discrimination, I feel deeply that no one should ever be discriminated against again. Faced with violence, I genuinely feel that all violence should cease. I don't know if you understand.

I have come to the conclusion that we are all products of our history and that history constructs us: our little, personal histories inscribed within the larger history of a society, of a country, of a continent, of the world. And that little, personal history is the only one you can influence. I can't tell my son how to live. I can't. I shouldn't. He has to make his own decisions and has the right to make his own mistakes. As a mother, I can only give him the best tools I can to make those decisions. That's our struggle. The more tools my son has to keep him from falling into the Mexican trap, to keep him off drugs, to keep him from the world's current wounds (drugs, violence, etc.), the better off he'll be. Truth be told, the deepest wounds in the history of humanity stem from a lack of love. It all happens because there is no solidarity, no love.

What is the status of your militancy today? And how do you feel about those who were militants back then (1970–73)?

I'm not a militant in any political party. I want to repeat that I still hold many ideals from back then. My country's well-being interests me very much. I aspire for all people—for the men and women of all countries, of every age, race, and creed—to strive for a more just world in which respect for all people matters, in which we all learn to respect each other and the world that shelters us, in which people care for natural resources. In short, I've still got many personal dreams to realize.

I feel good. My life hasn't been easy. I've known achievements and failures, strength and weakness, pain and joy. However, I've been privileged enough to remake my life and to continue learning how to live.

I knew that my collaboration had happened during an extreme situation and that it wasn't entirely my decision. Other people and factors intervened that weren't entirely clear at the time. But something told me I had to enter into it completely. I felt like I would never be able to keep going if I started down the path of feeling like a victim, even if everything changed at some point. I knew that others took different paths. The guards talked about "the fanaticism of those who died without talking." I always admired the MIR's militants for their bravery. Even in the worst of conditions, they got organized and found ways to get documents out of the prisons. I was never able to do that.

—*Luz Arce, The Inferno (1993)*

SANTIAGO, SIXTH DAY OF OCTOBER TWO THOUSAND, **MARÍA CECILIA BOTTAI MONREAL**, A CHILEAN, NATIVE OF SANTIAGO, 50 YEARS OLD, MARRIAGE ANNULED, ABLE TO READ AND WRITE, ORAL SURGEON, NATIONAL IDENTITY CARD NUMBER X.XXX.XXX-X, WHO LIVES AT FROILÁN ROA NUMBER XXXX, HOUSE NUMBER XXXX, IN THE COMMUNITY OF MACUL, APPEARS BEFORE THE COURT, AND HAVING SWORN TO TELL THE TRUTH, STATES:

I know why I have been called to testify, that it is about providing details regarding the period in which I was detained by state agents, in 1975–76, and held in different detention and torture centers . . . They also detained my mother, Teresa, and my sister, Carmen. OSVALDO ROMO carried out all the detentions. Carmen and María Teresa were taken to Villa Grimaldi, where they stayed for about ten days. ROMO and LUZ ARCE tortured them.

2

Collaboration, Critiques, Remorse

I'd like to talk about collaboration. How did you start collaborating with DINA?

When I was a political prisoner . . . when I had already begun collaborating . . . the image that came to me frequently . . . Oh, it still hurts . . . [*She starts crying*] . . . But don't worry.

As a prisoner, I felt like I was educated every morning in front of the toilet. There I was, and I was the worst of the worst. I was scum. And even still—I don't know if it was because of the education I received or because of my subsequent conversion to Christianity—I feel that, despite everything, God gave me two very important gifts that I've possessed ever since the day I was born: happiness and optimism. But when I was in that painful situation, I felt miserable. I can't think of any term more appropriate than miserable. As a prisoner who was considered a collaborator, I remembered my grandfather and said, "Well, at least you're dead so you don't have to see what your granddaughter has become." Do you understand? In other words, I even found something good in that.

Strangely, when I was a prisoner, I *always, always, always* maintained a certain degree of lucidity. There were many times when I was literally unconscious, either because I had been beaten, or because of hunger, or whatever. Consequently, I have forgotten entire days, weeks. I remember that when I'd open my eyes and see that I hadn't died, I would think that I had two options: to live or die. So I decided that I would act as if I were going to live. That was permanent. I kept listening. I kept trying to find things out, to gather information. I never dreamed I would testify later. Never! But I needed that information to survive.

I want to say that I lied to DINA about many things. In other words, my collaboration was never 100 percent. In fact, if someone were to take the time to examine who I turned in—unfortunately four people died, but it was because there was no logic in the detention centers—they'd see that I didn't even turn in a single party nucleus leader. What I'm saying is that I tried to find the least painful way to collaborate.

To answer your question, I didn't torture anyone.

You've just told me that you were responsible for four deaths as a functionary of DINA. Who were the four people who died, and how do you know that there

were only four? In other words, how do you know that the definitive number was four and not greater?

I've narrated all this in *The Inferno*. That information has been registered and investigated by the Rettig Commission (*Comisión Nacional para la Verdad y Reconciliación*, National Commission on Truth and Reconciliation) and by the tribunals and courts in Chile and other countries. I want to clarify that as a functionary I bore no responsibility for deaths linked to the detention of people or to torture.[1] Yes, they took me along on some detention raids so I could point people out or ask where they were—but all of that was as a prisoner, under torture, and with no chance to object. Later, as a functionary, I was never again taken on detention raids.

Thinking about those four deceased people, how do you experience them today?

Painfully! Situations like that shouldn't exist. I've referred extensively to this topic elsewhere. To summarize, though, I can say that during my whole experience as a prisoner (and I include within the category of "prisoner" the length of my time with DINA both as a prisoner and a functionary), I was *forced* to be a functionary of DINA/CNI. I have integrated that experience into my life little by little through the process of testifying, writing, learning about my strengths and weaknesses, and learning about life.

As a collaborator, who exactly did you turn over to DINA/CNI?

During those awful times, in the worst stage, August 1974, which is when I informed on people, I turned in people from the (Chilean) Youth Organization, people from the movements, that is, from the party's periphery. I was certain that if they talked, DINA wouldn't be able to penetrate the party structure using the information they provided. Moreover, because those people were young and hadn't been associated with any militarized aspects of the party or used weapons, I figured that at most they'd be kicked around a little and *chau*. But that wasn't what happened. That wasn't what happened! And today four of them are disappeared.[2]

It's just that I was never really ideologically committed to DINA. I couldn't be. There are people—militants from that era—who have come up to me and said, "Thank you." And I say, "Why?" And they say, "Because you didn't turn me in." "Ah," I tell them, "that was more than thirty years ago." But that's what they say. Do you understand? They certainly don't say it within the confines of the party because they'd be . . . It's because within party confines there's a clear position on these matters. Nor would I ask them to say it. That doesn't interest me today.

I have thought several times, Michael, that my wanting to talk with you might be interpreted as an attempt to unload, to avoid responsibilities. But it's not that way at all. That's not how it is. I'm not going to waste energy. I have clarified certain personal feelings and I'm not going to fight that fight, because to defend myself I'd have to say . . . well . . . things that I don't want to say.

Are we really dealing today with a realistic vision of what we lived? I get the feeling that there is still so much subjectivity in the air. I think that when all of us are dead—and when I say "us" I am referring to my generation—younger people will approach this history, read about it, look at it, and they'll have the right to evaluate. Although they may never have lived through political prison or torture directly, they'll be able to deal with the issue without emotional involvement or prefabricated judgments.

Other survivors with whom I've spoken have told me that, among detainees, collaboration was the norm rather than an exception. Does it bother you that you have been labeled a collaborator without there being a more realistic vision of the scope of collaboration during the dictatorship?

Right. The scope of collaboration still doesn't get discussed—although it's mentioned much more often today than in the nineties, for example. In the 1980s and 1990s, it was just Marcia, Carola, and me. Period! No one else collaborated. Do you see? In this country, no one else collaborated! We were the only ones.

You three were the only collaborators . . .

Exactly! Everyone else was a hero, and the three of us were traitors. Everyone who died was a hero!

So does it bother you that you've been used as a scapegoat?

It's that . . . You know what? . . . I think that what I did will pain me forever. I feel that the people I turned in . . . in my mind, following the party's protocols, following what I was taught . . . because . . . strictly speaking, first I informed on the dead, then on those who were already prisoners, then on the exiles . . . and they kept figuring me out. Of course! It was logical! I would give them three or four names, tell them how to locate people, and then the DINA agents would go and discover that the people were murdered some time ago. Then the agents would come back, and I'd swear I had no idea.

Because I didn't start collaborating for six months after I was captured, I could tell my repressors that I didn't know things—even though I really did know many of those things. Curiously, as a prisoner, unconscious, beaten as I was, I was always listening. Do you understand? I was always filing away information, not knowing that someday it would be valuable in court, as it is today. As a prisoner, I was always keeping track of information because I had to know if someone got captured who knew my name. As I stated in my book, I withheld my name for three days to give my family time to clear my room so they wouldn't become accomplices. And when I figured that they had had enough time to clean my room out, that's when I gave up my name. Until March 20, I was Isabel Romero Contreras. They beat me because they had already discovered that I was using a false name and that the address on my ID card didn't exist. Throughout the coming months, until mid-August, I didn't give up any information at all. Never, never, never! And when I eventually broke, I started by turning in those people whom I already mentioned.

Also, it turns out that I helped secure asylum for many of the people I turned in before they fell. I knew that they'd never be detained because they already had asylum. They were either still inside an embassy or in another country. In that sense, they were not at risk. That strategy bought me little windows of time.

DINA's teams would go out and do their work, and with any luck, MIR militants would fall. If that happened, they'd leave me alone. That's how bad it was in DINA's dungeons! And when they'd finish with their line of torture and questioning, they'd go back to my list only to discover that those I'd named had achieved asylum. The whole time I kept insisting that my information was more than six months old. I kept reciting the *Combatant Manual* to them. It was then that I discovered that DINA's agents didn't understand what I was saying. For example, I would talk about the *caleta,* and they'd ask me, "What's the *caleta*?" "Well," I'd say, "it's where people hide." That's when I discovered a pos-si-bi-li-ty. But I had to create the possibility of collaborating in a different way. And obviously Krassnoff told me to go to hell because he was a man of action. He was one of the few intelligent DINA leaders at that time, and he knew I was trying to buy time.[3] For Krassnoff, detainees were for sending to the *parrilla* (the grill) so that they'd give up information that might lead to other detainees, or to MIR's central committee, or to the political commission. Krassnoff never listened to me! I got the feeling that he knew I was lying. But fortunately they soon stuck me with Cirro Torré Sáez, a police officer who I doubt had two functioning neurons in his head. I then figured out that Torré felt discriminated against within DINA because the superstar officers were Krassnoff and Lawrence.[4] The guy didn't have a big vocabulary either, so I told him that if he were going to be an "Intelligence Officer," he'd have to learn Marxist terminology. So I started writing him a leftist dictionary. He gave me paper and a typewriter, and I wrote pages and pages. Later I wrote a sixty- to eighty-page "Communications Manual" that never existed with contents I invented based on spy books I had read, or on my memories. In other words, I devised strategies, within my realm of possibilities, to avoid being out on the street turning people in.

For these reasons, if you were to take the time to investigate who fell in September, October, November 1974, and later, you'd see that no one else fell because of me. I benefited from the officers' stupidity! If I had been captured by a normal secret service operation, made up of trained individuals, I'm positive I would have wound up rotting in a detention camp. The fact that I resisted torture for six months, coupled with the incidents that happened at the Military Hospital with Rodolfo González Pérez (who remains disappeared), made them assume I was a MIR militant or that I had more extensive preparation than I actually had.[5] (Also, my time as a prisoner was lengthened because I had a bullet wound in my foot.) But, in early September 1974, when they determined for sure that I wasn't from MIR, I had already been detained for so long that I knew various DINA officers and personnel. I know they thought about eliminating me on several occasions, one of which was early in November 1974. But I managed to survive.

Strategies like these served me well because I managed to stop having to identify people in the street. I managed to stop turning in my comrades. In other words, I wasn't just a traitor; I was a traitor who tried to be the least traitorous I could. That helped me to sustain myself, because I think that if they had broken me completely, I would have even ratted out my own father! And that's not a metaphor, because my father was active with the left in his workplace. But DINA never found out about my father!

I also managed to get my brother out of there. I broke when I saw them torturing him. I just couldn't take it. I lost all capacity to reason.

We started off with a question about whether you feel you have been used as a scapegoat or as an emblematic traitor figure.

Look, I don't feel like I have been personally targeted as a scapegoat or a traitor figure. That is, I don't particularly feel that those labels have been directed against me. I think that in any process of this nature, the human mind has a tendency to wander in certain directions. I see it as a natural human response. Also, I feel like if I had not lived through it, I would never have understood the experience of someone like me.

You know that there are two things I never like to do: one is to speculate, the other is to assume or judge another's intentions. These two things are very common in Latin American countries. I tend not to think about what someone else is supposedly thinking. But to answer your question, I am going to speculate even though I don't like to.

Let's assume that after the coup repressive forces were looking for me. The Socialist Party offered me asylum, but at the time I made a personal decision to stay active, although I asked for a change of assignment. I knew that if I kept working in the street as a communications liaison I would undoubtedly fall. Everyone knew me in the neighborhoods because I was an athlete. If anyone were to run across my name, I could be located. I was even known as an athlete in the press. So I said to my boss, "What if instead of acting as a permanent liaison in the street you send me to work on some project for the masses in a place where no one knows me, like in a shantytown?" And he said to me, "If that's what you want, I'll agree." I speculate that had I managed to switch assignments, maybe I never would have been detained. But I was detained before I ever managed to switch jobs.

Speculating a bit further, I dare say that had I heeded my boss's suggestion and sought asylum, I wouldn't be either "the traitor" or "the informant." (At the time my boss was Gustavo Ruz Zañartu, a member of the Socialist Party's central committee for whom I acted as a liaison.) I would probably have returned to Chile years later and in very good shape. All this is speculation. And if upon returning I had run into Marcia or Carola or someone else who experienced what we did—especially considering the way I was back then and knowing the testimonies of those who lived in exile—I doubt I would have understood anything.

Therefore, I start with the assumption that all I've had to face is part of a process. I don't feel that Luz Arce is being targeted in particular. I feel that people's feelings are directed toward someone who did certain things and who is naturally going to be attacked given the circumstances.

On the other hand, I have certain defenses within myself that I've already explained: all the fighting I did that no one values, knows about, or imagines. At first, as I've told you, it was just the three of us who were traitors: Marcia, Carola, and me. And the accusation was, "She ratted people out! Traitor! Informant! Never forgive her!" Later, when evidence arose that we weren't the only ones, the argument changed to "She received a salary from those people!"

Diamela Eltit is quite representative of that line of criticism.[6] Don't get me wrong, I very much admire her as a writer, and I try to read everything of hers that I come across. I have nothing personal against her—quite the contrary. But Diamela's reading of me is always from the outside. She can't do a reading from the inside because she didn't live my experience. So I have to suppose that she does her reading from the outside relying on everything she was told by her exiled friends—who probably suffered much need, or their mothers died while they were abroad, or maybe they suffered millions of painful things—and that her suffering is no greater and no less than mine. I am absolutely convinced that the cause of one's pain doesn't much matter. What matters is how one lives that pain. Maybe someone living in exile suffered just as much for not eating Chilean bread as I did for informing on people. It's possible. They are totally different things, but maybe someone exists for whom that pain is comparable to mine. And that's what matters. So I don't dare say that someone's opinion doesn't matter because that person is outside the situation. I think that everyone acts, offers opinions, and reacts according to her own history, her own emotional baggage, her own personal capacity, and her own upbringing. And Diamela and all the rest who are extremely critical of me have *their* histories and *their* suffering and *their* baggage. Do you understand? But I have mine.

So I'm not going to start a conflict with Diamela Eltit or anyone else. *They,* we all react with the tools we have at hand, just like I reacted with those I had. It hurts, sure. Sure it hurts! It pains me! And I'm not prone to drama. They have a right to say what they want because it's how they see it, how they feel it, based on *their* stories and in *their* contexts. I know I could have done a lot more damage, and I tried desperately to avoid it. That, as I see it, is like a bit of balm for the wound. And that has kept me going in the worst moments.

As I've learned more over time, I have come to discover that even if the schooling that I had as a child, as an adolescent, as a prisoner, or as a functionary of DINA wasn't desirable for anyone, it was—quite simply—the schooling I had. I'm not crazy. I don't have kids who are drug addicts. I've been able to have a family and a job. All of that gives me strength. In other words, I derive strength from those little successes.

You've mentioned Diamela Eltit's writings about your testimony. How did you react to her specific criticisms of you?

I don't remember exactly what she said in her article, despite the fact that I read it several times. But there's one thing I'll never forget: she assumes my intentions. She says something like that I was with the left because the government was leftist, and then I changed over to the military because the military was in power—as if I had wanted to do all that! Do you understand? And now supposedly I'm going to run for political office or some such.

So all I could say was, "This woman is crazy!" If she had sought me out just once—even for half an hour . . . (And she could have done that because we both published with Planeta and the publisher knew where to find me . . .) If she had just dialed Planeta's number and said to our common editor, Carlos Orellana, "Look, Carlos, I want to speak with Luz Arce," and had he called me, I would have gone running to meet her, because I respect Diamela Eltit as a person. If she had just spoken to me, asked me some questions for 15 or 30 minutes, I would give her a lot more credit. But she never did that. Never! Never! Never! Never! She doesn't know me. And if it's true that she wouldn't have really known me after 15 or 30 minutes, at least I would have said that she was a serious individual. She never even called to interview me, to say, "Look, I want to find out who this woman is."

As I read it, Diamela Eltit's critique does not have as much to do with the fact that you collaborated as with what we might call the subsequent

"bureaucratization" of your collaboration—that is, becoming a functionary of DINA and accepting a salary.

That's right. On May 7, 1975, when they took Marcia, Carola, and me to General Headquarters—without telling us where we were going—I thought they were going to kill us. Frankly, we had no other alternative than to be there. Later, Contreras called us each into his office and added that soon we would be leaving Villa Grimaldi, that the three of us would be given an apartment to share across from the General Barracks on Marcoleta Street, and that we would each continue working just as we had been up to that time. I would keep working as Rolf Wenderoth Pozo's secretary.[7] Man, was I mute! I only managed to ask Contreras if I had any alternative. I went into the office first, then Alejandra, then Carola. And when we left, the three of us looked at each other. It was really strange. I got the same feeling I got when I informed on comrades and realized that DINA could find them and torture them.

Soon the three of us went back to the car and Carola, who was always very practical, said to the officer who was driving, "And will you pay us a salary? How are we going to be functionaries if we don't have clothing?" She was worried about practical matters. I felt pangs of conscience . . . strange . . . like . . . like everything was spinning . . . like . . . lethargy . . . like . . . I don't know . . . it's really weird . . . and so I started thinking, "What does all this mean?" That moment meant never sleeping again at Villa Grimaldi. It meant never sleeping in that shithole again!

I started seeing what the changes would be like, and I was relieved that according to Contreras I would keep doing what I had been doing, that is, taking dictation from Wenderoth. That meant I would be able to move forward without sacrificing my objective of not informing on anyone else. All the people I knew had already fallen. (Really, I wasn't the one who turned in many of the comrades I knew who were captured.) The rest had left the country. I no longer knew where they lived. It had been more than a year since I had known. In that sense, I was relieved. I started thinking, "OK, what do I do now? What's next?" I was always asking myself, "Where am I going?" But there was my son to think about, and my mother. Threats against my family were ever present.

It seems as if there were several junctures during your time as a functionary in which it could have been feasible for you to leave DINA/CNI. Why did you stay for so long? Why didn't you get out sooner when you had the chance?

As time went by, as days passed, I started thinking, "I have to get out of here." But also, I thought, they have to *let* me leave. If at first my main objective was not to turn people in, later my objective became figuring out how to leave. The first thing I did after starting to work for Wenderoth was to ask him if he'd allow me to take a secretarial course. Wenderoth had already authorized Marcia and Carola to do it, but he didn't want to let me. He wanted to keep me there with him. He didn't let me take the secretarial class for the simple reason that he wanted to keep me seated there at his desk! At that time, the three of us would leave work at 5:30 and Wenderoth would put us in his car and drive us home. We'd get home, make tea and toast, and Wenderoth would have tea with us. Then he'd leave and we'd double lock all the doors. In addition to what was normal for Santiago homes, we asked for them to put a chain and a peephole on our door.

On May 7, when they made us functionaries, I said to myself, "Well, at least I'll be able to walk through the neighborhood park again." But the truth is that months went by before I dared—or the girls dared, or all of us together dared—to go out on a Saturday or Sunday afternoon for a walk in the park. It was such a sick situation that even if they did give us a chance to go for a walk, it took a long time before we took advantage of the opportunity. I wouldn't have dared!

I didn't leave DINA, flee, or hide because I was perfectly familiar with what had happened to Marco Antonio and Lucas, the two boys from MIR who were involved in the "press conference."[8] They had gone through the same process of collaboration that we had, and DINA gave them their freedom "with surveillance" even *before* we got ours. Behind DINA's back, they established contact with MIR and sent some self-critical letters. It turned out that DINA was intercepting all the mail MIR was sending abroad. They read the letters and sent for the boys. I saw Marco Antonio and Lucas come in blindfolded and handcuffed. And they died! Later, I found out that the boys, when they discovered they were being pursued, had gone to the Vicariate of Solidarity and Cristián Precht, the leader of that organization that was giving aid to victims, wouldn't receive them. He wouldn't receive them because he was scared. I suppose that part of his job was to take care that the Vicariate wouldn't be infiltrated by DINA. That seemed logical. So I said, "If I flee, nothing will come of it! What would I do? Where would I go?" Fleeing wasn't a solution. I had no resources to hide from DINA. I had to create a situation in which they'd *let* me leave.

The amount of money they paid us at that time was enough to buy deodorant, toothpaste, and toilet paper to share. They only raised our salary a little when Wenderoth noticed that we didn't have clothes to wear. That new salary was no great shakes either. It was enough to pay my son's school tuition, and after that I had five hundred pesos left for his transportation. That was it! For years I had eaten only what was given to me at lunchtime in the General Headquarters, and not a morsel more. If I was lucky, I'd also get a cup of tea and a piece of bread at home. Wenderoth even bought the bread for teatime. So sure, of course I had to receive a salary. I had to educate my son and everything else. What's more, I certainly wouldn't have worked for those *milicos* for free.[9] Nor did my family have resources to give me.

So I understand. I understand what Diamela Eltit is saying. But I feel like she did not live the situation I did—not even remotely! I'm sure she is a great person who, if placed in the same situation, could have left DINA with her head held high. I'm sorry I couldn't. Yes, there was bureaucratization. But the only answer I can give—without trying to defend myself; I can only articulate what I lived and felt—is that at every stage I did what I was capable of doing, nothing more.

I'm telling you all this because people on the outside might think, for example, that if you go today to an army or air force office and see the women functionaries doing their jobs, that that's what our life was like. But that's not how it was. Do you get it? It's not like I kept working for them like Carola did, for example. (I know—it's bad for me to compare because she has *her* process and *her* life, which I understand. I just talked to the judge about that last week.)

I was a functionary of DINA/CNI for four years and five months. The whole time I was looking for a way out. I found it on November 2, 1979.

Would it be accurate to say, then, that you had no choice—that you had no choice but to remain a functionary of DINA/CNI for so many years?

In all honesty, I'm not going to utter the sentence "I had no choice." That's not the exact phrase. The exact phrase is "The three of us were terrified." I think, to this day, Carola is still terrified. Marcia stopped feeling that way when she decided to testify in November 1992. And I stopped feeling that way when they finally accepted my resignation, and throughout my whole personal journey that came later on. Our fear was so profound that it took months for us to go out into the street! I only went out when I was able. When I tendered my resignation, my boss said, "You're giving up a stable salary. You're giving up the house that you'll soon be able to afford. You're giving up a lot of security." And I told him, "Yes, I am, because none of it makes up for what I'm feeling right now."

Today everyone knows that Carola retired as part of DINE—that she stayed there for the twenty-some odd years she needed to retire. Today she has an apartment where she can live. Every month she gets a certain sum of money, her pension. If she loses a tooth, she can go to the Military Hospital. And if she needs medical attention, she doesn't have to walk around with her hand out like I do. But none of that matters.

In your book, the place from which you speak is clearly that of a victim of state repression. Have you ever thought of yourself as anything other than a victim?

Yes. The first time I heard that I was not what I felt I was—a "traitor" who was incapable of defending what she stood for—was from my friend, a psychologist, in early 1985. I didn't accept what she told me. Then a second psychologist who gave me therapy for six months—also in 1985—told me the same thing. I still didn't accept it. Then the Dominican priest, Father Cristián, who heard my first confessions in 1988, pointed it out again.[10] It was only with him that I finally started to entertain the idea that I could be considered a victim during the period in which I resisted torture without giving up information.

When I testified to the Rettig Commission, I heard again that I was a victim. Not only did the lawyers who recorded my testimony mention it (Carlos Fresno Orrego, Jorge Correa Sutil, and Gastón Gómez), but they repeated it over and over, but I still couldn't accept it. Nevertheless, little by little, I started assimilating it all. And yes, now I feel like I was a victim too.

Obviously everyone is responsible for his or her actions, but there are factors, other considerations that also influence one's thoughts and actions. While I was detained, none of what happened—giving up information, informing on comrades, working as a functionary—was a decision made with even a minute to reflect. At various junctures, I didn't even make decisions. The brutal force that was exercised over prisoners was permanently disconcerting. I know now—and I always knew—that there were comrades who didn't talk. I don't know the details of their experiences. I suppose that for whatever reasons they must have been better people than I. But in my case, that's how it is, or that's how it was.

What factors contributed to your collaboration?

I suppose that there were several factors ranging from those that were my own responsibility to others that have to do with genetics, upbringing, life experiences, and so on. I couldn't resist indefinitely. Not even the functionary stage was a good one. I was still scared. I always wanted to leave that place. I just couldn't do it until I mustered the strength to stand up to them in 1979. That decision was a process too. It wasn't a decision that I just made one day and that was it. I left when I was able—and scared to death! I had to learn how to walk in the street again. I had to learn how to take my son to kindergarten. Even if my kids couldn't have gone to school on their own, I wouldn't have taken them. Little by little, my life normalized in that sense.

1991 was a decisive year. When I testified to the Rettig Commission, I was liberated from the weight of the factual information I possessed. It was like I could finally breathe. Being with my two kids in Europe, managing to work and support myself while I was there, studying theology in a Chilean university and other institutes, managing to improve my family situation: a lot of factors made me feel like I could do things, like I could have goals. I didn't realize until I returned to Chile that I could have a future. I don't know exactly when it happened, but one day I figured out that I could set long term goals. Before that, I would never commit myself to anything, not even for the following week. I had no idea whether I'd be there or not. I think that at some point in prison I started living from day to day. Only by 1992, did I understand that my life didn't have to be that way.

My decision to go to the Rettig Commission at some point in 1990 didn't make me happy. It was the result of a process. It was so evident that I should go; I couldn't deny it. Friends and priests counseled me. They told me I was under no obligation and that if it was going to be as difficult as I felt it would be, then I shouldn't do it. But I felt it was necessary. I couldn't fool myself into thinking that I had a choice. I felt it was something I had to do. But if I could have convinced myself otherwise, I wouldn't have done it. In fact, I didn't go when the commission was first established. I thought I would wait until the university school year ended. Then my husband got sick, so I waited until he had been operated on and was recovering at home. That was when the Rettig Commission's lawyers came to my house and I told them I would testify. I didn't seek them out.

I'm telling you this because at that point in time I still felt guilty, despite the fact that theoretically I knew that I wasn't "guilty," but "responsible." Understanding that was a step I could only take in time. Later, I understood that I had been subjected to a cruel experience and that I responded as I could. Some people have said my decisions were intuitive. I don't know. I don't have the knowledge to figure it out. Maybe someday I will—or not. I don't know. If I had time or money, I would love to study psychology.

So you assume complete "responsibility" for informing on several of your comrades and, indirectly, for their deaths?

I'm not trying to say that I'm not responsible. Undoubtedly, I am. But it wasn't a decision or a choice. I don't know if you can appreciate the difference. I'm not exactly sure; I only know what I lived and felt. I only know what DINA/CNI took away from me.

At the same time, I do have problems with the term "victim." That's because in Chile there's a way of using the term victim to refer to people who attribute everything to fate, people who are incapable of recognizing their own responsibility. As a prisoner, I fought hard not to wind up in that state. I saw it happen to many "detained and disappeared" people. I could never understand the question "Why me?" that I heard every day from detainees who were close to me—the attitude that for some reason things just happen to some people and not to others, that one has nothing to do with what happens to him or her. I don't know either why these things happen. A lot of things are hard for me to grasp. But I know that they are still happening—and more often than we'd like—in many countries. Although I knew that what was happening in the detention centers was horrific and unthinkable, I also knew that I was there because I was a militant, because I was a clandestine member of the opposition at a time in my country when the military had enormous power—the power to decide who lives and who dies.

Naturally, there is no justification for what happened—not then, not now. If you're asking if I feel like a "victim," understanding by that term that I was subjugated by force, that I couldn't oppose myself to that force or even preserve my normal senses, that—without avoiding responsibility—I was obliged to do the things I did because of direct threats against me and my family members, including my son, then yes, yes I was a victim, a tortured person, a person who still harbors physical and moral scars.

DINA/CNI took so much away from me. Today I even feel like the fact that I was a collaborator was, in some sense, also their responsibility. Collaborating was my responsibility, but it was also theirs. That affects my life to this day. I think that that's what it means to be a victim.

Quite simply, I broke. I think it happened because of the aggregate effects of torture over time, coupled with other emotional factors. Not everything implied a decision. Collaborating didn't even assure I would stay alive. Every day was a kind of mortal game, like Russian roulette. I was just not capable of leaving until I was able. For that, yes, I am responsible.

There are people in Chile, Michael, who say that collaborating under torture was understandable, but that staying on as a functionary wasn't. I haven't dignified that with a response. Never! On one hand, I wasn't capable of leaving immediately. And on the other, I needed to live. I received a monthly salary from March 1976, until October 1979. I went to the Military Hospital to cure my ailments that stemmed from torture. I'm responsible for all that. I accept that. I had to send my son to school, to feed him, and so on.

Nor have I defended myself by falling back on the nature of my work as a functionary. The public information with which I dealt was so inconsequential that I think the DINA agents didn't event know what to do with it. The repressive units worked independently. Those are aspects of DINA that no one considers. In my case, all I had to do was summarize some press articles to do my job.

At the end of the day, no one has bothered to verify whether what I've said is true. (In fact, many details of my life never figure into the larger narrative because they're not relevant in court.) Additionally, many survivors who were detained only for a fraction of the time I was—people I knew were there and who saw me—have maintained that I didn't apprehend them, torture them, or do anything at all to them.[11] At the same time, there are others who have not said anything voluntarily, only with reticence and when directly asked. Their testimonies could exonerate me from various accusations. I've learned something important in all this: it's easier for people to just believe any old thing than to pursue the truth. I don't buy that attitude—especially when it's spouted off by people who continue to categorize others as traitors or heroes. Those labels still exist in Chile. Oh well, it's all part of this reality and, consequently, I have no choice but to accept it.

You have referred elsewhere to two people who maintain that you tortured them personally. Later, you denied having said that. First, what are those two people's names? Second, where did they get the idea that you tortured them? Is it just a blatant lie or could there be some other explanation?

Like I said before, for ten years I openly answered questions about this and other topics for any person or institution that asked. I never dodged a single question, no matter how it was posed. I won't do that anymore, Michael. It's not my place to judge these people. Every person has his or her process, his or her timeline, a manner of dealing with all this, of confronting the facts. I will not say anything about this, not even the people's names.

I respect your decision not to mention names, but if you have already mentioned them in *The Inferno,* it would be useful to reiterate them here for the purpose of this final extensive interview, particularly because doing so adds a dimension of reliability to your responses. But if you still don't want to name those people, perhaps you can answer the second part of my question: Where did they get the idea that you tortured them?

If, over time, instead of doing things and trying to become a person again, I had dwelled on everything that had been said or published about me, in addition to being drained of all my energy, I would have achieved nothing. On one hand, personal experience has taught me—and I've pointed this out several times in our conversations—that everyone has his own timelines and rhythms. I can say something a million times, but it will only be received if the listener is willing and has the tools to understand, to take into account what is being said, or at least to give someone the benefit of the doubt. It is often said in Chile that people are innocent until proven guilty. I was condemned before I ever had the strength to present myself to the Rettig Commission—long before.

Oh, I just remembered something that I think I mentioned to you before we started this interview. A woman, in the 1990s, someone more or less my age, a little younger than I am, a respected professional, a university professor and a survivor, told me, "You killed Lumi Videla."[12] I responded to her in the most respectful way I knew how that I didn't do it, that I didn't turn information over to DINA so that Lumi could be located and detained. I said that all the facts about Lumi's detention had been ratified by more than one court of law. When I told her this, the woman said to me, "It doesn't matter. In my mind, you killed her."

I thought about that a lot. I came to the conclusion that what I thought was unjust at the time—because until that time it had been so hard to accept what I was responsible for, let alone what I was not—was precisely what that woman *needed* to think at the very moment she was seated in front of Luz Arce. I have my pain, my rage, and so on. I'm sure she has hers.

Faced with situations like this, do you think people can get anywhere by talking? Do you think it would make things better if I told you the woman's name? I don't think so. I understand where she was coming from. I even think I understand the scope of her pain.

So what for? Those of us who survived the dictatorship's repression have enough to do. After that experience, I got away from my initial, erroneous idea that I would someday be able to reconcile definitively with others. That's not how it works. I have reconciled with myself. I still have a lot to learn. I have reconciled with a lot of people who are important to me, and oftentimes I have had support while doing so. In large part, what I have achieved, I have achieved by myself, but I have also had a lot of support. These are processes. And others' processes also matter.

I also want to point out that personal healing, reintegrating into society as a productive individual, requires involvement in national matters. I have found healing in many ways: by testifying in court, by returning to crime scenes with judges or sometimes even with the same people who tortured me, through trials, by seeing DINA/CNI officers put in prison, by reading certain news stories in the paper or hearing them retold by a friend. These things have been important in addition to the love of my family and friends.

I used to say that I only trusted individuals. Today I can also say that I trust my country's institutions a good deal more than before. I didn't do much. I merely testified. And I wasn't the only one. Every man and woman who testified added something—as did judges, family members, lawyers, and many others. The day in 1991, that President Patricio Aylwin received the Rettig Commission's report from the hands of Executive Commissioner Jorge Correa Sutil was very special for me. I felt better. When I heard on the radio that the detention order against Pinochet, issued by Judge Garzón and the Spanish courts, had been carried out in London (1998), I healed a bit more—and so on with each successive resolution. Many people have played important roles: Judge Juan Guzmán, Judge Solís, Judge Cerda, Judge Raquel Lermanda, Judge Dobra Lusic, and the "Special Judges" who have been appointed to expedite human rights cases. It's not right for me to mention only them. I testified before various others too.

In short, I'm not going to speak about others' motivations because I don't know anything about them. I would be speculating.

You say that you have "friends" who helped and defended you in the face of accusations by others. Who?

I won't answer that question. I am not looking to justify my actions, defend myself, or be defended. I think that's a product of my personal maturing process. I've reached a point at which I don't need anyone's approval. I have had neither the time nor the occasion to pause and reflect on whether or not people accept me. From the very beginning, I've had to prop myself up on my own. As a prisoner, I had to try to maintain my sanity alone. Later, during the time period in which I had to face myself—which was hard in my case—I accept that I was given lots of help. I was helped, yes, but I was free. Right now, I still get lots of help from my friends, from those who are close to me, because no one is entirely alone.

I am thankful every time someone defends me, and I value greatly when someone calls himself or herself my friend. I prefer to keep the names of my friends
relatively private—and that's how it should be. I say "relatively" private because
some of their names are already known. You don't go around publishing your
friends' names, do you?

**Have you ever doubted your decision to survive rather than withhold infor-
mation and accept the consequences of that decision?**

As a detainee, in my case, there wasn't time to think. No decision I made was
thought out. There was never a moment in which I said, "I am deciding to survive."
I just reacted. Everything that happened made me feel like I was falling down a
toboggan slide. Much of it happened under torture, subsequent loss of consciousness, or in a state of consciousness that I've never again experienced.

During the period in which I was tortured, wounded by an AK bullet in my
right foot, hospitalized, operated on various times, at every moment I felt like
dying would be liberation. But I didn't die. My intention was to resist. In fact, I
endured daily torture for six months—the longest months of my life—without
giving up information. For example, after having been interrogated and tortured
at 38 Londres Street, before becoming a collaborator, I was asked under torture to
sign a statement saying that Rodolfo Valentín González Pérez, from the air force, a
man who remains disappeared to this day, was a traitor to DINA. I refused to do it.
Krassnoff seemed like he was in a hurry, and he pressured me to sign to avoid pain.
I refused again. When he grew tired of my antics, Krassnoff ordered me to put my
fingerprint on the document. I was naked on the *parrilla* with my hands and feet
tied when someone ran to get an inkpad. They forced my thumb onto the pad and
then onto a piece of paper that I never saw or read. I have no idea what happened
to that document. I never saw it again. Could it be in the air force archives? Or was
it just meant for Krassnoff's superior? Had they already killed the soldier? I don't
know. Lots of stuff happened that way in DINA. And of course the next day they
kept torturing me just to teach me a lesson.

I accept that I decided to survive, notwithstanding the levels of normalcy or
consciousness I may have had at different moments. But there are two things that
are important to clarify when we're talking about collaboration. The first has to do
with how one arrives at the "decision" to collaborate; the second has to do with the
level of commitment one assumes. On one hand, you have an expressed commitment that you verbalize to them; on the other hand, you have an internal attitude
that helps you withhold certain things. These are not the same. I think this was the
case for others too.

I suppose the idea is still widespread that those who died or disappeared are the
people who didn't collaborate. That's not true. I know cases in which people gave
up information and died anyway. I wasn't aware of that when I went to the Rettig
Commission. The lawyers were the ones who showed me that some disappeared
or executed comrades informed on others before they died. Not all survivors collaborated, but certainly more did than people admit.

It might seem brutal to "saddle" the memory of those who are no longer with
us. I'm not going to name names, but generally speaking, those involved in the
legal cases know that many survivors collaborated. I even know about the case

of one mother whose son is disappeared and who found out that he informed on his comrades before disappearing. The lawyers told her the truth once certain information offered by other families was proven valid. She reacted poorly. What's interesting is that the mother later changed her attitude; she took a more humane approach to the facts of our violent past. But there are still many Chileans who think that dying at the hands of DINA was always synonymous with noncollaboration.

Death was a constant possibility in those days. Not even collaboration could take away that possibility. One could die fortuitously on the *parrilla* or have a heart attack. In my case, the possibility of death was always present, even when I was a functionary. It's not an exaggeration. It's the truth!

Sure, when asked today, of course I would like to have escaped from DINA without informing and collaborating. But that's not how it was. Any other consideration would be speculation and wouldn't get us anywhere. For that reason, now, since I'm still here, I try to keep learning in order to understand and correct what I can—if it's correctable. At this stage of the game, I think that—more than necessary—it's interesting to observe how people in my country have been learning the facts, and how facts translate into justice, forgiveness (God willing), and hopefully reconciliation.

What is your relationship today with your experience as a victim and collaborator?

There were times in which I felt like there was no path for me. At least I couldn't identify one. There were even fewer sources of support. It was then that I felt I needed to construct what I didn't have. And if I didn't have the tools to do it, I had to create them.

In 1988, when I started to tell Father Cristián about what had happened to me, I felt it would be very difficult to go back to not only *being* a person but also *feeling* like I was one. Many times I thought I wouldn't get there. Nevertheless, I'm still here with my baggage—not as something I can cast aside, but as something that over time I must integrate into every aspect of my life: chewing on the experience, crying about everything.

At first, one feels horror about what one is; one feels incapable of resisting. In time, horror morphs into tenderness at the sight of how small one is—tenderness toward what one could potentially become. I learned to accept that in my country some of us were disappeared from our families; some still are. I keep trying to understand it because I know that such things are still happening in this world of ours.

It's about accepting, recognizing, verbalizing, and incorporating the past into one's personal, daily memory. It's about admitting that I betrayed people, that I collaborated by giving up information and comrades, four of whom are still disappeared. It's about admitting that I was a functionary of DINA/CNI. All of that is part of my life today. It's a memory. It's sad. It often makes me quite sad. All of that was the most painful thing I've had to recognize in my life and to carry with me to this day.

My husband and children have accepted my past and have supported me lovingly. In some sense, that support and all that I've experienced have taught me that living a "limit" situation requires one to rebuild what has been damaged, open doors that have closed, and if one can't open them, one must create others.

Confronting one's personal limitations is hard. What's irreparable is the disappearance of those four comrades. I have no choice but to accept that. All of that helps me understand who I am as a person. I knew I couldn't resist in those moments. Over the last few decades, many people have told me that there's a point at which no one resists, that I wasn't the only informant, that there are others who still have not admitted it. I understand that, but it doesn't take away the pain I feel inside. I think I'll always carry that pain in my life—always.

Only one argument has sometimes helped me assuage that memory in my daily life: the disappearance of those four comrades was in no way logical. I learned that lesson late, and the hard way. There was no logic within the world of DINA/CNI!

I want to reiterate that I never turned in my superiors, nor did I give up any of the Socialist Party leadership, or that of other leftist parties. That has been established in my country's courts. When I felt I had no alternative and thinking that the people I named would get out alive, I informed on those who were on the periphery—people who would not lead DINA to the party leadership. I don't want you to take away from all this, Michael, that those people were less important than others. I only remember that when I felt I was about to inform on someone, I did it thinking about how a militant would do it.

I still remember the MIR manuals we read clandestinely, even though we were socialists. I remember the voice of the comrade who read them to us. We read those photocopied texts to learn them, and we talked about the increasing repression that was happening during the dictatorship's early days. The exercise of reading those manuals made us think of our comrades who were being detained. We'd say, "If there's ever a moment in which we can't resist, we have to turn in our most peripheral comrades." That's what I did. I turned in supporters, sympathizers, people from the propaganda brigades who had merely painted signs during election times. I sincerely thought that aside from being knocked around a bit and maybe spending some time in prison, nothing major would happen to them.

I was wrong. Those comrades are disappeared today.

For years I thought they were in some detainee camp, somewhere in Chile, or that maybe they had been freed. It wasn't until I was a functionary and managed to read in *La Segunda* newspaper the so-called List of 119 that I saw their names.[13] The article claimed that 119 former militants had killed each other abroad in leftist infighting. I couldn't believe it! Even so, after reading that newspaper, I kept holding out hope that those comrades were still alive. I think it was a defense mechanism for my guilt. I had to think that they had found asylum, or had gone into exile, or were hiding in the provinces, or, as a worst case scenario, that they were in jail.

It was in 1978, that I found out that the courts were doing investigations and that they were looking for me to testify. Before that, in 1976, I knew that they were looking for me to be a witness, but I didn't know it was because of those people's deaths. It was in 1978, then, that I became aware that they were gone—not only because of the court cases I could access but also because when I worked on the computer I could see the list of disappeared that the Vicariate of Solidarity had published. That was definitive. I could no longer doubt the written information. *La Segunda,* or any other paper, published what the dictatorship wanted. But I couldn't doubt the Vicariate's report. Shortly thereafter, I tendered my resignation to CNI because obviously it was impossible for me to stay there.

Thinking about it today, I recognize that informing and collaborating were things I was capable of doing. The idea that I was acting according to militancy manuals doesn't serve me anymore. I think about many things—even about Carlos Marighella, his life, his death.[14] All of our manuals in Chile were based on his teachings about guerrilla warfare in Brazil, and on those of our Tupamaro comrades.

He pressed me down into the tub. The water kept rising, almost covering my cheeks. I was frantic and I closed my mouth. Water started going down my nose. I opened my mouth, more water. I reached out with my hands and tried to remove his, but he put the hose in my mouth. Water started filling my stomach. I swallowed it and felt like vomiting. I was suffocating. Suddenly he took me out of the water, held me, and started to kiss my thighs. I tried to breathe, to speak, to reason, but I couldn't. I wanted him to take away that disgusting mouth that was slithering all over my body and sliding between my legs like a sickening slug. I managed to sit up and grabbed him by the hair. I wanted to get him out of there. The water kept filling the tub. His damned tongue felt so cold, or was I the one who was cold? I kept vomiting water. I started hitting his head with my hands. He stood up. His eyes were red . . . I started begging him, "Sergeant, please, please, you're hurting me . . ." Again that face and he started touching me once more, searching for my clitoris with his hands.

"I want you to feel pleasure, did you hear?" he shouted as he bit me. Then, looking at me, he added, "Stay still," as his hands reached my breasts.

"Enjoy it! I want to see you feel pleasure!"

—*Luz Arce, The Inferno* (1993)

There was a place called "The Tower" at Villa Grimaldi, and one time they hung me naked and interrogated me in "The Tower" ... At that moment, they beat me, cut up pieces of paper, and placed them all over my body, especially around my stomach. They lit the paper on fire and burned me because I wouldn't talk. I didn't know anything about the young guard who was doing all of this. [Another] man was beating me and savagely kicking me on the ground. He told me: "Now you'll know what fascism is, but not foreign fascism; this is Chilean fascism."

—Luz Arce, legal testimony, January 7, 1990

3

Trauma and Writing

Readers of *The Inferno* understand how difficult it was for you to tell your story. You had to overcome many fears and personal obstacles. How would you characterize those fears?

It was hard for me to tell my story. I didn't decide to do it in one particular moment. It was a process that took years. From the time I managed to resign from CNI until early August 1988, all of my efforts were geared toward forgetting. Later, out of personal necessity, I started allowing myself to remember things, accompanied by my friend, the Dominican friar Father Cristián. By talking to him, I started to recover those years of my life. As a result of that process, I decided to place my story in the hands of competent authorities. I decided to testify to the Truth and Reconciliation Commission (also referred to as the Rettig Commission), created by President Patricio Aylwin when he assumed the presidency in 1990.

Before going to the Rettig Commission, my fears were many: fear of being recognized, fear of uttering my name, even fear of remembering. However, after deciding to testify to the Rettig Commission, my fear shifted toward what might happen to my family. I was sure that former DINA or CNI agents would make attempts on my husband's life or my children's lives. That was why I decided to leave the country after I testified.

The way I see it, after I decided to testify, my fears changed. I no longer feared for myself. It was as if accepting the facts and trying to take responsibility lessened my fear of what might happen to me. I thought that by leaving the country, by being away from part of my family, I would at least spare my husband and children.

My earliest fears were diffuse, generalized. I preferred to be alone or only with my immediate family. After testifying in 1990, I feared for my family.

What role did writing play in overcoming those fears and in recovering a sense of personal identity?

In my case, writing played a fundamental role. Maybe it's because of how I am or because there was so much to recover from my past as a prisoner of the dictatorship, but writing things down forced me to extract something concrete from myself.

Even though I never reread my writings or even had them in my possession until I started working with them in 1991 to put together *The Inferno*, the fact that I had written, and that those writings existed, made me feel like I had identified and drawn out of myself something that was harming me. I also thought that if something were to happen to me, if I were to die, the essential details would be preserved as a first person account penned by my own hand. I trusted that when the time came my Dominican friends would know what to do with my text.

Nevertheless, I wrote without thinking that my writing would someday be a book. I wrote motivated by my Dominican friends who suggested that writing my memories might help me to heal. In effect, that's what happened. I relived as I wrote, as I began to let some things out.

When you sat down to write, what audience did you have in mind? Did you fear the repercussions of going public with your testimony?

When I decided to publish my perception of the facts, I had some personal objectives related to the period of my life living outside of Chile in 1990. My feeling back then was that *The Inferno* could contribute—based on what I could glean from my memory—a narrative about the people involved and of whom I was aware (both victims and victimizers), information about the detention centers I knew, and information about how DINA and CNI operated. That's what the German publishing house that bought the rights to my book suggested, and it seemed like it was worth a try.

The book was conceived as an alphabetic index of people, a thematic index, and a detailed description of life within the repressive organizations. At one point, I thought I would include drawings that I had done of the detention centers, as well as organizational diagrams of DINA/CNI, but I didn't have time to do it before the book went to press because I was so busy testifying in court. I did the drawings and diagrams later for Chilean judges who ordered much more complete reconstructions of crime scenes. To do it, the judges counted not only on me but also on many other survivors who began testifying after 1992. The objective was to assist people from Chile's human rights sector.

Between the time when I began reorganizing my writing in 1990 and the publication of *The Inferno* in late 1993, things happened both in Chile and in my personal life that made me consider other objectives that I eventually incorporated into the book. When I left for Europe, I thought that testifying to the Rettig Commission would pave the way for judicial processes in my country that would establish the facts—the truth about what happened to various executed or "detained and disappeared" people whose cases I knew. I thought that for that to happen my testimony to the Rettig Commsion's lawyers would suffice; so I signed an authorization for my testimony to be used in court proceedings. During my stay in Europe in 1991, I understood that what I had done wasn't enough, that it wasn't helping. I understood that I needed to return to testify personally in the Chilean tribunals. Consequently, I went back, and thus began a long series of depositions that lasted for years.

I need to point out that during a meeting with attorneys that took place the day before I started testifying in court, both personal friends whose family members had disappeared and police investigators expressed concern that I would be pressured not to testify or that someone might try to harm me or my family. Everyone seemed to think that the best security I or my family could have was for the media to disseminate my story widely. I adopted that perspective and maintained a fluid relationship with the media, which told the story of what was happening in court step by step. I bring this up because there are many people who have commented publicly and privately that I enjoy giving interviews. I think that only the many journalists who asked me questions daily outside the courthouse doors, the detectives and police officers who protected me by court order, and certain family members and friends who supported me at the time know how hard it was for me to face those interviews—especially at the beginning when I constantly trembled, had physical reactions, or anxiety attacks similar to those I experienced in the worst moments. Regrettably, I found that on occasion the press would take things out of context or make up sensationalistic headlines about things that people who had never lived a "limit" experience would have a hard time understanding.

Nevertheless, as the months passed, I realized that it was good for the cause of human rights if I remained high profile in my country. So I assumed the responsibility of speaking with multiple journalists and students from different journalism schools who sought me out for articles, reports, and interviews. When they asked for information, I gave them not only an answer but also a vision of what DINA was, its structure, its changes in leadership, and even of the language used within it.

In those days, while it seemed important to protect my family from all that was happening—particularly because it was a period full of depositions, crime scene reconstructions, and hundreds of declarations in domestic and foreign tribunals, as well as to police and human rights organizations—it also seemed important to write a legible text, written in the first person, and geared not toward the human rights community (which had known since September 11, 1973, practically everything that happened during the dictatorship), but toward the people of my country. I did it so that readers could have a vision of DINA/CNI, repression, torture, and the annihilation of people and movements, told from the firsthand perspective of someone who had lived through it all for years. I knew at the time that many people in Chile who hadn't been directly involved really had no idea about what went on. Although it seems hard to believe, it's true.

I published my book without fear. Just like other human emotions, fear is something that must be worked through. It has to be worked through over time. I had to get used to the idea that fear would be there accompanying me in different forms throughout my entire life, or at least for a large part of it. My terrible fear of DINA, my fear of its irrational authority, that's what I had to work through so it wouldn't continue ruling my life.

In essence, the feeling I had back then was that there would always be a lot of people who wouldn't understand my experience as I had lived it. I could tell from their questions, their opinions, and their way of thinking. They didn't understand that people are products of their errors and of their whole story, that people are integral beings on whom even childhood issues sometimes have an effect.

Maybe if I had had an absolutely "normal" life I would never have learned certain things that today are helping me get my small business off the ground. I no longer feel guilty for having a few moments of happiness. What's more, I think that happiness is important, but it's not a permanent state. Along with love, happiness is the most important thing in life. But as with just about everything, one has to create it.

How was your book received by the government, the Catholic Church, the military, and the human rights community?

I don't have, nor have I had, contact with my country's government. The Rettig Commission's representatives were the closest thing, but they weren't government functionaries; rather, they were lawyers who were contracted to do a specific job. I testified to them, and to this day they are still my friends, although they no longer belong to the human rights world.

I don't have contact with officials from the Catholic Church either. However, I do know and have contact with various people from the church who are personal contacts, friends, teachers, or colleagues from the period in which I studied theology. I'm not in touch with anyone from the church's hierarchy, although the "church" isn't just its hierarchy.

My contacts in the military haven't existed for many years, at least since I resigned from CNI in 1979. I am not in contact with any human rights organizations.

I think that the reception of my text is something that people from each of the sectors you mention would have to evaluate on their own, that is, if they read it when it was published.

How did human rights activists react to you?

My contact with the human rights community has been limited to what is germane to proceedings in courts and tribunals, and to one or another event in Chile or abroad. I have been in touch with lawyers, primarily during my declarations for different cases. As soon as a case would close, I generally would no longer have contact with those people.

The people I met from the human rights community were always very cordial. Some family members of the disappeared are my personal friends and, for that reason, they shouldn't be construed as "contacts" within the human rights world. I suppose that there have been mixed reactions about me among victims and family members. But it's not up to me to comment on that. As I've said before, I like to talk about facts, not intentions.

I have crossed paths in court with many people from the human rights community (lawyers and family members), and they have always maintained an attitude proper to our surroundings. The most radical attitude I've encountered is indifference. In many cases, people have told me that they understand or even *thank* me for my contribution to their loved one's case.

As you say on the first page of your introduction to *The Inferno*, one of your motivations for writing the book was to debunk a "black legend" that had circulated about you in Chile. What was the nature of that black legend, and who fomented it?

I suppose that a "black legend" began to circulate between the time I was practically "disappeared" (in March 1974) and late September 1990, when I "reappeared" to testify to the Rettig Commission. People believed that I had turned over to the secret police the vast majority of militants who had been detained or disappeared. There was, therefore, a disproportionate expectation regarding how much information I could really provide about the disappeared.

When I returned to Chile and started testifying in court in early 1992, Manuel Contreras, former director of DINA, testified that I had given up the names of practically everyone from all the leftist movements. Even worse, when military officials or subordinates appeared in court or went to be deposed, they made claims that I had been a key figure in the repression. Later, when the judges didn't find their arguments credible, they tried to discredit my testimony by saying that I had voluntarily approached DINA to offer information. These types of arguments started cropping up in the 1990s around the time that I went public with my story.

It is important to point out that there were people who knew exactly when and how I had been detained and who kept that information secret until 1990. Because of what I had said in my own testimony, the Rettig Commision's lawyers asked them specifically about me. The person who turned me over to DINA on March 17, 1974,—a Socialist Party militant—was set free without being detained by DINA at the time. Apparently, the agents who detained him tortured him and cut a deal with him to give up people who came to his house or, as in my case, people who he contacted by phone to meet him at a particular place. That person never admitted that he turned me over to DINA. He went on with his life, participated in human rights activities, and even wrote books on the topic.[1] I found all of this out when I testified to the Rettig Commission.

When I testified as to how I was detained, the lawyers sought this person out on their own. He denied my claim. Nevertheless, months later, in 1991, when the summary of my testimony that the Rettig Commision put together was published, the media located this person to ask him about my accusation. The person called a press conference to say that I was lying. Prior to the press conference, the Rettig Commission's lawyers had already told him that if they found out he was lying, he'd be in trouble. When he was interviewed, he changed his tune, but only said, "What she claims is true." Years later, I ran into the man in court. He explained that he tried to warn me of my impending detention, that he gave me a signal. That wasn't true. But I accepted his apology. Considering that it takes courage to recognize all that he had covered up about that period in his own life and mine, and especially considering what it means to be terrified (because I lived it too), I accepted his apology. I told him, though, that I did not think he had given me a warning sign, but I also told him I was happy to see him alive.

Later, there were other experiences. The Rettig Commission told me that there were people, even in other cities, who had testified to the Vicariate of Solidarity that I personally detained them, that I tortured them, and so on. Fortunately for me, my trajectory as a prisoner of DINA and CNI is well established in other survivors' testimonies. The lawyers clearly understood that it would have been simply impossible for me to be in other cities detaining and torturing people.

At the present time, there are a couple of people in Chile who claim that I tortured them. There is a woman, for example, who says that I hit her. I met her in 1992 when I returned to Chile. Honestly, I had not met her in the political party prior to the coup. I didn't even know her name. To date, I have no idea what part of the Sociality Party she was from, nor did I see her in the José Domingo Cañas torture center, where she was detained. What's more, even though I saw her several times in court, she never said anything to me personally.

I also know about another guy, a man whose last name is the same as that of the woman I just mentioned (although I'm not sure if they're related), who also says I tortured him. When I tried to express my interest in talking to him—always via third parties—he refused to meet with me. To date, I have never met him.

I have not done anything about these situations. I feel that it's difficult to get people to change their minds just by talking to them, especially after they have been making the same claims for years. That's why I so appreciate that the person who gave me up in 1974, has recognized that he lied, covered up the truth, and ascribed responsibilities to me erroneously. (By the way, because my testimony proved that that person had given me up and covered it up for decades, he wound up being absolutely marginalized from the human rights world. I don't know if it was because of how people in the human rights world felt about him, or if it was because he marginalized himself. I even found out that he moved out of Santiago.) I also want to say that at the time I testified to the Rettig Commision, I had no idea how my testimony would affect this person. I never thought that any of these things would happen. Over time, I have assimilated all of this by reliving, thinking about, and reflecting on my experiences. This is the kind of collateral damage that state repression causes that doesn't get captured by any statistic.

I know that my life and actions have been interpreted by—as we say colloquially—everyone and his brother. Sometimes I feel like people think that they know what I should have done back when I was in prison. The media has published perspectives by valuable intellectuals who comment on my intentions. I don't pay any attention to those things, because it has taken me years—decades—to understand what happened. Even today, I'm still learning, integrating my experiences. I wish I had had the clarity about my own thoughts and feelings that other people seem to have had about them.

It really doesn't depend on me, then, to correct these "black legends." It depends on others to speak. On many occasions, I assumed my rightful responsibility: in court, with respect to human rights organizations, and in my personal healing process. Frankly, I don't care what people say about me. What I do care about is making it so that others don't have to live through the situations that I had to live back then.

In the pages of *The Inferno*, there are profoundly painful moments in which you describe in great detail the torture you suffered while detained by DINA. While writing, did you discover any parts of your experience that were impossible to narrate?

No, I didn't. I think I talked in my book about my most painful experiences. Obviously there were some things that I found harder to write about than others. But I forced myself to give the most complete accounting I could of my memories. I had decided to do that with my first manuscript in 1989, though I didn't plan to show the material publicly to anyone other than my Dominican religious friends. My Dominican friends read it, and then we talked about it. When I testified to the Rettig Commission, I relived it all, so naturally I had a lot of sad times. But by the time I wrote *The Inferno*—which was the third time I relived the experience in depth—I had processed many things.

At the same time, I have often felt that the language I possess is incapable of representing the pain, terror, panic, and impotence I lived.

Do you still have flashbacks of the torture that you experienced or witnessed? How do you face those memories today?

I have suffered *many* flashbacks of those experiences, throughout the 1980s and even in the early 1990s. But I would say that for every flashback about torture, I had two about rape. The torture that army major Gerardo Ernesto Urrich González inflicted on me had a huge impact. He hit me, nearly drove a truck over my legs, swiped my left leg with the tires, hung me, burned me, and left me isolated for days in "The Tower" at Villa Grimaldi.[2] He did all that just to get me to say that I hated him. I couldn't do it! I also have no idea why I acted as I did, because if I had just said that I hated him, maybe things would have been different. I don't know why I didn't say it. I have no idea.[3]

Beatings, electroshocks: at a certain moment, I remembered those things *irrationally.* But I think that my irrational memories of torture and rape at Villa Grimaldi disappeared in 1988, when I got sick and received treatment from a neurologist and from my psychologist friend. At that time, I was laid up and had to spend three months in bed while I was being treated with drugs. They diagnosed me with multiple forms of depression that, until then, I had managed poorly.

During the 1990s, and particularly in 1992, when I suffered from chronic fatigue syndrome, I had some flashbacks, but not as intense as before. Since then, I haven't suffered from such irrational experiences. I'm talking about the experience of reliving a past traumatic event that is triggered by some everyday occurrence.

The memories of torture are still there, and they're very vivid. But they're not irrational. They are just that: sad memories—but I never lose sight of the fact that I am remembering, although I do still have physical symptoms resulting from anguish and anxiety. When I verbalize those experiences, my hair still "stands on end," as they say. Sweat. Heart palpitations. Dry mouth. Even right now when I'm talking to you, or when I testify in court, I have those physical sensations.

For example, in 2001, I went to testify in France. It was my second to the last deposition. On that occasion, testifying affected me in the same way it always did: pain, flashbacks, exhaustion. I was so exhausted, in fact, that I had to go back to the hotel and sleep until the next day's session. Curiously, the feeling I had was similar to how I felt when I saw the Twin Towers fall on television on September 11, 2001.

Bad migraine headaches that accompanied the flashbacks lasted for years and generally put me out of commission once a month. These problems were usually in synch with my menstrual cycles, and made it so that I couldn't make any commitments. I couldn't do anything! In 1998, a doctor friend gave me seven sessions of NLP (neuro linguistic programming), which helped me to manage my pain because I could detect the causes. Until I learned those techniques, any extremely stressful situation triggered a migraine. Thank God I have happily been headache free for nine years.

Michael, I want to share something that is very private, that I haven't ever ver-balized until now. I suppose I haven't talked about it because the information hasn't been necessary for my testimony in court. And even though I have talked with people who are curious about that period in my life, I guess they haven't dared ask, or they haven't asked because of how personal this is. But here it goes . . . The hardest moment for me was when I started dating my husband, and it had to do with having intimate relations. In those first years, in the early 1980s espe-cially, those intimate moments were often accompanied by memories of repeated rape. Nevertheless, my husband's patience and love helped me heal. Because I have never had access to an integrated course of therapy (just a bit of sporadic help from a psychologist friend), it has been by studying and reading about the topic that my husband and I have learned to resolve these problems alone. We have resolved them over time, based on mutual trust and affection.

I think that if I was able to have sexual relations with Rolf Wenderoth, it was just a task. It wasn't—it never was—like it is with my husband. Even as a detainee I thought that a woman who was raped even once would always have difficulties getting over it. I said to myself, "I doubt that I'll have the possibility of seeing a doctor, or a psychologist, or of receiving treatment, help, or kindness; so I'll just have to figure it out on my own." However, I couldn't help fearing that I'd be raped again. I tried to suppress those feelings, but I never really managed to do it. The pain and impotence were always there.

I feel today that my life with my husband, building a family, and some personal achievements have helped me to leave all that behind. But the memories still make me cry, like I'm crying right now. I can will myself not to cry. I don't cry in court, for example. But at home, when I'm alone, yes, I cry. I suppose it's from all the pain—so much pain! My throat constricts. It hurts a lot. It's a reminder of some-thing that is hard to forget, but that I won't let incapacitate me again. Sometimes I tell myself that I'm not as bad off or as crazy as I could be, given the circumstances. So I keep walking. I keep trying. My family, my studies, understanding: those con-tinue to be my main strategies for achieving normalcy.

Let's change topics and talk a bit more about your book, *The Inferno*. You started writing your first manuscript shortly after meeting the Dominican priests. Later, fearing reprisals by DINA, you burned it.

Yes. In the end, I wound up befriending the Dominicans.[4] I studied with them and we talked for hours. At a certain point, I remember Father José Luis saying, "We could talk about this for days. Why don't you write it down?" Thus, the first manuscript was born. But I ripped it up! I burned it! I was scared to have it in my apartment. I didn't have any place to keep it under lock and key. The kids used to get into everything. And I thought: oh, what if the kids see it? What if they find it? What if DINA gets ahold of it? So I burned it!

How long did it take you to write it?

It took me six months to write the manuscript. I never reread it. One of the priests had given me a huge stack of envelopes and a bunch of legal-sized paper, so I wrote and wrote. When I'd run out of time, I'd staple what I had written that day, put it in an envelope, seal it, sign it, tape it up, and place it in a cabinet that was in the Dominicans' library.

While you were writing *The Inferno*, you were also participating in Gonzalo Contreras's literary workshop.[5] What was that experience like?

When I went to Gonzalo Contreras's workshop, my book had already been published. The workshop was excellent. Gonzalo Contreras is one of the best Chilean writers. I didn't continue in his workshop because I didn't have the money to keep paying for it, and also because the time I spent testifying in court kept me occupied most of the time.

Why did you attend the workshop if you didn't consider yourself a "writer"? When did the workshop take place, and what did you do while you were in it?

I take great pleasure in writing. It's something I love. I know that I'm ignorant about many things, but I still hope to have the time and resources to learn about what I don't know. When I can, I'll go to a workshop again.

Like everyone in the workshop, I listened to the teacher. I learned much from Gonzalo Contreras. I did all my reading and wrote what he asked us to write. During the workshop, I managed to write a short story and Gonzalo gave me his opinion.

Did Planeta, your publishing house, suggest any particular changes to your manuscript that you didn't like?

No, only my lawyer did. He had read the book from a legal standpoint, and he said, "The things you say about Lauriani are really harsh. He could sue you."[6] But I told him, "Look, Carlos, Lauriani is an idiot. The manuscript goes as is." And that was that.

When my editor, Mili Rodríguez, finished her corrections, she handed me a manuscript that was all marked up and that had tons of suggestions for footnotes. I had just written. But what I eventually discovered is that I had written like I speak, and that many things could be stated using fewer words. I also discovered that I tend to use lots of synonyms for emphasis. In some cases, I took her advice; in other cases, I didn't. Without the changes, though, it would have been a drag to read it. I began to discover that I could craft sentences in other ways. I even started to make suggestions.

In the end, it was Carlos Orellana, editor-in-chief of Planeta, who came up with the chapter divisions. But just as the book was about to appear, Carlos called and told me that the publishing house was experiencing some economic problems and that publication would be delayed. I didn't believe him. "Oh no," I said. "Someone is pressuring them not to publish it."

So you're saying that you doubted that there were economic pressures.

I thought that maybe there were political party pressures. I never found out what went on. I just figure that someone didn't want the book to see the light of day. I don't know. It's all speculation. But, at any rate, it eventually came out.

Carlos suggested that we publish it for Santiago's annual International Book Fair. He said that we'd have a best seller! The fair took place on November 17, 1993, and the launch was at the Galerías Hotel, a pretty place in downtown Santiago.

How did the book sell?

The first print run sold out. It was the second most sold book in the country for about a year. Then it dropped to third place, moved up to second, dropped to fifth, went up again, and so on. It sold out and they never did a second edition.

Later, there was a German edition that was published for the Frankfurt World Book Fair in October 1995. I didn't attend the launch, but between January and March 1996, I went all over Germany giving talks to promote the book in universities and event centers.

And here in Chile, what repercussions did the book's publication have?

Everyone had an opinion! The press! The people! Everyone! I reviewed what was being published about my book on a daily basis. It was all horrible! Horrible! All of it! The most radical perspectives were the worst. It was around then that Diamela Eltit wrote her critique. But that was one of the decent ones. Because even though she is critical and makes assumptions about my motivations for acting in certain ways, she's not offensive. Do you understand?

But other things were published that were really ugly, especially in more radical media like *Punto Final* or some Communist Party publications. Lots of ugly stuff—all personal! No one said anything about the book. No one said if it was good or bad, or if it was terribly written, or mediocre. No one said I should forget about writing and go home to care for my grandchildren. No! No one said anything about the book! They all just attacked *me*. Do you understand? At any rate, there were all kinds of reactions.

Did you receive any threats from the military people you name in your text?

On one hand, I sensed a change in attitude when I saw them in court. Fernando Lauriani and Marcelo Moren Brito seemed very perturbed.[7] They acted differently toward me, that is, if I were to compare their attitude to the way they treated me before I published *The Inferno*. On the other hand, I did receive some threatening messages on my answering machine. But, by that point, I was well enough on my feet that they didn't bother me too much. I was being protected. In fact, the protection was smothering me. I longed to move about freely. Father Cristián protected my kids at school. So nothing really bad happened—just those offensive, ugly phone calls.

In December 1975, they transferred me from Villa Grimaldi to DINA General Headquarters on Belgrado Street. There, I assumed the job of department chief within the Sub-department of Domestic Intelligence, which was dedicated to the investigation of subversive activities on a national level. I stayed in that job until 1977. The job was very similar to the one I had at Villa Grimaldi, for which I had the collaboration of ALEJANDRA MERINO and LUZ ARCE, who had already lost their status as detainees and had become functionaries of DINA and were keeping regular office hours . . . My relationship with ALEJANDRA MERINO was always one of boss and subordinate. With LUZ ARCE, however, in addition to our work relationship, we also had a romantic relationship.

—*Rolf Wenderoth Pozo, legal testimony, November 28, 2001*

The "I will or will not go to bed" with someone "if I want to," allowed me to consent to only those relationships that I intuitively knew wouldn't be traumatic. That was the only way for me to receive affection, which I needed a lot. It wasn't an interest in sex, and I'm not even talking about feelings. I wanted someone to be there who could chase away ghosts and fears. I wanted the illusion of someone showing me some affection, even if only for a few minutes.

The knowledge that I was having difficulties led me to tell myself [that] sex is just another form of communication, something I can choose to practice or not. Then I made up or adopted a saying as my own, "I'll give myself to someone, if I want to, but I won't sell myself."

—*Luz Arce, The Inferno (1993)*

4

Masculinity and Femininity

In the course of your narration about being a functionary of DINA, you highlight the importance of seeming more masculine (and consequently, less feminine) to survive in a hypermasculine, hierarchical military space. What details can you provide about that experience?

I started to feel that way in March 1974, when I first became a prisoner of DINA. The feeling intensified during my time in the Military Hospital, which was during my third stay at 38 Londres Street, in August 1974. I think the feeling stemmed from being at the mercy of the guards. It wasn't just being beaten and tortured that made me feel that way. What hurt the most—at least at the time—was the sexual abuse. Later, as a functionary, it wasn't as important to seem more masculine. How I *seemed* didn't really matter at all, because I didn't really belong to their world. They would do what they wanted with me, whether I liked it or not. However, I do have to recognize that at certain times while I was a functionary I was not forced. I could even have said no to some demands.

I have not talked about this topic much—pretty much only in intimate circles, among close friends and family. Feeling that things would go better for me if I seemed less feminine is something that I felt outside of DINA too—even before DINA. Because I'm from the 1960s generation, I guess that my feelings have to do with certain attitudes that prevailed back then in my country (or at least in my city or in the spaces I inhabited). Today I understand that my generation, starting in the sixties, achieved certain changes through a battle with my parents' generation. We were the ones who broke with certain norms that governed family life; we challenged certain concepts of authority, and so on. Our children were raised differently than we were. Here, in Mexico, many of those arcane repressive attitudes toward women are still around, especially in the provinces. They are attitudes linked to the cultural moment that communities are living.

At various times in my life, I have suffered specifically because I am a woman. In the case of DINA, I was living a dramatic "limit" situation. I was always trying to avoid rape or other forms of sexual abuse because I was a woman in a man's world. Outside of DINA (before and after), I suffered discrimination in the workplace. I had fewer possibilities to achieve certain positions because I was a woman. If you can believe it, all of this even has to do with the education I received as a child.

It was always hard for me to claim my femininity. When I was young, ever since I can remember, I have been a happy, optimistic, naturally smiley person. I just couldn't avoid it and, as a child, I was often criticized for being that way. Later, when I discovered that boys wanted to approach me, I had some problems. Even though I wanted to be their friend or form affective relationships, it was hard for me to accept those relationships. I didn't dare. I was petrified of my father because he and my mother raised me with so many restrictions, even more than my friends had. Those experiences shaped my life and made me extremely insecure.

It was through sports that I started to understand that I could do things on my own, alone. Studying was the same. What's more, I always worked and paid for my own education. I left home very young, before finishing college, and I got married. It never occurred to me to live alone. Getting married meant to be free of my father's house. I felt I really didn't have any other options—maybe because living alone would have been frowned upon back then. Living alone just wasn't on my drop down list. It was as if I had been weaned for marriage. If I paid for my own education, it was because my father said he would only pay for my brother's schooling. His logic was that my brother would have to support his future family, whereas I would get married. Consequently, I didn't need a career.

I never felt like I was the daughter that my parents hoped I'd be. I always tried my hardest because I felt like I owed them a lot. But no matter what I did, I could never repay them. Later, in DINA, having intimate relations didn't help me to resolve any of my issues. (I understood, too, that those relations were often motivated by not wanting to be alone, by wanting to escape, by not wanting to feel afraid, by wanting to be caressed—although I knew that the caress I received would be devoid of any affect.) But, like I said before, this all started before DINA, and it included feelings of guilt about boys approaching me. I felt like something about me was motivating them, although I supposed it was inadequate.

I remember that even in the 1990s I felt guilty—though not responsible—for a thousand things. One day I was talking with some friends whose family members were disappeared, and they told me, "You've got to stop feeling so guilty. We all had pretty complicated love lives. It was a function of the times. We were young. Times were tough. Now listen, and get this through your head because we're not going to say it again: back then we were with this guy, and this guy, and this guy, and this other guy." Hearing that was incredible! It really had an impact on me—not of revulsion, but of admiration for their attempt to help me accept myself.

Really, even before DINA it was hard for me to be a woman. As a youngster, I did just about everything that my parents tried to restrict. I went to college. I was an athlete. I competed in athletic events that in Chile were not thought of as feminine. In fact, I was of the first generation of women to run the 400- and 800-meter events. Incredible, isn't it? I enjoyed reading about topics that weren't considered particularly feminine. In short, lots of things proved how hard it was for me to be a woman: having professional aspirations, changing grammar schools when I thought I should, leaving home, getting married when I wanted to and without going through all the typical rituals, being a militant in a leftist party, wanting to change lots of things, wanting to raise my son like the pediatrician told me I should and not according to my parents' wishes. It wasn't easy!

In DINA, I wouldn't say that being a woman was ever a plus, except for helping me to survive. That's because I still think that DINA let me get away with things that never would have been tolerated from a man. Besides all the things that are already known because they have come out in my testimonies and interviews—things that have to do with humiliation or resisting torture—on some occasions I resisted just because in those moments I was incensed; I couldn't put up with it any more, and I just lost it. Sometimes I said some pretty strong things in font of DINA agents. As a functionary, I refused to do certain things they were asking me to do because, at the time, they seemed uncalled for. Even during my years as a detainee, I challenged certain officials by refusing to do things because I wasn't going to put up with it! Later, from 1976 forward, I progressively dared to say things.

Nevertheless, in other circumstances, it seems like you were playing the gender card—that is, that you were using your female gender as a way of relating to power. How do you understand the complex relationship between the masculine and the feminine within the context of Chilean political repression?

I wasn't playing the gender card. I never sought relationships with them. They weren't even relationships like those one would have in normal life. Oftentimes, what one couldn't stand, what one feared, was being alone, or being massively and indiscriminately harassed. That's what happened with Rolf Wenderoth. His presence saved me from the harassment of others, among them guards and other officials. It was either him or many others. The choice was obvious—at least it was for me in those days. I didn't seek him out. It took me months to accept a kind of relationship with him that was never devoid of fear. But it was less fear than I would have felt with others. He sat me down across from him at his desk. He didn't force me. He asked and asked, and talked and talked until I eventually gave in. More than giving in, I didn't know what to say. By that time, Rolf was protecting me from lots of other violence, as he did with two other detainees. He protected the three of us. Because I was always with Alejandra and María Alicia, he protected them by extension.

I'm not beautiful. I never was. But I'm also not the Hunchback of Notre Dame. I have often felt that if I had weighed a ton when I appeared in the media, or if I had been wearing tattered clothes, many people would have said, "She deserved it; she got what was coming to her." But I didn't conform to that description—though I certainly wasn't pretty or really young. I wore my forty years well, with gray hair ever since I can remember, with my wrinkles, but I was always optimistic and happy to have reestablished a life with my family, my kids, and my friends. I got the feeling that that bothered people. In fact, not only did I feel it; people pointed out to me that I'd never be able to be happy. But that's not true! It hurt to hear those things at the time, but like lots of other things, I was able to assimilate and understand them.

Although it hurt me when people pointed out that I had used my femininity to gain advantages, I eventually learned how to situate myself in what I now feel is my place: that of a woman who loves her family and who respects others just because they exist, because they are people. I refused to be belittled in the ways that some people wanted to belittle me. At the present time, I feel good about my personal life. I think in certain ways and act accordingly. I think that maturity, age, life experience, my family, and so on, have given me these gifts. I am a woman and that's all—without problems.

When I read about your affective relationships with some members of DINA, particularly with Rolf Wenderoth Pozo, I couldn't help thinking about the difficulties those relationships must have presented for you at the time. Looking back, with the distance of years, what reflection can you offer?

Like everything else, it was. It happened. The truth is that I tried to leave DINA and CNI many times, sometimes even risking my life. Eventually I got out. In reality, I had resigned earlier, in 1978, but I wasn't capable of following through with that decision, so I continued. Nevertheless, after 1976, I was trying to get out. That's why whenever I could I studied computer science behind CNI's back, that is, until they caught me. I was also on the verge of leaving in 1977, but the transition from DINA to CNI left me in a dangerous situation in relation to the new authorities. I was more fearful than ever.

I couldn't free myself from Wenderoth until the army put physical distance between us by stationing him outside of Santiago. I cut the relationship off with him many times. He kept begging me. He kept me under his thumb at work, and of course in his office; he was always close by, protecting me, or at least that's how it seemed. In some cases—not in all, but definitely in some—I think that perhaps he controlled me. I don't know. I'll never know. Later, when my oldest son came to live with me, Rolf protected him too. He helped me send him to school; he helped him with his homework, and so on.

The relationship, or whatever it was, had problems—obviously. We weren't a couple in the same way that I now understand the idea of a couple. Ours was a relationship of a superior and his subordinate—a bit off the wall, but a subordinate nonetheless. I felt badly. I didn't have romantic feelings for him, but his attention, his care, his concern that I was eating, his concern about my health (I still suffered lots of physical repercussions), all permitted me, for brief periods of time, to forget what I was, who I was.

When I became conscious of reality, I asked Wenderoth many times to help me get out of DINA. He refused, just like he refused to let me study secretarial skills, as María Alicia and Alejandra had done. I told him many times that he wouldn't always be there, that I wouldn't tolerate him, and that things couldn't continue as they were. But he wouldn't accept it.

Today I have no problem with that time in my life. I think that at some point he really had feelings for me. And I learned how not to be fearful in his presence. In fact, when he would go on vacation or travel, I would go back to feeling the terror I had always felt. It was a strong contradiction, but the terror of his absence was worse than that of his presence. I think I felt gratitude and also some form of affect because I worried about his problems; I was concerned when he was sick.

I saw him again years later, in the 1980s. I even introduced him to my current husband. Wenderoth located my family in 1985, and, through my relatives, he went to meet my son. He showed up like a friend and he was happy—at least he said that he was happy—that my life was normalizing. Nevertheless, at that moment, I felt differently. It bothered me that he looked for me, that he knew my address.

But I understood, or thought I understood, that that's how it would always be with those people. If they wanted to find me, they'd find me.

My trial by fire was when I testified in court about what Wenderoth had done as a member of DINA. I didn't have a problem testifying. Later, in face to face confrontations, I managed to make it through my testimony without a problem. I even talked to Wenderoth. He asked me why I had testified publicly about our relationship and written about it in *The Inferno*. I told him what I honestly thought: that if I didn't say anything, if I kept it to myself, they, the ex-DINA and CNI agents, would use the information against me to discredit me later. He said nothing. I think his silence acknowledged that "Yes, that's what would have happened." Because I didn't and don't want to withhold anything, even if what I say is misinterpreted, it hurts me that all the information I gave about our personal relationship has affected his daughters negatively. But I felt like I had no choice. That's why I spoke up.

I think it's fair to say that Wenderoth gave me what I needed most in those years: some moments of tenderness—but only moments, short periods of time, false tranquility, but even still, moments that let me breathe and continue.

Another of the positive effects that derived from my time as a prisoner of DINA is that I never speculate about what I would have been had I done one thing or another. So, as with everything else, I accept that quasi-relationship as real. It's part of my life. It had some very ugly parts, but also some positive ones.

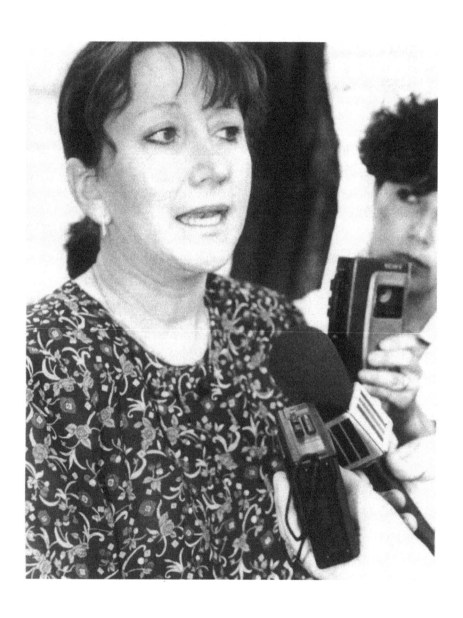

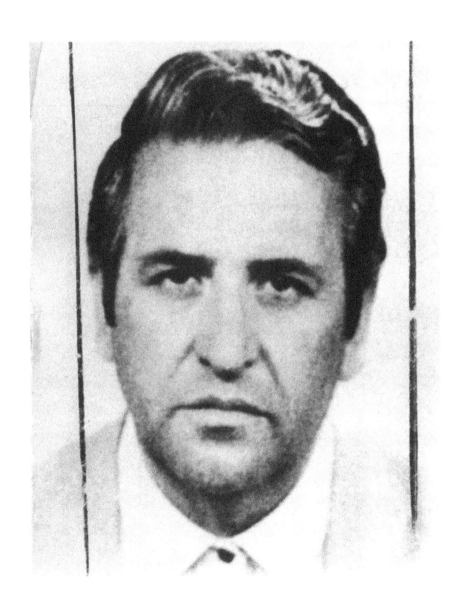

For a long time, [La Flaca Alejandra] was a "thing," formless, malleable, a zombie active in the military's hands, suited to their whims. No one will ever be able to compensate for what happened to her: the eternal black hole, "evil" stuck to her skin, impossible to erase, her survival that meant wounds for the other prisoners, electric shocks, death.

Today I can still hear her telling her truth to the world. This is it, unpolished. I'm a coward. Death, I feared death so, the unbearable pain, I had to stop it, I had to do anything to survive, I broke, I gave up, I obeyed the orders those men gave me, I told them everything I knew, when I went out into the street to point people out, I trembled, they knew it, I am responsible for the deaths and disappearances of many comrades, for a long time I had no idea who I was, the mirror revealed an unknown face to me, never again a song by Silvio Rodríguez, or Mercedes Sosa, nothing that could awaken an emotion from that time, I'd spend nights in my room doped up on tranquilizers and would fall asleep listening to Beethoven's Fifth, I'd do anything to avoid remorse, I fell deeper, I lived day to day. General Manuel Contreras, the creator and master of DINA, known for his perversity, was for me a good and fatherly man. For a long time, I thought he had allowed me to be reborn, he proposed that I be a DINA agent, receive a salary, a house, missions, he said he was doing it to save our lives because MIR had decided to eliminate the three of us— Carola, Luz, and me—I accepted. Some years later, I met an officer in the north, he invited me to dinner, I told him my story, he was impressed, I fell in love with him, sex wasn't important to us, he protected me, but he was married, and we separated.

They sent me back to Santiago, I attempted suicide again, the doctor hated me, they forced me to continue, under watch, I went back to my work in DINA's analytical office, sometimes I'd find little pieces of paper with promises to "collaborate" written by the "detained and disappeared," those whom DINA has not recognized as such to this day, I was so scared again, I didn't say anything to anyone, especially not to the families that I knew were looking for them. I was scared of them too, every night I tried to forget a bit more, time passed uniformly, but one day they stole my television, I went to file a report, the police detained me, there was an order for my arrest for complicity in the Bill Beaussire case, he disappeared in 1975, remorse assaulted me again, violently, obsessively, I plunged again into fear. Captain Miguel Krassnoff Martchenko took me out of there, he decided to distance me from DINA, they "froze" me, I only kept distanced contact with them, I worked in a station, using my real name. I sought refuge in the Church, during confession I cried and the priest said to me, "Why don't you love yourself?" During a trip to Easter Island, I met a native of the island, he hardly spoke any Spanish, we got married, I couldn't get pregnant, I wanted a child so badly, but I couldn't have one. I always steered clear of the courts and the subpoenas. Manuel Contreras, head of DINA, gave me a new house, I started taking tranquilizers again, I kept working on my own, I was trying to live a normal life, I didn't tell any of this to my husband, or my mother, never. One day the judge who was investigating the case of Alfonso Chanfreau, the young man [from MIR], the only one whom I truly loved, sent me a summons, I didn't respond, not even for him, I didn't even do it for Lumi Videla, my best friend. Later, two weeks ago, I read in the newspapers that the courts were reopening the Chanfreau case, I saw the judge's tears on television, I sensed Erika's desperation, his wife, I saw, I felt within me an incredible force welling up, it tore through me brutally. Lautaro Videla, Lumi's brother, who had returned from exile, sent me a message, I accepted a meeting with him, I was so scared, I shook while I waited for him to show up, but he spoke to me as if we had just seen each other yesterday, without reproach, he listened to me, he said: "Speak up, Flaca, tell what you know, it will do you good, it will help us to get at the truth and convict the real criminals." The next day, he showed me a photograph of Lumi's cadaver, her broken body, tortured, the body that DINA agents had thrown onto the front lawn of the Italian Embassy, at long last I could see the past, I saw myself, me, the other, in that past, little by little I started piecing things together. No one can understand except us, the ones who lived the daily experience of a torture house . . .

A torture house wound tight like a watch, one can go crazy there, she enters and the trap closes. One survives, sometimes, if she buys time, one hopes to save herself by cuddling up, by letting herself be shaped; adapting implies forgetting the outside, the time prior to detention, tomorrow. One forgets the concept of colors, of day and night, of good and evil. In the José Domingo Cañas torture house, the game plays out, no one knows who has the other, or who has fallen into the trap.

One has to invent herself in the darkness, despite everything, a line. To be, to keep being who one is. Octavio fakes dementia. Diana knows nothing until the end. Lumi feigns collaboration. Others blurt out fragments of information, they guard what is essential, some even manage not to see pain again. They have almost all died. Flaca Alejandra, Luz, and Carola became traitors. But Gladys Díaz and Miriam Ortega managed to keep quiet despite abhorrent suffering. All five survived. There's no logic in these places. One can speak without betraying. One can start to betray without giving up anything important. But she has crossed over to the other side; she belongs to them.

—*The experience of La Flaca Alejandra as imagined by Carmen Castillo, former MIR militant, Santiago-París: El vuelo de la memoria (2002)*

SANTIAGO, EIGTH DAY OF SEPTEMBER TWO THOSAND FOUR, **MARÍA ALICIA URIBE GÓMEZ**, IDENTITY CARD NUMBER X.XXX.XXX-X, NATIVE OF CALERA DEL TANGO, 56 YEARS OLD, SINGLE, RETIRED FROM THE ARMY (A CIVIL SERVANT), TELEPHONE NUMBER XX-XXXXXXX, WHO LIVES ON SANTA ROSA STREET NUMBER XXX, APARTMENT NUMBER XXX-X, HAVING SWORN TO TELL THE TRUTH, STATES:

There's a period while one is detained in which one doesn't speak at all. Later, because of pressure and torture, one is broken absolutely. That's what happened to me in late 1974. When I broke, I decided to collaborate. It was voluntary collaboration; they pressured me just the same. What's more, I had very few names of Miristas to offer because I worked with MIR's special intelligence structures. The government's security organizations obtained information from the detainees. I don't think there is one detainee who didn't talk or turn someone in. It was like a chain in which one person would turn in another. In fact, my best friend was the one who turned me in. They called her "Flaca Alejandra," MARCIA MERINO [. . .] When GENERAL CONTRERAS left DINA and CNI was created, GENERAL MENA sent me to work on an antidrug program that the military government wanted to implement. So I went to work at the University of Chile's psychiatric clinic. Later, I went to the *Intendencia* of the Metropolitan Region where I worked to set up drug prevention centers for adolescents at the community level. When the military government ended in 1990, and all of CNI's functionaries became employed by the army, they contracted me too. So I went back to working in intelligence for DINE until I retired in 1998.

SANTIAGO, TWENTIETH DAY OF MARCH TWO THOUSAND TWO, **MARÍA ALICIA URIBE GÓMEZ**, CHILEAN, NATIVE OF CALERA DEL TANGO, 54 YEARS OLD, SINGLE, IDENTITY CARD NUMBER X.XXX.XXX-X, WHO LIVES ON SANTA ROSA STREET NUMBER XXX, APARTMENT NUMBER XXX-X, SANTIAGO, RETIRED, HAVING SWORN TO TELL THE TRUTH, STATES:

I didn't participate in the interrogation of detainees, much less in torture. Nevertheless, because I was so physically proximate to the interrogation room, I could hear the cries and screams of pain of the prisoners being tortured. I imagine that in those interrogation rooms they had the same torture tools that they had at José Domingo Cañas, but I never saw them because I never went into that area . . .

The truth is that Luz Arce and I shared a mutual mistrust of one another. For that reason, we didn't communicate much. Nevertheless, in a book she wrote, she recognized that I had been the most tortured of all of us. Luz was friends with Marcia Alejandra [Merino]. The truth is that living together was very difficult, and we wound up with a strained relationship, not because we had done anything to each other, but because of the conditions in which we were forced to live . . .

LET THE RECORD SHOW THAT THE WITNESS CRIES AND POINTS OUT THAT SHE DOESN'T REMEMBER MUCH ABOUT WHAT HAPPENED AT VILLA GRIMALDI BECAUSE SHE HAS BEEN IN PSYCHIATRIC TREATMENT AND HAS FORGOTTEN ALL SHE LIVED THROUGH DURING HER TIME IN DINA. SHE ADDS THAT HAD SHE KNOWN WHAT HAPPENED TO THE DISAPPEARED, SHE WOULD HAVE SHARED THE INFORMATION.

. . . I kept working for the army because I was forty years old when the military government ended, and I had no work experience. Consequently, I chose to continue my service because, by that point, I didn't care about politics. I didn't have any political position.

The best time in my life was when I worked in MIR, but that brought severe consequences.

I always had the idea that Marcia Merino, "Alejandra," wanted to commit suicide when Miguel Enríquez [the leader of MIR] died. But in 1992, when we both testified in court, she told me that her suicide attempt had to do with the death of another MIR militant, alias "Lautaro," who died in a confrontation in late October 1974.

—*Luz Arce, legal testimony, June 9, 2000*

5

Luz, Marcia, Carola (Ana María Vergara, Marta Vergara, Gloria Vilches)

I would like to talk a little bit about Carola (María Alicia Uribe Gómez). Unlike Alejandra (Marcia Alejandra Merino Vega) and you, Carola remained a functionary of DINE (*Dirección de Inteligencia del Ejército*), the Chilean army's intelligence service, even after the 1990 return to democracy and the formal dissolution of DINA and CNI. Have you ever felt any kind of rejection toward Carola because of how she ultimately decided to confront the common situation that the three of you lived?

Most people don't like to hear what I'm about to tell you. I'm sorry, but I can't say anything else, because this is what I feel, even if it bothers people.

I want to say that I love both of them: Marcia and María Alicia. Deep down, I feel tenderness for them, affection. We shared far too many moments, hours, months, and years together—scared to death—for me to feel otherwise.

One day, for example, after we had just arrived at the apartment where the three of us lived together—the one in front of DINA headquarters—María Alicia was crying in her room, on her bed, and Marcia and I heard her. We went running to try to console her. There were other things that happened, but that instance impacted me deeply. We shared so much pain, a huge bond forged in pain. That's what wins out. It translates into feelings of tenderness.

I feel affection for María Alicia, just like I feel affection for Marcia. On one hand, we share in common that we survived the dictatorship's repression. On the other hand, I feel like destiny joined us together and forced us to share the worst moments of our lives. But the affection I feel for each one of them is different. I have to admit that, if I'm going to be honest. I have no idea how any of this will evolve, because I'm still waiting for María Alicia. I am telling you sincerely. I feel that if she doesn't take a leap and leave DINE (Intelligence Directorate of the Army) [successor to CNI], I'm going to die waiting for her.

Anyway, now that María Alicia has retired, I just don't know. Perhaps too much time has passed. Now isn't the time for her to go to the courts to testify. I just don't know. But I want to think that María Alicia, too, can free herself from the horror, just like Marcia and I managed to do.

On the day María Alicia takes that leap, if I'm anywhere nearby, I don't know what I'll feel. I sincerely don't know. Even though I'm aware that time has passed, if she had taken that leap, I probably would have felt immense happiness, enormous satisfaction. It would have meant that the three of us, at last, were free. I feel like Marcia and I are free. And it's so beautiful to feel free from the slavery that DINA imposed on us. I wish the same for María Alicia, but I understand that her process is personal. Without knowing her reasons, I respect her decisions, even though I feel differently.

How did you feel when Marcia Alejandra Merino "took the leap," severed her ties with DINE, and started testifying in court in November 1992?

That happened at the behest of Judge Dobra Lusic Nadal. Her honor asked me to explain to Marcia, as honestly as possible, what my experience had been like between the time I testified to the Rettig Commission and the present. I didn't have a problem doing that. That's how we started talking. Our conversation took place with no press, privately, without any strangers hanging around.

I arrived at the courthouse first. Judge Lusic sent an investigative police team to Marcia's house with a subpoena for her to appear in court. I assume the judge did that so that Marcia wouldn't know about the meeting ahead of time, because Marcia was still connected to DINE. At the time, Marcia wasn't working directly for DINE, but she was receiving a salary and living in an apartment owned by DINE. I suppose that because Osvaldo Romo had recently arrived from Brazil (he was detained at the time), and because it was so difficult to get him back to Chile, the court decided to take precautionary measures related to upcoming proceedings, testimonies, face-offs, and so on.[1] It was also a touchy situation because if Marcia decided to testify, obviously she couldn't go back and live in the DINE apartment. In that case, she'd need to be given protection.

In those days, I also took some precautions to protect my family at home. I would say that I was locatable and available to the courts, but my lawyers and close friends recommended that I spend some days in hiding, even though we were living in democracy. Certainly my new clandestine life wasn't as anguished as my previous life had been. I didn't face the same risks or have the same problems that I had when I lived clandestinely (from the time of the coup until my detention in March 1974).

That same day, November 22, 1992, Marcia arrived at the courthouse and agreed to testify. Judge Lusic carried out her inquiry and, afterward, Marcia and I talked for a long time. We drank coffee and smoked a lot of cigarettes together. And almost immediately, despite the fact that Marcia still depended on DINE, I trusted her. I trusted her enough to give her my home phone number, and I told her that I had no problem going with her to court if she thought it necessary or if she wanted me to.

To this day, I'm still in touch with Marcia. Even though, because of time constraints, we're not in daily contact, we still write to each other pretty frequently.

And you don't maintain that same kind of contact with Carola or feel the same kind of affection toward her?

I get very emotional about this subject. I feel like Carola probably wanted to take the leap and that she would have done it under the right circumstances. But those circumstances never presented themselves, and time passed. I feel like taking the leap to testify in court honestly opens a path of hope, a chance to reconnect with oneself first and, later, for reintegration. At the same time, it also signals an important new beginning, a new chapter for finding oneself and for reengaging with family and friends in a different way. It also opens the possibility for a peaceful life, a life in which one feels human. Of course, I'm not talking about forgetting, but rather of integrating everything in a healthy way, as an experience, as a learning experience.

Marcia, María Alicia, and I truly lived through hell. Marcia and I lived through everything I've just been outlining for you—the process of reconnecting and becoming human again—each in our own way, each at our own pace. But even still, to be frank, even though I feel affection toward María Alicia, if she were to take the same leap today that Marcia and I took before, I don't think I'd dare say, "Why don't you come over to my house?" In other words, my point is that I'd have more security concerns with her. Maybe it's just because so many years have passed. Remember, she *retired* as part of DINE! I just don't know what happened with her.

In 2004, I saw María Alicia in court when I traveled to Chile from Mexico to testify. The same day I was going to return to Mexico, I had to attend a couple of depositions. My encounter with her was nice. It wasn't like I expected it to be; I thought I would have to keep certain things to myself. María Alicia simply walked into the judge's office and we embraced spontaneously. We talked, and I managed to see . . . well, at least it seemed that she embraced me tenderly. We hadn't seen each other for more than a decade. I can only say that on that occasion, yes, I gave her my home address. Even though I didn't think it was totally safe, sometimes you just have to trust people, right? We exchanged phone numbers and went downtown together just like two people would do, two friends who have followed different paths in life and who have not seen each other in years.

Even though Carola didn't give as much information in her deposition as I might have liked, I give her the benefit of the doubt that maybe she didn't remember, or maybe she didn't know much about the case we were discussing with the judge that day—although it's likely that she just didn't want to testify to anything beyond what was in her personal interest. But I also feel that if I remain faithful to my principles, I can't expect her to change the way she feels. At the end of the day, it's her process and she'll live it at her own pace.

That day, when we left the courthouse, we went into downtown Santiago and had coffee. We talked without fear, without reservations, and later I said good-bye to her from the airport. I called her on the phone before I boarded the plane. We said we would write to one another. Through a third party that both she and I hold in mutual confidence, I sent her a letter from my home. I haven't received a reply. Maybe now isn't the time. But now I have the patience to wait for her to reinitiate contact. Our conversation was nice. She told me about her mother. I told her about my family, my granddaughter, my son, but a lot remained pending that day. I gave her my silver earrings, and she gave me one of her rings and a sweater to cover myself because it was raining. That exchange was nice. It implied something like: even though the two of us chose different paths, the fact that the three of us lived through the inferno, the fact that we shared so much pain (even though we didn't always express it), bonds us in sisterhood, reconciles us, and permits us to grow as people. The three of us were, and perhaps still are, so different and, nevertheless, despite it all, we can still feel mutual affection. We can still respect and accept one another, tenderly.

Once, at one of the proceedings to which María Alicia and I were called to testify, she said to me, "You have no idea how much I hated you when I found out that you testified to the Rettig Commision. I hated you even more when you published *The Inferno.* You exposed me, my pain. Later, with time, I understood you and realized that you humanized me in your book." The truth is that I simply wrote according to what I felt, according to my memory, nothing more. But based on what she said, I felt like María Alicia understood my process, that she intuited something—Marcia too, because Marcia lived through the same thing from the time she started testifying in court. The three of us know the personal costs involved, we know the horrendous fear, we know what pain is, and we know how to walk a mile in another's shoes. That's valuable, very valuable.

From an ethical perspective, do you feel capable of judging María Alicia?

No, because I understand her. I am certain that the fear she still feels is the same fear I felt. Also, I feel that, over time, María Alicia's practicality, in combination with other factors, left her hands tied. When I saw her last November, she told me that her mother had cancer and that the only possibility of getting her treatment was through the Military Hospital. I think that María Alicia—although she never said so—was also thinking about her mother at the time she made certain decisions. I'm not justifying her actions. I'm just telling you what I know about her and about the factors I think influenced her decisions.

Notwithstanding the conditions we were in, I feel like the three of us reacted in every moment according to our temperaments and personalities. María Alicia always was—and I think still is—the most practical of the three of us. Her practicality stems from her life experience. Her personality dictated that she would never move from her position with DINE until she retired. Now that she's retired, her house and her daily life are taken care of. María Alicia always needed personal security; Marcia and I were more irresponsible. For us, if there was no food, there just wasn't any food. Marcia and I would see it as an opportunity to lose some weight. But not María Alicia. She was always interested in securing her future. She could only think about herself, and perhaps that's what makes me trust her less.

Maybe I'm being unfair to María Alicia, but my attitude has changed over time. Maybe in the course of her process she has changed too. But what I honestly feel today—and I would say this to her face—is that I can't trust María Alicia one hundred percent. If the occasion arose, we'd have to reconnect gradually.

Carmen Castillo's documentary film, *La Flaca Alejandra: Vidas y muertes de una mujer chilena* (Skinny Alejandra: Lives and deaths of a Chilean woman) (1994), attempts to explore some of the dilemmas that arise from collaboration and limit experiences. What is your opinion of that documentary?

I only saw it once, and in interrupted fashion, because while I was watching it with Marcia, we talked about a lot of personal issues. One day, Marcia told me that she had the video and suggested that we go to her house to watch it. We had coffee and talked, but because of the distractions, we didn't have a chance to watch it very carefully. But based on what I saw and remember, I didn't like it.

Why?

I remember it as a film that was made in late 1992, early 1993. Consequently, it was a product of that moment. Marcia took the leap on November 22, 1992, and Castillo started filming her documentary after that date.

I only know Carmen Castillo quite superficially. I have met her in person, and she has always been very nice to me. I can't say anything bad about her. I am not familiar with the rest of her work. I've only read one of her books. I'm not sure if she has written more.

And the documentary?

I felt it was implacable. I thought it was really harsh on Marcia. Anyway, that's how I felt.

Did you feel like Castillo was trying to take an objective look at Marcia?

I never felt like her gaze was objective. I don't think she can be objective with Marcia, nor with anything that has to do with the dictatorship or DINA. I don't feel like I'm objective about those subjects either—obviously.

Did Marcia like the documentary?

Marcia is different from me in that sense. I think she is guiltier than I am—and I'm quite prone to guilt, or at least I used to be that way. Now I don't feel quite as guilty as I once did.

Marcia feels—or, to be more exact, I should say that she felt—guilty about everything. I think that if Marcia and I were here talking to each other alone, not about this, but socially, she'd be fine. But suppose you can't find your wallet and you honestly think it was stolen on a bus, Marcia would jump up and say, "It wasn't me." Do you understand? Well, that's how I remember her, even though I feel she is different now. She has been going through her own personal process for a long time.

I spent many years in the same state. I feel like my whole childhood, my whole adolescence and youth were racked with guilt. My time with DINA was absolutely guilt ridden. But I think that taking responsibility for everything that has happened has helped. Verbalizing to Father Cristián what happened to me in DINA had the effect of relieving my guilt—though not to such an extreme that I don't feel any responsibility. I want to make a distinction on that point. In other words, I feel . . .

Responsibility but not guilt . . .

It's that they're different. What am I supposed to do with guilt? On the other hand, taking *responsibility* implies assuming, repairing, making, recognizing, and a ton of other stuff. Just harboring guilt doesn't help anyone—not you, not anyone.

Yet Marcia feels guilty.

I haven't seen Marcia since she left Santiago. Her husband moved away before her, and obviously they didn't want to live apart as a couple. So a bunch of her friends got together and we bought her a plane ticket. I helped her pack her personal belongings. Before she left, Marcia stayed at my house for a few days and I took her to the airport. That was in 1997. Since then, we haven't seen each other.

Now that she's home, I suppose Marcia is continuing her process. I don't know how she is now. From her messages, it seems like she has been able to overcome many things. I don't know what her present "guilt level" is, but she did feel quite guilty when Castillo filmed her documentary.

To be honest, I have always mistrusted artists who fancy themselves part of an elite class. I am really critical of any works that pose as intellectual. They inspire mistrust. I'm not saying that that's how Carmen Castillo is. But based on what little I remember, on the fragments I saw, her film gave me that impression. And that makes me mistrust her.

Fine, I hit a woman. Yeah, I hit her. Sure! I slapped her around because, if I didn't, she would have died. Luz Arce. Luz Arce, the one who went from being a traitor to a collaborator, because she couldn't bite the hand that fed her. Luz Arce worked for Allende; she was a telephone operator for Allende. She worked for DINA and slept with high-ranking DINA officers. Ah! She slept with them. She earned a salary from DINA, and now she's mixed-up with the other side, with the *Rettig Report.* So, she's already played for three teams. She's worse, though, right? She's worse than a soccer player who has played for seven different teams, because soccer players play for love of the game. But she didn't play for love of the game; she played for personal reasons, with her weaknesses, thinking of what she could gain, with a personal agenda. La Flaca Alejandra was the same. La Flaca Alejandra is now in . . . Now they're all victims. No way! You can't sell me that line!

—*Osvaldo Romo Mena, DINA torturer, interviewed by Chilean journalist Nancy Guzmán, Romo: Confesiones de un torturador (2000)*

Former DINA agent Osvaldo Romo Mena, remembered as one of the military regime's cruelest torturers, was buried this morning. The burial took place on Patio 39 of the General Cemetery in the most absolute solitude.

As Radio Cooperativa reported, not even the priest officiating the ceremony spoke because no one was there to bid farewell to Romo's remains.

"Fat Romo" was buried in slot 32 of the Sisters of Charity mausoleum.

Tulio Guevara, director of the General Cemetery, indicated that in his many years in charge he had never seen a burial that no one attended.

Romo died Wednesday morning at age 69 in a prison hospital. He was serving a sentence for kidnappings and human rights violations.

"Fat Romo," or "Commander Raúl," as he was known in DINA, suffered from diabetes and pneumonia, in addition to a heart condition and the repercussions of a stroke.

—*"Osvaldo Romo Mena fue sepultado en la más absoluta soledad," La Segunda, Thursday, July 5, 2007*

6

Shame and Reconciliation

At various points in *The Inferno,* you talk about feeling shame: shame that stemmed from being tortured, or from having been a collaborator and functionary of DINA/CNI. How do you understand the different faces of shame, and what mechanisms have you employed to mitigate it?

I believe today that any action that is painful or difficult to overcome, that one only submits to out of obligation (in this case after being tortured repeatedly), or that introduces strong contradictory feelings that totally alter ones life, produces shame. Knowing that one's life has been broken, shattered, or halted, also generates feelings of shame. If I had to define it, I would say that shame is the feeling that one's actions are out of sync with one's beliefs, with what one feels or loves.

For example, I felt shame when I was raped. I knew that what happened wasn't my fault. I knew I wasn't seeking it voluntarily. What's more, I never imagined that such things could happen to me. Even when I was detained, I thought they would beat me and pressure me, but I never thought they'd rape me. Like many survivors I know, none of us even remotely imagined the things we'd live through.

I can't list for you the reasons I felt guilty for having been raped. There were so many! When I was raped was when I most wanted to disappear. I wanted to be invisible. I suppose that everything I heard when I was a little girl, or later as an adolescent, about women who "provoked" rape weighed upon me at that time and for many years after that. Intellectually, I knew that rape was a form of aggression that a bunch of "beasts" had exercised against me, but I couldn't help but feel shame and guilt.

The clearest example I can cite is when I was raped by an on-duty officer on New Year's Eve of 1974–75. The day after I was raped, Pedro Espinoza Bravo called me into his office and asked if it was true. I didn't dare say yes. There I was, seated in front of Espinoza Bravo, and I felt like I was turning red, like I was going to become speechless.[1] I wanted to run away, to flee. My previous experiences had taught me that if one wanted to complain about an officer, even though that officer's actions may have been censured at the moment of his transgression, later, when the authorities weren't present, the soldiers would take it upon themselves to beat us in retribution for having complained. For that reason—but also because of shame—I said nothing.

Even in the worst moments something existed that might be called "conscience." I never asked: Why me? I knew exactly why I was there. It was because those people wanted to assure, at any cost, the dictatorship's permanence and supposed governability. And, whether it was a reality or not, according to them, we, the detainees, were a threat. When I perceived directly that they considered me a danger, I began to feel that they would annihilate us. But before doing that, they'd have to saddle us, belittle us. And more than to "save the country," they had to do it to stay in power. But even still, living in such a state of belittlement makes one's conscience shrink, as if one were fading away.

When I was aware of my collaboration, I would sometimes get desperate. Other times, I'd feel extreme pain. I tried to avoid those feelings. My salve was withholding information or giving irrelevant information. It also helped that, ever since I can remember, I have always been a fun-loving person. I think that my good character, the joy with which I was born, my perpetual optimism even in the worst moments, and my physical strength, were all factors that helped me get out of there alive, without going completely psychotic. Those traits helped me to not lose my sanity, to want to get out, to survive.

I never felt like I was part of DINA or CNI, neither as a collaborating prisoner nor as a functionary. As a functionary, I was aware of the situation I was living. I knew what many comrades who had been held in the same detention centers were living. I knew that they kicked María Alicia until they broke one of her ribs. I knew about the abuse of detainees. There was never one second in which I considered myself part of that world or in which I wanted to stay there. I was there "in transit." That idea got me through. But, just the same, being there made me feel ashamed: ashamed because of what my son would think of me, or of what anyone would think for that matter.

In the most difficult moments, I sought refuge in myself, in my memories of the outside world, in my country's landscape as I knew it prior to September 11, 1973. During my time at Villa Grimaldi, I could see a little bit of the Andes from Wenderoth's office. I memorized that image and replayed it over and over again for hours. During that ugly period at Villa Grimaldi, I remember that occasionally they'd open our cells and let us take our blindfolds off for a while, unless they said differently. When the door was open, I could see a tiny bit of sky amid the foliage. I saw the moon. It was beautiful and light blue on a Chilean spring night. I remember gazing at it and thinking that maybe my son was looking at it too. I got a beautiful feeling.

I think that remembering the beauty of my country and of human beings was a way to escape from that atrocious reality, from shame, from an awareness of what I had become there. It was a way of mitigating what had become unbearable. I don't know. I'm just guessing. There were people who made fun of me and who asked, "How's your imaginary forest doing?" I didn't care. I didn't bother to explain it to them. What for them was a joke, was for me like an inner wellspring that made me not forget the beauty of the world and people. I started to reconcile with my parents on the inside. That internal reconciliation (which I couldn't communicate to my parents directly for a long time after that), coupled with my love for my absent child, kept a certain quota of humanity alive in me that dictatorship's brutality tried to take away. They couldn't do it.

The Inferno emphasizes the importance of forgiveness and reconciliation, which have been key words that the media and the government have repeated infinitely during the transition to democracy. Your book appeared in the early 1990s, at a time when these concepts weighed heavily in the public discourse of the *Concertación*. Have you ever thought of your book as an extension of *Concertación* politics?

I didn't decide the book's publication date. Planeta, my publisher, decided. Forgiveness and reconciliation were born in me during the personal process I started living in 1988—a process that continued as I wrote during the first semester of 1989, my testimony to the Rettig Commission, my yearlong trip to Europe, my study of theology, my conversion to Christianity, and my attempt to keep my family stable and intact in the midst of it all.

My book is not an extension of *Concertación* politics. It's a stage in my life and my personal process, situated in a specific moment of the life of my country. Every person is a product of his or her times. It's undeniable that if I hadn't been a rambunctious adolescent who was touched intellectually by the beauty of the 1960s, perhaps my life would have turned out differently. Every person is a product of the history of his or her times.

How do you understand the idea of reconciliation? Is it something that has been achieved or that is achievable in Chile?

Reconciliation has deep meaning for me personally. It is something I have lived intensely. I have fought for it, for years, starting with reconciling with myself.

For me, reconciliation is more than a concept; it is something that is lived, learned with difficulty, and, on a personal level, is part and parcel with a fulfilling life. On a personal level, reconciliation *can* be achieved. But this implies many things. It means forgiving oneself and those who have caused harm; it means understanding the facts of one's circumstances (either those one is living or those one lived); it means knowing oneself; it means recognizing one's own weaknesses, mistakes, and limitations. It also implies having the humility to see oneself as one really is, without preconceived or idealized images. Only such a raw encounter with oneself can make reconciliation permissible. At the same time, reconciliation means being able to look upon another person with the same love with which one sees oneself. All of this is possible, but it takes time, willingness, and resolve.

And what about reconciliation on a broader, societal level?

I don't know how reconciliation functions on a societal level, but I maintain hope that it is possible. Time, truth, and a willingness to come together are key ingredients, in my opinion, for societal reconciliation.

I think reconciliation is necessary for both individuals and societies. I suppose that in the worst of cases, reconciliation will be achieved in my country when all of us who survived the dictatorship period have died. I hope that other profound societal divisions can also be overcome, like the gap between rich and poor. That would be a good thing for Chile or any country that has suffered such a profound division.

Certainly reconciliation is not easy. But it's possible. At least it seems possible to me, since I am living it today and have been for some time. Maybe someday I'll discover that it can't be. But this is what I think.

Do you forgive those who tortured and mistreated you during the dictatorship?

I harbor no resentments regarding either the past or the present. I harbor no hatred. I managed to heal over time by attempting to take responsibility, by repairing myself, by testifying, by facing those who mistreated me, by living my personal processes intensely in an effort to achieve understanding, by learning of Pinochet's detention in London, by reclaiming my life.

But Luz, anyone who considers your situation logically would want to know if the reconciliation and lack of resentment to which you refer have limits? For example, wouldn't you feel hatred if, theoretically, you bumped into Romo or Contreras on the street? How can you forgive people like them? I am trying to understand the extent to which reconciliation is a political fiction and the extent to which it's real.

I don't think I ever felt hatred, although I must admit that I never figured out whether all the fear I felt impeded me from hating. I accept that it's probable that I felt hatred but that I just couldn't identify it as such. In the late 1980s and throughout the 1990s, I managed to feel rage, lots of it, as if it had been welling up inside of me. But I never felt anything like hatred. I am a person whose fits of rage are very short-lived. As soon as I become aware that I am mad, my rage is dispelled and I find myself asking forgiveness.

I sincerely believe that people can reconcile. I assume that there are different moments or stages, and it is through day-to-day living that I have been able to discover the prejudices that guide my actions.

Regarding Romo, I was deposed with him on November 23, 1992, but I had seen him before in the courthouse corridors. My first impression when I saw him was that he wasn't the same person I remembered. In my memory, he appeared tall, monstrous, imposing. That day he seemed smaller. Someone suggested to me later on that people like Romo may have seemed bigger than they actually were because, as prisoners, we were always flung on the ground, strapped to the *parrilla*, or living in a precarious state. Years later, when you see them from another perspective, they look different. Even though Romo was still just as disgusting as I remembered him, with greasy hair and gnarly, dirty fingernails, on that day, dragging a leg behind him, he seemed hunched over. He seemed to have aged much more than I had in those intervening years. When he approached me, I didn't feel anything akin to hatred. Rather, I was amazed at how I was now able to perceive him, and by how deteriorated he looked. He was in bad health. I remember thinking, "Is this the man who terrified me so?"

Later, with time, through different encounters in front of different judges, I came to understand that Romo hadn't changed much. He was the same. It's just that he was plagued by sickness and age. Nevertheless, at a certain moment, he asked to speak to me after a deposition while he was still interned in the infirmary on Pedro Montt street. That day, during his deposition, he lied, just like he always did. But I agreed to speak with him. People from the Investigative Police were

protecting me, and the judge and various comrades were hanging around wait-ing for him to come out. I didn't have room to feel hatred. I didn't rationalize my feelings; it's just that I didn't hate him. During our conversation, Romo asked me for toilet paper and for stationery to write letters to his wife. I told him "yes," that I would send him those things. He asked me for money because he said he didn't have deodorant, soap, or other essentials. Since the authorities were going to drive me home, I handed him everything I had in my purse. Later, I sent the other things he requested via the Investigative Police: toilet paper, some envelopes, and a writ-ing tablet for air mail letters. I genuinely wanted to do it. I wouldn't deny those things to anyone, not even to the worst of criminals. I know what it means not to have things, especially when one is in prison.

I wouldn't have failed to help Romo because of what others might think. Natu-rally, I would never be his friend, nor would I be Contreras's friend. I don't think that I could feel affection for them either. I want them to be punished for their actions insofar as Chilean law allows. That would help me to recover a lot of what I still lack. But I'm not out for vengeance—and much less toward their families. I also have no idea what these people feel when they're alone with themselves. I only know what I feel when I'm alone with myself. I am talking about personal processes of introspection, although I have discovered with time that not everyone probes his or her soul in hopes of achieving personal discovery or self-knowledge. In fact, I tried not to do that for years. Oftentimes, rooted in my Christian faith, I ask God to help those people admit what they did and repent, even if it never hap-pens publicly, even if it happens only in the very last seconds of their lives.

In Romo's case, even though he tortured and violated me personally, it's easier for me to forgive him than to forgive Contreras. I think that Romo had fewer tools to defend himself within the world of DINA. In fact, I feel that, for DINA, Romo was a disposable man who was used and violated too. He just didn't know it. Some people say that Romo was tortured as well—although apparently not by DINA. But I'm not sure if that's true. I think that, in his case, his very difficult life as a young man is a factor. I am not trying to exonerate him, much less justify his actions. I am just trying to understand him.

So I guess I would change your question about reconciliation. For me the question is not "Is reconciliation possible?" but "Do we want to reconcile?" I sincerely think that not everybody in Chile wants to reconcile. And I suppose that those who don't want to, even though they may not be aware of it, have tons of reasons—too many, and all of them understandable—but these can also be addressed and overcome. I join with those who think that these questions—forgiveness and reconciliation—are not by decree. They can't be.

Forgiveness and reconciliation won't rain down from heaven. No one can bestow them. First, one has to become conscious—normally with the help of others—and then work toward what he or she desires. Sometimes I think: Who am I not to forgive? Or I think of Augustine of Hipona's sentence that I used as a chapter title in *The Inferno*: "How can I hate someone who could someday be my brother?"

I think if we could all understand each other, if we could assume a critical attitude toward ourselves—healthy, not rigid, perhaps like the attitude I had when I was young—it would be a lot easier to forgive.

I'd like to talk about the French documentary *Chili: Des borreaux en liberté* (Chile: Torturers at Large; 1999), by Tony Comiti and Emmanuel D'Arthuys. In one scene of the film, you are seen confronting your former torturer, Marcelo Moren Brito, in the parking lot of a Santiago grocery store. What details do you remember about that confrontation, and how did it affect you?

The emotions I experienced were incredible. The encounter wasn't totally casual. We already knew where Moren lived, and the film crew asked me to accompany them. They asked me if I was willing to speak with him, and I said yes. Pinochet was detained in London in those days, and there still hadn't been any convictions in certain emblematic human rights cases that are now resolved. To make a long story short, seeing Moren in a state of absolute normalcy enraged me a lot. He was buying avocadoes in a supermarket, on a Sunday, just like any grandfather who was about to have afternoon tea surrounded by his family, children, and grandchildren.

When Moren saw the camera, he turned violent. His voice got louder, and he started to shout, "Marxist! Communist!" It was a really sudden change. So even though we had planned many things, there was no script to follow in that instance. The situation simply unfolded. I have the feeling that words were just bandied about in the moment. Moren's family even got aggressive with the cameraman.

I think that standing in front of Moren, I really felt my loss for the first time. Some people lost their lives; some lost family members; some lost their jobs. There were so many losses. And throughout the whole journey I had made up to that moment of encounter with Moren, I had never stopped to think about what had happened to *me* in the process, about what *I* had lost, left, or gained. And that day it happened. That day—without denying my responsibility and regardless of whether I had alternatives, because I am certainly responsible for things—my outlook changed. I felt a mixture of rage and sadness. Even though I bore some responsibility for my losses, I understood that *they* were responsible too. They forced me. I wasn't looking for a job from them. I didn't join DINA voluntarily. It was like, at that moment, facing Moren, everything merged: the six months of torture, the moment at which I broke, and everything that came after that. It wasn't a complete film. It was like a bunch of scenes, flashes, or moments that added up to a kind of summary. I felt like DINA had completely taken my world from me, the world to which I belonged. All of that enraged me, as if Moren symbolized at that moment everything I would never again have. And when I felt like I would never have it again, I felt sad. I couldn't stop crying.

Your encounter with Moren leaves me with a question. If, in *The Inferno*, you propose reconciliation as a utopian project, as a goal to be achieved, doesn't your lived experience with Moren contradict that utopia?

Totally! At many points I have felt like sometimes reason and emotion are at odds with one another. I still maintain that we should reconcile with one another. Commander-in-chief Cheyre's statement in *La Tercera* today, for example, is a step in the right direction.[2] When I was writing *The Inferno,* I honestly thought that the process of reconciliation would be more viable in the short term than it has turned out to be.

I still think that it's good for Chile to bridge its divisions. We continue to be two countries in one. Yes, I feel like Chile has advanced in many ways, but the divisions still exist.

In the days following my encounter with Moren, going over it in my head, thinking about what happened, I felt ashamed for having let my emotions get the better of me. I felt rage first, then pain, but I still don't think I felt hatred. Or did I? I don't know. Moren was detained for acts he committed while in DINA. I think that he has already been convicted in some cases. Around that time, a lawyer friend of mine wrote to me from Chile and told me something I'll always remember, "Justice takes a long time, but it eventually comes."

Chilean sociologist Tomás Moulián argues that societies are characterized by struggles and divisions, more than by consensus and reconciliation. He reminds us that democracy is founded on the idea of differences of opinion and perspective. He also holds that the idea of reconciliation is rooted in a religious or mystic conception of society, that it's not grounded in reality.[3]

I'm ignorant of the subjects I would need to master to respond to Moulián, but I feel like in Chile, at least once a year, the country becomes reconciled. I am thinking about the Telethon, for example.[4] Reconciliation is possible.

To reconcile, one has to learn to act for the common good. We may not even be talking about doing good works on a national level. Maybe it's enough to act at the level of individuals or small communities. Reconciling implies many things: agreeing, reaching consensuses, and establishing common goals.

And is that attainable in Chile?

I hope so. In the worst case, when all the survivors have died, I hope that then the country can be reconciled.

But isn't reconciliation, at the same time, forgetting?

How do we understand the idea of national reconciliation? It doesn't mean that everyone in the country thinks alike. It implies a country in which every person is able to take a stance toward life. But in the interest of living collectively, every individual must be willing to take into account the greater good of the group. I still hold dear the crazy Bolivarian dream of a united America. When I look at Mexico's enormous riches next to its poverty, or when I look at Argentina's riches compared to its current state of affairs, I feel like our problems come from fighting over a few square meters of land on the border. This is our plight, because we aren't capable of uniting.

There are certain things that aren't short-term goals. We have a lot to change both as individuals and collectively. But I do hope that reconciliation can be achieved.

I value difference. I'm not even so sure that today's divisions are really about left and right. But I do believe that we can't remain divided.

Regarding forgetting the past, I was really happy when I saw Cheyre's statement. Maybe it's true, as people from the Families of the Disappeared organization claim, that Cheyre's declaration is nothing more than a band-aid on a deep wound. Maybe it's just a strategy for mitigating the harsh impact that the *Valech Report* will have.[5] But it's a step. All eyes are on the military, so some change will have to occur.

Another thing that strikes me as important is that Pinochet has now abandoned his men, which isn't being looked upon favorably within the armed forces. Maybe this doesn't seem like such a big deal to us civilians, but Pinochet betrayed certain arcane concepts that still govern military life, concepts like "honor" and an "army that protects its own."

That's true, because just recently, on September 11, 2004, Manuel Contreras stated in an interview with *El Mercurio* that "Pinochet left us totally abandoned."

See? Even Contreras is mad at Pinochet for that! Miguel Krassnoff's new line of defense, for example, is admitting that things happened, without accepting responsibility. Krassnoff's argument is that his superiors are the guilty ones because they gave the orders. Krassnoff says, "Ask Moren." And Moren says, "Ask Contreras." And Contreras says, "Ask Pinochet." What happened to the soldier who takes responsibility for his men?

I'd like to think that some good is going to come from Cheyre's statement. There have been changes. Some military people are now testifying. The scene today is much different than it was in 1991 or 1992. But, at the same time, I think Cheyre will let certain people testify in exchange for upholding the 1978 Amnesty Law.[6] I don't think Cheyre is making these public statements without asking for something in return. As always happens in power relations, everyone is playing his hand. And I sincerely believe that, up until now, the army has played its hand poorly.

I think that forgetting has to do with failing to stay active in human rights or memory work. Say what they will about me, I think that as long as the human rights organizations remain active in these issues, there won't be forgetting.

In addition, I think that the specially appointed judges for expediting cases have been excellent. These dedicated judges have made it so that cases don't languish—because all of this can't go on forever! It's not good for a country for these processes to be eternal! I hope that justice will come soon—with investigations, truth, and convictions. But I honestly don't think that there will be forgetting.

One day I awoke and knew that God existed. I couldn't believe it. It was like awakening on a sunny day. I got dressed happily, and I went to the window. God was everywhere shouting out the joys of the immense wonders of his creation. I could sense His divine presence in the trees, in the cloudy sky, and everywhere I looked was like a huge book outlining a plan for a life, for a full life.

Knowing God changed my life, feeling that God is love, that His word is the word of love, that, as Christians, we are called above all to obey His word. That made me think about who I was and who I am, and, of course, it also meant coming to terms not only with myself, but also with my relationships with those around me. The Luz who had been unfaithful so many times, who felt so miserable, started wanting to be able to say yes to the Lord.

—*Luz Arce, The Inferno (1993)*

7

The Present Time

New Critiques and Pending Questions

There has been an abundance of essays and academic articles written about your "case." This reality, coupled with the fact that *The Inferno* is taught both in Chilean and foreign universities as a paradigmatic text on collaboration during the Pinochet regime, compels me to cite some critiques I have read and to give you an opportunity to respond.

Professor Stacey Alba D. Skar, who translated *The Inferno* into English, recently published an article in which she poses two rhetorical questions related to your book: "Can [Luz Arce's memoirs] be read as an innocent portrayal of her desire to reconcile with her personal past and on a national level? Or should we analyze [her text] as a manipulation of dominant discourse so that the [author] can garner the protection of human rights organizations like the Vicariate of Solidarity, or the courts, to protect herself from judicial reprisals by people who consider her a traitor or accuse of her of the torture and deaths of her comrades?"[1]

Every person who writes a book makes conscious decisions about how to present and frame her experience. In the case of *The Inferno,* why did you decide to frame your experiences through the lens of your conversion to Catholicism? Can doing that be read as a survival strategy, as a way of explaining a life trajectory that, without such a framework, might remain unexplainable or, perhaps, intolerable to you in the present? Or did you have some other reason for focusing your text in the way you did?

Regarding why my conversion to Christianity figures so strongly and prominently in the text, I can only respond by saying that anyone who, after reaching forty years of age, feels profoundly that she believes in God, particularly after having denied God for years, knows that the experience of knowing God permeates, or should permeate, every second of her life. I just wrote about what I was living. I never intended to make instrumental use of my faith to gain special favors. If, in 1993, when I published *The Inferno,* I had had the experience I do today, perhaps I would have reserved much of what I revealed. Because if there's one thing I would never want, it's to use my faith in God or my friendship with people from the church for personal gain.

The reality is that today I believe in God, and I thank him infinitely for the many blessings he has bestowed upon me, even for having shown me some of the darkest aspects of life—and I'm not just referring to my time as a prisoner of DINA.

I was blessed in my conversion process to have the support of people who live a Dominican lifestyle. The Dominican friars are an order known for not forcing people to be a certain way. Being accompanied by Dominicans meant not being forced to subscribe to one discourse or another. To the contrary, it meant being allowed to discover freely which decisions to make and how to make them. It meant learning how to take responsibility before myself, others, and God. Having faith in God doesn't mean that one receives automatic enlightenment; one isn't a saint by virtue of being a Christian. Being a Christian is a daily struggle with oneself to live a life coherent with God's Word, with the gospel. My decision to be a Christian continues to guide my life. It has given me strength to discover hope in the world, for us all, because the Lord has already forgiven us.[2]

Professor Patricio Quiroga Zamora published another critique in his 2001 book *Compañeros: El GAP, la escolta de Allende* (Comrades: GAP, Allende's personal guards), a research project on Salvador Allende's "Group of Personal Friends," based on interviews with various former group members. Toward the end of the book, the author mentions you. He writes, "Siblings Luz and David Arce are surrounded by a black legend fraught with doubt, horror, rejection, and recrimination, but also with mercy . . . What happened with Luz Arce? This is the question her former comrades ask when they remember her being a member of GAP from May to September 1972. Three questions arise: (1) Did she belong to military intelligence services, and was she already working for the armed forces? It's possible, because Martín, one of the traitors, was in GAP. (2) Was it all just an adventure, the folly of placing oneself in the eye of the storm? It's possible. But how can we explain the deaths that she left in her wake? Not only did her comrades from GAP die but so did Alfredo Rojas, director of Chilean Railroads, for whom she served as his personal secretary, and Wagner Salinas, at whose orders she served in GEA [*Grupos Especiales de Apoyo*, Special Support Groups] . . . (3) Why did Manuel Contreras visit her regularly? Maybe Luz Arce was a frightened, isolated, and abused victim who just opted to survive."[3] How do you respond to these rhetorical questions and musings?

About whether I belonged to military intelligence services before being detained or while I was in prison: absolutely not! My forced participation as a functionary of DINA—under coercion—began on May 7, 1975, and ended on November 2, 1979, the day on which I tendered my resignation, which was accepted on March 16, 1980.

A while back, I decided that I wouldn't respond to questions like these because they are perverse, sick, twisted. These new questions make me react similarly. Nevertheless, assuming that agreeing to be interviewed implies voluntarily exposing myself to these lines of inquiry, I am going to respond to you for two reasons. First, I'll do it out of responsibility to you, since I made a verbal commitment when I agreed to be interviewed; my agreement implied that I would answer any questions you asked, and I never requested that you not touch on certain topics. Second, I think that every person, including those who have not lived through experiences like I have, has a right to seek explanations that go beyond the surface level of what happened. This is one of the fundamental rights every human being should enjoy: freedom. Nevertheless, what I have learned over time is that this freedom should go hand in hand with responsibility, something that doesn't seem to proliferate as much as the imagination when it comes to asking questions that I find disrespectful. Assuming another person's intentions is quite censurable in my opinion, especially when one doesn't even know the other person. Even if I were the worst person in the world, it's not right to obviate with one stroke of the pen the torture, pain, and suffering I lived for years, all of my struggles to continue growing as a person. I am not going to defend myself against every line of the text you have read to me; I don't wish to even attempt a self-defense. These days I don't have the time or the desire to do that. For some time, my efforts have been geared toward personal matters that require tons of energy. That's what I choose to concentrate on. Also, the accusations you have mentioned are clearly based on ignorance of what my country's court system established long ago.

I guess that deciding to testify voluntarily to the Rettig Commission (1990), authorizing the commission to use my testimony in court (1990–91), making the decision to testify in my country's courts (1990–present), writing a book (1993), and keeping an open relationship with the media for a decade (1990–2000), just to mention a few of my activities, makes it so that I have opened myself up to the opinions of whomever wishes to chime in. Some time ago, when I realized that my actions also played a role in shaping this reality, I decided to accept the consequences. That's why, Michael, I've been talking about closing a chapter, about this being my final interview. That's why I'm responding today.

Why did you decide to talk about your experiences with me, then, when you could have easily refused to grant this interview?

In the first place, I agreed to be interviewed because the theme of human rights is part and parcel with my life. I am—and I will be—available for whatever my country's courts require of me. On a personal level, granting this interview is a way of closing a chapter, the public chapter of my life. The second reason is that I met you over the Internet when you were working on your doctoral thesis. You seemed to be the kind of person who would approach these matters seriously.

Let's tackle a pending question that I've heard others ask. When CNI sent you to Uruguay and Argentina (1978–80), I suppose it was to carry out tasks related to what we now know as Operation Condor, the coordinated alliance of security services of various Latin American dictatorships. What, specifically, were your tasks as a CNI operative in Uruguay and Argentina?

I didn't work in the Republic of Uruguay or in Argentina. The period in question, in 1979, is also narrated in *The Inferno*. What's more, I returned to Chile with the expressed intention of resigning, specifically so I wouldn't have to work in Argentina, Chile, or any other country at the behest of CNI.

But you say that you were sent with false names and everything to Uruguay and Argentina. There has to have been a reason. Why would CNI send you for no reason? I don't understand.

I went to Uruguay, as you say, "with false names and everything," to get away from Chile, to study there and earn a Uruguayan professional diploma, to learn to speak like a Uruguayan, to learn Uruguayan history, to find out all the things that, generally speaking, a citizen of that country knows—about sports, literature, folklore, and so on—if he is university educated or a professional. The infrastructure I would create for myself would serve me well in the next phase, if I had to get out of Argentina. Certainly, at some point, I was supposed to obtain Uruguayan documentation. I *never* got that far. During that time period, I never went to Argentina. I went back to Chile first and resigned.[4]

What's your view of the Chilean armed forces today? Do they inspire confidence or mistrust?

I look upon the armed forces today with goodwill, but I've had to force myself to do that. Every day I understand a little more clearly that those institutions, in some ways (though not in every way), differ from the institutions that carried out the dictatorship's repression. I want to believe that the armed forces won't ever again plot a coup, that they are living their own process of integration into democratic life and institutional order, beholden to the civilian powers that we aspire to have lead us.

Pinochet's death in December 2006, shocked the country and dragged old divisions to the surface. What did Pinochet's death mean for your personal healing process?

At first, I felt frustrated because it would have been healing for me to see the Chilean courts charge him for human rights violations while he was alive. The initial news of his death, the coverage of the funeral, and of what went on before and after it, brought back my days in prison, torture, everything I lived back then. The sadness associated with the memory of so much loss, so much pain—the pain of so many—came with it. Days went by, and because I was certain that Pinochet would be remembered by the world as a coup plotter—a dictator in whose prisons many were violated in countless ways that we are still today discovering—I started to feel that his death no longer held any special meaning for me. Death is part of life. He died, just like we all will at some point. In that sense, it was like turning a page. My husband and I used the occasion as an opportunity to talk, to look fondly on all the strides we had made, to remember our journey together. Despite Pinochet and the dictatorship, we have advanced. We have grown as people, as a couple; so have our children, family, loved ones, good friends, and Chilean society at large. With all its problems, Chile is learning and moving forward, not just in human rights matters. Sure, there's a lot left to do, but the journey continues.

What is your evaluation of Michelle Bachelet and of the future of truth and justice in Chile?

I especially value that Michelle Bachelet is a woman and that she is from the *Concertación*. I'm joyful and proud of the Chilean men and women who voted for her. I don't know her personally, but in the media Michelle Bachelet comes across as a capable, intelligent, and sensible woman. Who has forgiven like she has?[5] So yes, she has important and evident merits. I see her as willing to make enormous commitments. But her government is just starting, so I think it's premature to pass judgment on her administration or particular aspects of it.

On the question of justice in general—independent of any particular government—there is a lot left to do in Chile. I think it's Bachelet's intention to work in that direction. I am talking about her expressed intention to improve the quality of education, health, housing, employment, welfare, and other programs, especially when they concern the most disadvantaged sectors of society.

Specifically in the area of human rights, the most important thing to consider is that, to date, the *Concertación* governments, at least as far as I can see, have been taking steps to establish truth and justice. Trials continue. There have been convictions. And there have been advances in reparations for victims and families. There's more to do, but they're working on it.

But there is a huge debt pending: the disappeared. The remains of the disappeared men and women must be found and the facts surrounding their disappearances established. As I said before—and it bears repeating—the *Concertación* governments have gradually generated the tools and institutions for achieving truth and justice. But they haven't yet been achieved. Those who remain indebted in the matter are the armed forces. They are the ones who know what happened, who ordered that people be killed and their murders covered up. They have testified falsely in court to keep the truth at bay. Those who have information and those who today are their superior officers need to share what they know with Chilean society so that this matter can be closed responsibly.

How has your return to Chile from Mexico been? Today, in 2006, have you found it possible to disconnect from your past, or have you found that there are still people who don't accept you in Chile?

My return to Chile, my country, and to Santiago, my city, has been beautiful. I have not tried to disconnect from my past. To the contrary, my personal struggle over time has been to incorporate the past in the present in the best way I know how. I have not had occasion to meet anyone who doesn't accept me as a person. Nevertheless, it's clear that there must be people who don't hold me in high regard. But it hasn't been a personal goal to be accepted or held in esteem; I have just tried to piece myself back together, grow, empower my family, and work to live freely. That's all working out, so I'm happy.

I want to ask a couple of questions related to an article called "*Delatora exiliada*" ("Exiled Traitor") that Carlos Sánchez published in the now defunct magazine *Plan B* in 2004.[6] The author claims that you were "protected" by the Dominicans. I'm interested in his choice of verb. To what extent is his claim valid?

I have to say that I met the author you're talking about because I was obliged to help him with a project he was doing on the Valencian priest Antonio Llidó, who disappeared from the José Domingo Cañas detention center. There was a period of time in which he'd come to my house every day. We'd have lunch together and then we'd work. So what he claims in his article is based on what he observed during the time we interacted. But I'm compelled to add that he is talking about isolated things, and much of it isn't true. He claims, for example, that no one in the human rights world forgave me. But later, in the same article, he says that Erika Hennings, Carlos Fresno, and Frei Betto, all of whom are leftists and representative figures of the human rights world, call me daily. So you can see that the author contradicts himself. To answer your question, then, I'm not exactly sure what Sánchez is talking about. Since you're asking about it, it seems like an exaggeration to say that the Dominicans were "protecting" me. I have friends in the Catholic Church, both lay and religious, not just in one order or congregation. I also have friends in other Christian churches and other institutions. My friends love me and support me in the difficult moments, just like they share my joy in the good ones.

The same article states that today you live in Mexico City and that you "teach human rights classes there at the university level."

I have no idea where he got that idea! I don't live in Mexico City, nor do I teach classes on human rights. The guy must have heard some things while he was at my house, and based on that, he wrote. In those years, he used to write for the Communist Party's newspaper. He even used to dictate some of his articles to me so that I could type them for him on the computer.

The part I find most laughable is when the guy claims that I approached him seeking "respect and a point of contact to participate in social movements." I never approached him. A priest who knows him called me and asked me to collaborate with him at the Father Antonio Llidó Foundation.

In reference to the same lack of forgiveness within the human rights world that you mentioned a moment ago, the *Plan B* article states, verbatim, "The human rights world never forgave her or accepted her catharsis. Moreover, people like Sola Sierra, the deceased president of the Group of Families of the Disappeared, felt that her testimony had not contributed anything new."

Forgiveness arises through a process, at one's own pace. There are also external intervening factors. There aren't recipes for forgiving or being forgiven; nor can we speak of collective forgiveness. I understand that people from the human rights world, when asked, say they haven't forgiven me. But others have.

I also know there are people who think that my testimony hasn't contributed anything new. Indeed, someone once told me that that's what Sola Sierra thought.

I feel like, for many years, the Vicariate of Solidarity already knew everything I said in the early 1990s about torture and DINA's repressive tactics. At present, I believe there are many people who know much more than I. What I did have, however, was a perspective that no other prisoner had within DINA. I know it's nothing to brag about, but it's true.

It's also necessary to add that between my detention on March 17, 1974, and my liberation in March 1980, there were times at which I had greater possibilities of knowing things than at others. For that reason, I feel like the only thing of value I could contribute—and mind you, I'm talking about the early 1990s, because today there are people much more versed in these topics than I—was an overall vision of DINA and many names of people. I met Krassnoff, for example. I met Troglo. I met Moren. And, naturally, I knew Contreras.

So I think Sola Sierra was being quite frank when she said that I didn't contribute much, because, in reality, it was true. It wasn't because I held anything back, but rather because ever since 1973, Cardinal Raúl Silva Henríquez's Pro-Peace Committee (*Comité Pro Paz*), and later the Vicariate of Solidarity, were functioning. By 1990, so much was already known without my testimony.

Nevertheless, to this day there are people who seek me out because there are things that I saw that no one else saw. For example, there are entire detention centers—small ones that were open only a very short time—about which there are no testimonies.

But if someone wants to approach the topic of the dictatorship's repression seriously, he can't just refer to my testimony alone. I sincerely wish I knew the whereabouts of the disappeared, but I don't. Maybe certain things that are obvious to me aren't so obvious to those on the outside. I think that much more was expected of my testimony. That's understandable. At least I understand.

Part III

Forum

Collaboration, Dictatorship, Democracy

Pedro Alejandro Matta

Some months ago, Professor Michael Lazzara asked me to write some reflections on the topic of collaboration during the Pinochet dictatorship. I could foresee the complexity, the difficulty, the painfulness, the delicacy of the subject I was asked to address. What I couldn't foresee were the hours I would spend in front of my computer screen figuring out how to develop my ideas, choose the right words, avoid hurting feelings and, at the same time, give the most complete vision I could in a limited number of words. What follows is the result of my efforts, which the reader will judge.

Forced collaboration under torture is undeniably one of the most destructive experiences to which detained or imprisoned people can be subjected in contexts of brutal political repression, military occupation, or armed conflict. In some cases, like in Chile, we use the term "low intensity conflict," though for victims that term is absolutely irrelevant.

In Chile, "collaboration" started to be talked about after Pinochet's 1973 coup, an event that set in motion one of the most brutal periods of political repression in Latin American history. The de facto authorities not only bombed the government palace and murdered its defenders but also declared a state of "internal warfare." From that moment forward, everyone associated with the deposed Allende government was labeled an "enemy" from the military's standpoint. The declaration of a state of internal warfare against a population incapable of resisting resulted in the capture of thousands of civilian prisoners. These prisoners were classified as "prisoners of war," even though the Geneva Conventions did not apply to them. Instead, they were subjected to brutal torture: inhumane, cruel, and degrading treatment. Many were shot without trials; others disappeared, never to be found again. The Pinochet regime's objective was to destroy the Allende government's support base while simultaneously generating a widespread state of terror that would deter any attempts to organize opposition to the new government.

All branches of the armed forces participated in the repression. But in 1974, Pinochet created DINA (National Intelligence Directorate) as a specialized secret police organization whose task was to locate, detain, torture, and eventually kill or disappear enemies. DINA was given all the logistical support it needed to carry out a low intensity war completely devoid of legal frameworks and ethical principles. It is with DINA that the phenomenon of collaboration began.

Collaboration can be defined as the extraction of information under torture with the purpose of using it to identify and eliminate pockets of political opposition. According to Luz Arce, one of the prisoners forced to collaborate with DINA, shortly after its creation, DINA carried out a statistical analysis that revealed that a person would normally be detained within a maximum of six months from the time DINA first learned of his or her existence. It is difficult to define the limits of the word "collaboration" precisely. This is because if we choose to define it as "any information obtained under torture that has the potential to cause harm to people or the opposition's political structures," then we'd necessarily have to conclude that the vast majority of prisoners collaborated from the very moment at which, as a result of physical or psychological torture (or both), they admitted their association with a political organization or entity that had supported Allende.

According to the traditional definition, derived from the French experience during the Vichy government, collaborators were understood to be those who aided or abetted the enemy. Based on that idea, collaboration was considered a form of treason because it signaled a person's cooperation with enemy forces, in this case the German army.

In the Chilean case, foreign military forces did not invade the country. Chile suffered a military occupation by part of its own military. The declaration of a "state of siege" (and almost simultaneously of a "state of internal war") created a legal framework similar to that which exists in a country that has been occupied through foreign invasion, complete with imposed war tribunals and summary justice. Torture was a commonplace practice supported by the state that was carried out systematically and regularly. Collaboration was a byproduct of torture, either psychological or physical.

Torture was carried out through various cruel methods and in increasing degrees of intensity. Its aim was the psychological dismantling of the subject. Among the most common forms of torture were the "grill" (the repeated application of electroshocks to sensitive parts of the body like the head, mouth, genitals, anus, abdomen, and extremities); brutal beatings (sometimes including the use of chains or metal whips); suspending people in the air; the "dry submarine" (placing a hood on someone's head to induce asphyxia); the "wet submarine" (immersing someone's head in excrement or decomposed liquids to induce loss of consciousness); torture with animals (like introducing rats or spiders into women's vaginas, or the raping of women by a German shepherd); various forms of sexual torture (group rape, rape with objects, women being obliged to perform fellatio on their torturers); forcing prisoners to witness the torture of family members, loved ones, or political comrades; mock executions; extraction of teeth or fingernails with pliers; and running prisoners over with heavy vehicles or mutilating their bodies.

Torture had various objectives: to destroy or annihilate a prisoner's capacity for resistance; to obtain valuable logistical information or information that might permit the capture of other "enemies"; to transform the prisoner into a terrorized and cowed human being; or, in the event that the prisoner survived various months or years of torture, to return him or her to society transformed into a kind of zombie with the goal of instilling fear in other people or groups.

Therefore, collaboration (giving up valuable information) is a direct result of terror and isolation, of the prisoner's absolute defenselessness in the face of an omnipotent, shameless, and implacable enemy—an enemy that recognizes no ethical limits. It is also a result of personal insecurity and of a survival instinct that prevails under extreme duress. Prisoners were expected by their torturers to "give up" their comrades who, in turn, would be detained and tortured. A seemingly endless cycle ensued.

It is extremely complicated to issue value judgments on collaboration because of the unique circumstances of each individual case. Generally speaking, we can identify four types or degrees of collaboration, although it is not always possible to determine where one type ends and the next begins. The first type, which encompasses the vast majority of detainees, includes those prisoners who had information extracted from them as a result of unbearable physical or psychological torture. (As an example of psychological torture, we can recall the case of a young couple that was forced to witness the torture of their 6-month-old baby so that they would "talk." Another example might be the case of a father forced to witness the group rape of his 16-year-old daughter.) A second type of collaboration, which encompasses a much smaller group, includes those who continued to offer information even outside the torture chamber—undoubtedly terrorized by the experience they had just lived. A third type, which encompasses a still smaller group, includes those who tried to "negotiate" the information they possessed in exchange for assurance of their survival. A final type, which applied to the smallest percentage of prisoners, included those who, as a result of the extreme torture methods applied to them or the destruction of their subjectivity, became active members of DINA and later took part in detentions, interrogations, and eventually the torture of former comrades.

During torture sessions, the pressure to collaborate was constant. *"Coopera, coopera, cabrito"* (Collaborate, collaborate, man!) is a phrase that every former prisoner remembers. Faced with this situation, the clandestine resistance organizations came up with various recommended response strategies. One such strategy required militants to promise not to give up useful information to their torturers for at least 24 hours after being detained. In theory, this would permit those linked to the detainee to take necessary precautions to avoid their own detentions. This stall tactic was well known by DINA and, as a result, it is easy to deduce that the first 24 hours of detention were a living hell for prisoners. To buy time, prisoners gave up names of people they knew to be out of reach. Another strategy was to give names of people who had already been captured. All of these strategies aimed to alleviate pressure on prisoners temporarily while DINA agents investigated the factuality of the prisoners' claims. Torture would often abate until DINA agents discovered that the information was not useful, in which case the prisoner would be subjected to even harsher treatment.

To "give up" comrades is one of the most difficult experiences to acknowledge, deal with, and accept for those who collaborated, especially in cases in which someone disappeared as a result. It is often considered a form of betrayal. Given the gravity of the accusation, in certain cases the "weakness" of prisoners whose collaboration caused the "fall" of a comrade has been erroneously attributed to other detainees whose collaboration was already proven. This is a form of displacing blame onto others in the interest of social healing.

But collaboration did not just take place in the torture chamber. In many cases, detainees would be taken out of detention centers to *porotear* (bean count), that is, to ride around the city with DINA agents and point out comrades for detention. It was also common for DINA agents to transport prisoners to a "point" (*un punto*), that is, to a particular place where the detainee could physically locate and establish contact with another member of his or her political organization. This was a form of entrapment that would result in a new prisoner's immediate detention. Yet another common form of collaboration was the *encuadre* (framing). In this scenario, prisoners would give up information about other militants who were actively being sought by DINA. The information would be filed away so that it would be available upon the person's eventual detention. This type of collaboration also helped DINA to develop organizational diagrams of the political structures it planned to destroy.

Quite obviously, the most intense degree of collaboration was participation in torture sessions. This was an exceptional case that affected a very small percentage of prisoners. It generally happened only when detainees had suffered, as a result of torture, severe psychological damage or a destruction of subjectivity that altered not only their emotions but also their core values. For these prisoners, collaboration became a means toward survival. The more they collaborated, the greater they thought their chances of survival to be. Moreover, this "option"—complete collaboration as a last resort for assuring one's survival—seemed like the only available option because, in many cases, the political organizations to which collaborators belonged had already publicly issued their death sentences. On some occasions, active and conscious collaboration was exacerbated when prisoners—both men and women—established romantic relationships with their captors in an attempt to guarantee survival. In the particular case of female prisoners, they sometimes became semiofficial lovers or concubines of military officers.

Some people, transformed by their circumstances, became semipermanent collaborators; some even became DINA agents. They were housed in the torture centers and kept separate from the other prisoners so that they would be constantly available to participate in interrogations or in the entrapment of new detainees. They also tried to convince detainees that resistance was useless or to infiltrate groups of detainees to glean useful information. These collaborators, because of the functions that they carried out, were the ones who remained in the detention centers for the longest periods of time. In contrast to the "common" prisoners who always wore blindfolds so they wouldn't recognize their captors, these collaborators carried out their functions with no impediment to their vision.

Serving as a "functionary" of DINA for long periods of time makes those collaborators who survived a great source of information—information that can be extraordinarily valuable for legal proceedings. They remember details about chains of command and responsibility, crimes committed in torture centers, the actions of individual agents and torturers and their roles in specific crimes, and prisoners who were murdered or disappeared. In cases in which former collaborators have testified in court, we have generally learned important information about the fate of victims of political repression.

What I have described here corresponds to Chile's experience under the Pinochet dictatorship, but it is also generally valid for other military dictatorships that were happening around the same time (those of Argentina, Paraguay, Bolivia, Uruguay, and Brazil), all of which were part of a secret consortium of terror—Operation Condor—whose goal was to eliminate political opponents who fled from one country to another.

Gloria Elgueta

In December 2007, on the occasion of the first anniversary of Augusto Pinochet's death, former right-wing presidential candidate Joaquín Lavín was called a "collaborationist" (*colaboracionista*) by former congressman Luis Valentín Ferrada, a well known member of the same political sector as Lavín. Ferrada was referencing Lavín's supposed complicity with the political coalition—*La Concertación*—that has governed Chile since the end of the dictatorship. The government spokesman at the time, Francisco Vidal, responded that "in contemporary political language, a collaborationist is a traitor to the homeland," adding that it was wrong to call Lavín a term more suited for the "citizens of occupied Europe who worked with Nazis."

Michael Lazzara's book, *Luz Arce and Pinochet's Chile,* would seem to contradict Vidal's statement, implying that acts of collaboration are not solely a "foreign" practice. As Primo Levi says in a quote that serves as an epigraph to Lazzara's text, "the harsher the oppression, the more widespread among the oppressed is the willingness . . . to collaborate" with the powers that be, regardless of their motivations or other mitigating factors.

The Chilean dictatorship was a very harsh one. It used the tactics of state terrorism to penetrate all spheres of society and affected more than just the individuals and groups that were victims of the most extreme and brutal repression. Aside from the kidnapping, torture, murder, and forced disappearances that were commonplace at the time, repression and control were carried out on a mass scale, as well as arrests, searches, and seizures, and many other practices aimed at threatening and intimidating the entire population. All of this took place in the context of a state of exception, whose everyday manifestation—the curfew—became naturalized throughout the country to the point that it seemed normal. Internal and foreign exiles, censorship, restrictions upon freedom of expression, gathering, and organization led to the destruction or weakening of the social bonds historically associated with popular movements.

The implementation of a system of that nature required a confluence of multiple wills, as well as material, financial, human, and technical resources. There were also social and political actors involved in the process—institutions, groups, and individuals—some who actively supported it, and some who simply adapted themselves to the new scenario at hand. As Pilar Calveiro has commented about the Argentine dictatorship—and things were no different in Chile—"terror enjoyed a certain degree of social consensus, which showed that our society probably was, and is, much more authoritarian than we are often willing to believe."[1] However, this type of social *collaboration* is less visible than the figure of the traitor or collaborator who, when considered individually, is often saddled, in the eyes of society, with all responsibility for what happened. In short, the figure of the individual collaborator ends up serving as a sacrificial lamb for individual or collective responsibility.

***

"Betrayal" is often considered the natural outcome of the "weaknesses" (be they ideological, psychological, or physical) of individuals who face moral dilemmas; these dilemmas take the form of a battle within the consciences of individuals when they are confronted with limit situations like prison and torture. Betrayal is not, however, considered to be the product of a system methodically and deliberately conceived and implemented to *produce* collaborators. This leads to a sort of analytical misplacement or disruption, in which the traitor, spy, or informant ends up taking all the blame for the defeat. Collective responsibilities thus become relegated to a secondary terrain filled with the white noise of procedural flaws, organizational errors, "security" problems, and the "conspiratorial methods" of the political organizations in question. In other words, responsibilities end up being understood primarily as an individual or technical issue, rather than as a political one.

Where there are traitors, so too are there heroes. In this dichotomous classification, the hero is an exemplary subject, always unquestioned, whose memory is a sort of cause célèbre. The traitor, meanwhile, is met only with social repudiation and condemnation. This is, by now, a completely accepted lens through which to look at a recent past scarred by state terrorism and the struggle against the dictatorship.

The problem with this way of understanding the complex relationship between political struggle, repression, and their many consequences, is that the issue becomes an exclusively moral one; opportunities are scarce to examine the phenomenon of collaboration in its proper political context.

***

Meanwhile, a similar phenomenon has occurred with two other concepts whose origins are in the legal sphere, but that are also used to analyze a broader and more complex series of subject positions and relations in our recent history: the concepts of "victim" and "victimizer." These terms acknowledge that a crime has taken place, and they define the relations among the protagonists of a repressive experience.[2] However, they obscure the conflict and the struggle at the root of that crime by defining the victim as nothing more than a passive subject, that is, the "person who suffers the harmful consequences of a crime," whether "by one's own fault or due to accidental circumstances."[3]

The use of these categories, which omit or diminish the fact that a very significant percentage of "victims" were political militants, obscures the political and social implications of the conflict, reducing it to the universe of those who recognize themselves in it—which is, as we know, a small minority of society.

That Chilean courtrooms—with all due respect—are the principal arenas in which our recent past is disputed is indicative of the limits of reflection and debate today. One might even say that there is currently no public forum capable of offering a real space to discuss the conflict and give those other than the direct victims an opportunity to express themselves. Broader areas of society, which would otherwise be able to expand and diversify the practices and processes that we use to come to terms with our past, are thus unable to participate.

In her excellent work *Traiciones: La figura del traidor en los relatos acerca de los sobrevivientes de la represión* (Betrayals: The traitor-figure in narratives about survivors of repression) (2007), the Argentine researcher Ana Longoni has stated that victimization and heroism are two constructions that "both end up depoliticizing the past, despite their differences." The former hides, or avoids acknowledging, one's political sympathies and militancy, while the latter skirts all the productive fissures that could allow for the analysis and critique of one's actions, or the ideas and concepts that sustained them.[4] This leads to the suspension of reflection and political judgment.

What about one's own responsibility with regard to the history of the dictatorship and our memory of it? Questions like this either have not been asked or have been relegated to the margins. And they are extremely important, because they allow us to situate ourselves more solidly in the political sphere. This is a central issue if we consider historian Steve Stern's analysis of what happened in Chile during the dictatorship as "policide," that is, the destruction of alternative ways to participate in and think about politics.[5] Our current problem, then, has to do with disputes over how politics and legitimacy are signified in the present. Although justice is an inalienable right, we must acknowledge that even if it were fully carried out—something that we have not yet seen—our debts to the recent past could still never be repaid. And those debts are primarily political ones.

Victoria Langland

Readers of *Luz Arce and Pinochet's Chile* will find much in the multiple texts that make up this fascinating book to move them, trouble them, and provoke them to reconsider how individuals and societies struggle to come to terms with the legacies of state terrorism, even long after the political order has changed. The intriguing contrasts of tone and emphasis between Luz Arce's official testimony before the National Truth and Reconciliation Commission, the scattered excerpts from her book *The Inferno,* and her extensive interview with Michael Lazzara suggest some of the many ways that people and communities interrogate their past to find answers they need in the present. Moreover, written memories such as these are more than mere *reflections* of broader struggles—complex and rich though they may be—but are also inevitably active *components* of the process. For the act of eliciting, arranging, and editing Arce's memories for publication—of literally making them public—implies a deliberate attempt to insert them into dialogue with others, thereby contributing to collective understandings of the past, even while acknowledging that the contours of this understanding cannot be foreseen.

Indeed, it is the diversity of forms of narration that most stands out in this complex and compelling book. Both by reading carefully within each section as well as by comparing across sections, we get a strong sense of the multiple ways in which a single person, Luz Arce, tells, understands, and shares her story. This becomes clear quite early on in the summary of Arce's testimony before the National Truth and Reconciliation Commission. Lazzara titles that section "Names, Dates, Places," an appropriate label for such a dizzying string of people, places and relationships, as Arce's testimony is clearly directed at the commission's investigation. Later in the book we come to understand how important it was to her personally to contribute with her offerings of names of prisoners, torturers, and guards, descriptions of detention centers, and so forth, yet what immediately emerges is the macabre underworld she calmly describes. Indeed the dry title, much like the formal proceeding itself, betrays (undoubtedly deliberately) the stirring emotional significance that pervades Arce's officious recounting of details. For no matter how much her narrative in this section seeks distant objectivity—to the extent that she herself often fades from view, as if she were the proverbial fly on the wall rather than both a subject and object within this tale—it cannot diminish the emotive impact of the stories she tells. Moreover, when she finishes her rich and detailed testimony, we are left with the lingering sense that her declaration has revealed to us not how much we now know about these events but how little. Among other impressions her testimony leaves, one is struck by her (and our) inability to understand or explain how the DINA officials she came to know found themselves able to participate in—and even create and sustain—this alternative and inhumane world. Perhaps nowhere is this ambiguity more apparent than in the seeming code of conduct vis-à-vis women prisoners and rape. For despite the official and systematic use of torture, including genital torture, the rape of female prisoners was still somehow considered off limits. And despite this reprobation, it nonetheless occurred frequently. Arce is able to bring the commission into this dark world, to *tell* them (and us) who was there and when, but she is unable to really *explain* it to us.

If Arce's testimony before the Truth and Reconciliation Commission was directed at an objective accounting of *what* she saw and did, then Lazzara's questions in the extensive interview that follows were all directed at subjective understandings of *why* she did what she did—both during the Pinochet regime and after—and what she came to think about those actions later in her life. In an apt reflection of the unsteadiness of subjectivity, this section loses the steady chronology and logical order that marked the commission testimony, and instead loops and swerves as Arce struggles to make the story her own. Despite editing for clarity, Lazzara has skillfully maintained the undulations of her answers that reflect this process. In some moments, she refuses to answer his questions, only to come back to the exact same point later from an altogether different context. She also refuses to name names, even though she has already done so, in print, in the past. And she maintains a strict silence about other collaborators—even going so far as to use vague, unnatural language to talk about the fact that collaboration, in the abstract, existed—while affirming that collaboration was common. Both of these features—the twisting chronology and the gaps in her story—suggest the ways in which the act of narration, even for someone who has told her tale so many times before, continues to be fraught with complications. Arce is both driven to speak (she seems to see it as both a personal release and a collective responsibility) and yet wary of it.

Another salient feature of the interview is the dialogical nature of the narration itself. Whereas in the Truth and Reconciliation Commission testimony Arce answers to an anonymous board, in the interview with Lazzara the relationship between them is fundamental and palpable. For the most part, there appears to be great mutual respect and trust between them. The directness of his questions is often striking, such as when he presses her explicitly on why she wouldn't name names. And she speaks to him candidly of her experiences of rape and later sexual intimacy—topics long taboo for public discussion, and even more so when between two people in a nonromantic relationship. Yet the interview also reveals an underlying tension at times. She evades his questions, only to circle back to them many topics later. She worries that he is trying to get her to say something that will get her in trouble, even as she repeatedly says she trusts him. And while she asserts several times that this will be her last interview ever, one she very carefully chose to grant exclusively to Lazzara, it is never entirely clear why. He, too, says this in his introduction. Perhaps, like the many silences she maintains, the vagueness of this decision is her way of holding on to the ownership of her story by not conceding how important Lazzara's role is to her, making it appear instead like a neutral gesture on her part, even as she is also invested in having a foreign male hear, publicize, and perhaps validate her story.

One clear lesson to take from the book as a whole is that the history of the military regime in Chile does not end in 1990. Lazzara's interview, and his careful and continued insistence on understanding the significance of Arce's story today, exemplifies the protracted ways in which the events of that period continue to be critical to Arce's understanding of herself, to the way she raises her children, and to her beliefs about political possibilities. The book also illustrates how Arce's words continue to provoke heated debates among others, and, circuitously, how her own consciousness of this directly influences the story she tells.

One other lesson, perhaps less clear, is that we still do not know how to reconcile our longing to know and understand the past with our repulsion at the acts of state terrorism that are central to that past, and that make us resistant to understanding the actors who engaged in them. A major argument of Arce's is that one cannot understand another's actions without knowing his own history, his own emotional baggage, his own personal abilities, and so forth. With this, she criticizes those who judge harshly her actions and those of others who collaborated. But she is unable to apply this same idea to the DINA agents themselves. They are always the one-dimensional forces against which she had to resist, even in her collaboration. Thus, we, too, never understand them. We still have little understanding of what drove people to commit these atrocious acts, and hence our vision for how to prevent them in future is likewise limited. And despite the fact that Luz Arce lived among and worked with the repressors for so many years, she cannot or does not explain them to us, or perhaps we don't really want them to be explained.

Patricia Espinosa

Luz Arce is a definitive part of our national history of infamy. However, the construction of that history is full of pitfalls, because any history that focuses on individuals ends up obscuring all the mechanisms of power and methodologies in the background—in other words, everything permanent, everything that inexorably continues to function. In these histories, everything happens in such a way as to concentrate all terror into a role call of wretched names, as if it were possible to channel it all into certain individuals, certain subjects, and then exorcize it. Reminiscent of the fantasy of success in neoliberal society, such histories allow for the fantasy of moral character flaws: the actions of particular subjects can simply be blamed on evil. Like the list of the "Ten Most Famous Chileans" who were just voted for and featured on Chilean television, these vile people, these traitors, must appear to us decontextualized, unhinged, detached from the social body.[6] They are left to languish as system errors, or defects; they are put to instrumental use to fill in the gaps in a moralizing narrative of the fundamental and the superfluous, of the transcendent and the momentary.

But things do not always have to be that way. Today, in the twilight of the *Concertación* years, the figure of Luz Arce appears to us once again in Michael Lazzara's work. She returns to make heard the plaintive cry of a betrayal that continues to unfold even at this very moment. Ricardo Piglia, in his novel *Respiración artificial* (Artificial respiration) (1980), states that "the traitor occupies the classic position of the utopian hero: a man from nowhere, the traitor lives in between two sets of loyalties; he lives in duplicity, in disguise. He must pretend, remain in the wasteland of perfidy, sustained by impossible dreams of a future where his evil deeds will at last be rewarded."[7] And so it is that the traitor seeks out a future in which his or her acts can finally be understood. For that to happen, evil must be individualized outright—subjects, rather than institutions, must be rendered to be the guilty ones—and institutions must inevitably negotiate positions and perceptions. Luz Arce mirrors the power of the *Concertación,* which has focused its efforts on resignifying and erasing all traces of similarity between itself and the figure of betrayal. Diamela Eltit and Nelly Richard, two of Arce's principal critics, seem to agree that after being "broken" by torture, inserting oneself into the machinery of power is fundamental for reconstituting identity.[8] When one accommodates oneself to power, the act of betrayal becomes complete. The discourse produced from this operation can provide a sense of redemption.

Collective memory in Chile has turned out to be fragile. As a result, impunity has reigned. The memory-story never ends because even when people serve sentences for their crimes, a hidden signifier persists, hidden beyond all words. This signifier is none other than the betrayal that operates at the core of the *Concertación* coalition's identity, an identity marked, on one hand, by consensus-based, collaborationist negotiations with the rightist opposition and, on the other hand, by the spectacle-based application of justice.

Written and verbal confessions like those of Luz Arce connote regret, self-absolution, and the refusal to face the consequences that society has in store. Kafka tells us that torture is the inscription of power on the body. Betrayal—one of torture's central objectives—is located in that murky zone of the words that emerge when the body is forced into extreme subjugation. Yet Luz Arce channels her betrayal by reinserting herself into the machinery of power; and this strategy requires constant discursive elaborations and reelaborations to seek validation. She thus uses her conversion to Christianity as a method of subterfuge—an abject use of Christian discourse that permits her to free herself from the burden of her participation in torture, betrayal, and collaboration with the dictatorial regime. In a similar move, the *Concertación,* meanwhile, cites democracy, the idea of material progress, the greater good, reasons of state, reconciliation, or any number of other rhetorical devices, as strategies for erasing the frenzy of betrayal that roots and sustains it.

In Lazzara's interview, Luz Arce does not hesitate to make herself out to be a victim. She somehow equates her pain with that of the victims she betrays, or with that of the families of those who were arrested and disappeared. Luz Arce's stated intention to collaborate voluntarily with the Rettig Commission in 1990, and her declarations before Chilean courts around the same time, are utterly self-aggrandizing. However, Arce also states that her interview with Michael Lazzara marks the end of an era. She points out that the great task remaining for the *Concertación* governments is to find the rest of the men and women who disappeared. As she indicates in the interview, from her perspective, truth and justice have not been achieved, and for this she blames the armed forces, which "ordered that people be killed and their murders covered up." Consistent with her other traitorous actions, Luz Arce places the blame for this genocide on its intellectual authors, and puts herself forward as nothing more than a pawn who had but a limited perception of what was going on, and who was thus unable to obtain information about a matter that was much larger than she was.

Luz Arce lives her life in disguise, in constant dissimulation, waiting for the compassion of others—of her victims—to redeem her. This is why revisiting Arce's figure should serve as a powerful interpellation of the direction that the *Concertación* and Chilean society as a whole have been taking. I must insist on how horrifying I find it when the practice of betrayal becomes naturalized—turned into state policy or into discursive practices that are strongly rooted at the center of political praxis. I must insist on how horrifying this is, because all signs point to the fact that *this* is our reality, here and now.

Jorge Arrate

Fifteen years have passed between *The Inferno* and Michael Lazzara's book. About *The Inferno* I only remember the most important aspects. As Sola Sierra, former leader of the Group of Families of the Disappeared, once remarked, Luz Arce's autobiography didn't teach us much more than we already knew about the facts of state repression. *Luz Arce and Pinochet's Chile* doesn't either. In it we find no additional *facts* about the brutal and systematic human rights violations committed during Pinochet's dictatorship. Michael Lazzara's book is not a journalistic investigation whose goal is to reveal secrets or hidden truths. Its value resides in *how* it revisits a place and a time that many people either have not wanted to revisit or they have revisited with great difficulty.

Postdictatorial Chilean society has shown great limitations—lies, euphemisms, and squeamishness—in dealing with the human rights violations committed between 1973–90. The political world has tended to silence that chapter of our history through timid words, flippant tones, and ambiguous pacts riddled with explicit and implicit statements. Rarely has the political world demonstrated a firm resolve to open a space for confronting the painful truths and conflicts of justice—as it should.

Truth and justice, forgiveness and reconciliation: these have been the axes around which competing visions have been organized in the postdictatorship. After the inferno, politics and its protagonists have fluctuated around these axes, while the human rights movement and its attorneys have taken the lead. Because of the efforts of the latter, more than fifty torturers and assassins have been convicted, starting with the leader of DINA, and more than six hundred others have been prosecuted for torture, murders, and disappearances. On balance, however, there have been many limitations: the frustrated attempts to try Pinochet in Chilean courts, meager reparations for the victims, the rejection of the Rome Treaty by the Chilean congress, and the 1978 Amnesty Law, which was passed in the same year in which Luz Arce started to distance herself from the secret police. On another hand, it is significant that, unlike other Latin American countries that have suffered dictatorships, Chile does not have a "full stop" law (*Ley de Punto Final*).[9] This has been a victory for the human rights movement.

Luz Arce and Pinochet's Chile challenges us. Lazzara's book signals that the episodes of inhumanity that played out under the auspices of Chile's armed forces have not been forgotten, that they are still part of a present that harbors within itself signs of the past, no matter how much people refuse to recognize it. Notwithstanding the truth of Arce's replies or the purpose of her reappearance on the scene, it is significant that she reaffirms her acceptance of responsibility for the events that she recounts.

Truth and justice? Forgiveness and reconciliation? I prefer to identity with the first axis because it is clear that the second loses its meaning without the first. After the inferno, what is needed is truth and justice. And that won't be fully possible as long as the Amnesty Law stays on the books and the courts can't fully investigate and convict the protagonists of narratives like *The Inferno,* and others.

Forgiveness and reconciliation: both concepts have framed Luz Arce's existence since her initial declaration to the Rettig Commission in 1990. For a long time, both concepts found great acceptance in Chilean society because they were given the official blessing of the Catholic Church and of high-ranking government authorities. Both concepts inspired various attempts, legislative and otherwise, to "close wounds," open spaces for "coming together," speed up legal processes for victimizers, and make forgiving and forgetting official positions of the state. Though unintentionally, both concepts placed pressure on victims and their families, certain organizations, political parties, and individual politicians insofar as they painted us as figures who held grudges or harbored hatred. This amounted to a second punishment for people who had already been unjustly punished.

The crux of the discourse of forgiveness and reconciliation is that "we are all victims." And, in a certain sense, if we go to extremes, I guess we all were—though to very different degrees of intensity. Yes, I am even talking about the victimizers, even about their leaders who, perhaps in a fit of insomnia felt pained by their guilt or like victims—of themselves, of course, or of their own circumstances. That's why reading *The Inferno* and now *Luz Arce and Pinochet's Chile* fills us with a mixture of revulsion and commiseration.

However, there is a fallacy in the idea that "we are all victims." If indeed this might be true in the aforementioned sense, it is equally true that not all victims were victimizers. Seventeen years ago, when the *Rettig Report* went public, I used a play on words in a television debate that has been repeated many times since: "Some committed errors, while others committed horrors."

The "gray zone" of which Primo Levi speaks can be narrow or wide, depending, and it can exist outside of concentration camps too. Faced with state terror, who didn't try to survive? Allende: not because he didn't love life, but because he felt a debt to his people and their future. But what did the vast majority do to survive? Hide? Change cities? Change their names? Flee? Seek asylum? Go into exile? Lie? Shy away from all political activity? Only a minority exposed themselves and confronted terror head on. Many lost their lives. To remember that minority, to honor it, doesn't mean to ignore the "gray zone" or unjustly "exalt" the martyrs. The point is that although those who confronted state terror were imperfect human beings; they had within them a moral force that sustained the struggle for human rights. Without them, forgetting, forced forgiveness, and a reconciliation imposed by the powers that be would have, I think, subjugated truth and justice. Chile would have suffered a lobotomy. We would all have wound up like the Chilean National Library's card catalogue, or Chile's public television archives: that is, with a huge silencing of the 1970–73 period and with an "official" version of the dictatorship's history. Only the ashes would remain of books, documents, photographs, and films from the years of dictatorship; only the ashes would remain of what was murmured in those years.

Forgiveness is an individual decision requiring each person to follow the dictates of his or her conscience. Bracketing the will of those who have promoted forgiveness in good faith, reconciliation has been a political formula for closing the human rights chapter of the postdictatorship. Luz Arce suggests in Lazzara's book that perhaps the deaths of the dictatorship's protagonists will bring reconciliation. I think that that's wrong. I *hope* that it's wrong. Let me explain with an example.

In recent days, a retired army general named Sinclair, who served as vice-commander-in-chief during the dictatorship and later served as a "designated" senator, was jailed for his responsibility for crimes committed by the dictatorship's agents in 1987. The news story caused a stir, but it was quickly eclipsed by another story: that of a young student named Música who threw a bottle of water at President Bachelet's Minister of Education when the minister refused to hear her complaints about how the student and her comrades had been abused while publicly protesting for a more equitable education system. The minister's proposal that Música be expelled from her school and accused formally in family court made it so that General Sinclair's capture took a back seat to the other story. In other words, an important episode in the history of Chile's struggle for human rights played second fiddle to a 14-year-old girl's irreverent whim and the government's fierce chastising of it. Santiago's archbishop called Música a "poor girl" when, in reality, had the story about the general gotten more air time, the archbishop's pious spirit would have made him wont to call Sinclair a "poor man."

Música's case continues to unfold. We've recently discovered that Música's parents fought against the dictatorship actively in the 1980s and that her grandfather, the director of a public institution during the Allende years, was an exonerated political prisoner. So the past returns in unexpected ways, even when the media power of conservative politicians and businessmen—those who have imposed forgiveness and reconciliation—don't want it to. This time, the past was buried at the bottom of a water bottle.

Michael Lazzara's book reminds us that the inferno has an aftermath. That aftermath hasn't ended. As he aptly points out, every reader will judge for himself. And, I would add that every reader will forgive according to his or her conscience. It is the state's responsibility to see that justice is carried out because what happened in the inferno—the *truth* of what happened there—merits neither amnesty nor a statute of limitations.

Gabriela Zúñiga Figueroa

Reading Michael Lazzara's book calls for a close reflection upon the different angles of one particularly vile practice that occurred during Pinochet's 17-year dictatorship and that has continued during our negotiated, collusion-based democracy: collaboration. In the case of *Luz Arce and Pinochet's Chile,* the interview, as a literary genre, is transformed into a tool that allows us to listen to one particular protagonist, Luz Arce Sandoval, and then debate the scope of collaboration as a phenomenon. Collaboration is a zone in which the roles of victims and victimizers become muddled and confused; sorting them out becomes a difficult task. I, for one, believe that there is no such thing as a chemically pure resistor or collaborator.

Collaboration with state-sponsored terrorism took place intensely and enthusiastically within institutions that, to this day, continue to go unquestioned, and are even venerated. These institutions include the press, the courts, political parties, and academia. Collaboration also affected society at large; we only have to think of individuals who chose to look the other way when something suspicious was clearly happening at their next-door neighbor's house.

Painfully and regrettably, I also have to mention the case of people who went from being politically committed leftist militants to collaborators. These individuals collaborated in different ways and to different degrees; some became enthusiastic cogs in the machinery of state terror, while others did the minimum that they had to do to save their hides. Each one of them followed some sort of culturally dictated code of ethics and morals. We have valued their testimonies, their memories, their forgetfulness, their mutations, their *aggiornamenti*, their myths, as useful tools in our quest to obtain truth and justice, and thus restore dignity not only to a number of men and women but also to a particular political project, Popular Unity, which has been silenced in the public sphere.

People of different political stripes tend to fault different groups for the human rights violations that took place. There are even some who have demanded apologies and mea culpas from those of us who were active leftist militants in the 1960s and 1970s. It's far too easy to dilute responsibility for the genocide that occurred in Chile—far too easy to say that because everyone collaborated with the dictatorship, no one did.

However, in the same way that jurists try to determine whether those involved acted knowingly—in the political, moral, and even interpersonal sense—so do we do the same, adjudicating more responsibility to some, and less to others.

The case of someone confessing while being tortured is not the same thing as someone who, after being tortured once, not only confesses but also chooses to collaborate with those who tortured her, receives a salary for doing so, and has an affair with her torturer. As the saying goes, "The road to hell is paved with good intentions."

***

The Press. One emblematic case of collaboration is the July 1975, headline of *La Segunda* newspaper, part of the *El Mercurio* company, linked to what we now know as "Operation Colombo." "*Miristas* Exterminate Themselves Like Rats," it proclaimed. The article falsely alleged that 119 leftist militants had killed each other in skirmishes and infighting that took place outside of Chile. The military washed its hands of all responsibility. The newspaper, in effect, spread a lie invented through the collusion of DINA, the *El Mercurio* company, and *La Segunda* newspaper. The journalists involved did not file reports, investigate, or compile information; they simply justified—falsely, shamefully—the disappearance of 119 of our family members.

People talk today about staging a public "ethical trial" for the professional class that participated in this and other efforts to maliciously manipulate the truth—professionals who, for the most part, continue to enjoy good health, by the way.

Later on, our democracy never hesitated to collaborate with these media outlets, advertising government programs on their pages, while letting newspapers that used to denounce injustices honestly—such as *La Época, Análisis, Apsi, Bicicleta,* and *Cauce*—go bankrupt.

***

The Courts. More than nine thousand court cases were presented and summarily closed without so much as an intention to investigate. From the comfort of their offices in the Palace of Tribunals, the judges refused to hear these cases. One president of the Supreme Court received the nickname "Sick and Tired" Bórquez (El "Curco" Bórquez), because of the response he often gave to those seeking justice for their family members: "I'm sick and tired of all this talk about the disappeared."

The judicial system continues to be the target of critique, given the fact that it ignored a sizeable amount of irrefutable information proving the existence of state terrorism. The imposition of statutes of limitations, amnesties, and sentences too light for the gravity of the crimes committed, have been—with just a few exceptions—the tenor of the legal system's response to the dictatorship's crimes, then and now.

And once again, our democracy does its part: judges like Alfredo Pfeiffer, who professed his faith in perpetrators of state violence, got named to the Supreme Court.

***

Political Parties. The dictatorship's ideological backbone is still present in the right wing of the political spectrum, which, during the Popular Unity period, did away with its pseudodemocratic façade and advocated for a coup d'état, actively engaging in the financial, political, and media support of the dictator.

That same populist right, which benefitted from the 1980 Constitution and the binominal political system, voted in November 2007, against the ratification of the Inter-American Convention on the Forced Disappearance of Persons.[10] Could anyone have any doubts about its collaborationism?

***

Academia. Those who refused to praise the dictatorship in the classroom were singled out, turned in, expelled, and marginalized. The university ceased to be an open, honest space for intellectual exchange, and the cultural sphere became obsessed with rooting out "internal enemies."

Our restored democracy carried out yet another act of collaborationism in this area by naming the historian, journalist, and lawyer Gonzalo Vial Correa—who coauthored the *White Book* (*Libro Blanco*) that justified the dictatorship's repression by invoking the Plan Z hypothesis—to the National Truth and Reconciliation Commission.[11] This inspires me to invoke a different popular phrase: the one about the fox guarding the henhouse.

***

I could continue on with a never ending list of both examples of collaborationism and the names of individual collaborators. The dictatorship robbed us of every trace of our humanity and sought to annihilate us. Whether or not it was successful in doing so depends on the angle from which each of us sees the facts—and there are as many angles as there are human beings involved. However, there have been figures all throughout history that have crossed over to aid the other side, betraying their principles. The historical treatment that these figures have received—Malinches, Judases, lackeys, or simply cowards—usually doesn't make reference to whatever virtues they may possess.

Without a doubt, we are shocked to the core by testimonies like that of Osvaldo Romo, or "Fat Romo," as he was known; no one can remain indifferent when hearing about the electrodes he applied to people's nipples while torturing them. And yet, in our world of things better left unsaid, no one takes responsibility for plugging in the device that administered the electric shocks; no one admits to having beaten victims; no one acknowledges having practiced waterboarding. Those who testify today admit to nothing more than being analysts, drivers, or administrators; they do so with the antiseptic language of those who disavow their links to the apparatuses of murder.

Collaboration is not a neutral word. Words are not neutral. Silences are not neutral. Memory is not neutral. And I cannot be neutral. And so, from my own lack of neutrality, let me say this, Luz Arce Sandoval: the words you have used throughout all these years of interviews do not exonerate you. To the contrary, they brand you as inconsistent, acquiescent, egocentric, and manipulative!

If I were to take your testimony seriously, I would have to believe that everything happened to you by sheer chance, through some strange twist of fate. I guess I would also have to assume that everyone was a fool—as you call some of your former superiors—except you. I am talking about the people you turned in—the people who are not with us today, apparently because of nothing more than "bad luck." I guess that what they say about taking responsibility for your own actions doesn't work for you.

But you know what, Luz Arce? There *were* alternatives. Carlos Contreras Maluje, for example, chose to throw himself in front of a bus rather than turn in his comrades. Sebastián Acevedo chose to burn himself alive to denounce the torture that was happening in Chile. These are only two very dramatic examples. We know of so many other men and women who found ways to stay true to themselves in the midst of all this torment. This may have taken place through nothing more than a song sung in one's head thousands of times, or a memory repeated to oneself ad nauseam. But there *were* ways to do it.

However, in a moment of clemency, and so that no one will think that I don't comprehend what happened to you, I will acknowledge what you did. You were imprisoned as an expert in Marxism; you were highly familiar with the *Minimanual of the Urban Guerrilla;* you could take AKA rifles apart and then put them back together as if they were Legos. So, of course, there was no way you could have known then what you know now, being the observant Catholic that you are. All this talk about free will—that is, the freedom to make decisions—meant nothing to you, because your decisions were made back when you were a dialectical materialist.

It's regrettable, and I don't think history will absolve you. But, then again, they say that the kingdom of heaven belongs to the repentant, so who knows?

In any case, I, Gabriela Zúñiga, the wife of Álvaro Barrios Duque, that "peripheral" militant, as you call him, the one you handed over—oh, that's right, it wasn't you, you only accompanied Patricio Álvarez to my house, because you figured that he wasn't important enough to be killed—and who disappeared on August 15, 1974, and who hasn't been seen since then, I CHOOSE *NOT* TO FORGIVE YOU.

Michael J. Lazzara

A first wave of reflection on postdictatorship in Chile (and other places in Latin America) foregrounded the tensions between memory and forgetting, and made memory an ethical imperative aimed at the politics of *"Nunca Más"* (Never Again).[12] Questions of trauma, representation, contested remembrances, positionality, the interfacing of individual and "collective" memories, among other topics, fueled debates from the late 1980s and early 1990s up to the present. In the wake of these discussions—which, of course, remain ongoing—a new phase of reflection on postdictatorship seems necessary for addressing still understudied topics like overt collaboration (in its variegated forms); the gray zone of bystander neutrality and omission; individual civilian and institutional complicities with the dictatorship's economic and ideological projects; the psychological transformation of citizens by authoritarianism; and the scope, reach, and limits of "justice," among other issues. In my comments here (and in the wake of my book project on Luz Arce), I would like to single out collaboration as one topic in need of further, serious investigation by scholars. I would like to refer here to two "scenes" that, I think, can shed light on the difficulty of having an open, honest, and productive discussion of collaboration in the Chilean context.

***

Scene one. On Monday, July 21, 2008, the Santiago, Chile publishing house Cuarto Propio organized a forum at Santiago's National Library to launch my book *Luz Arce: Después del infierno* and to discuss what in Chile has been—and continues to be—a silenced topic: collaboration and complicity during the dictatorship and transition. Intentionally staged in one of Chile's most centralized institutional spaces, the forum gathered a panel of speakers hand-selected to provoke the audience and generate a productive conversation about a painful and ethically tense topic that for the last 18 "transitional" years very few people have wanted to tackle head on. Patricia Espinosa, a cultural critic from the Catholic University; Jorge Arrate, a socialist politician, former government minister under Allende and 2010 presidential candidate; Gloria Elgueta, president of the 38 Londres Street survivors' collective, whose brother was disappeared by Pinochet's henhmen; and Gabriela Zúñiga, a former militant and prominent member of the Group of

Families of the Disappeared, whose husband Álvaro Barrios Duque, was killed by the military after Luz Arce knocked on his door and gave him up: these were the voices (along with my own) that weighed in on the topic. In their commentaries, the panelists agreed that truth and justice—however insufficient—have undeniably advanced over the years, but all were concerned that "pardon" and "reconciliation" have served as politically ordained formulae that have caused an inertia toward forgetting in the interest of restoring "governability" and of consensus-based politics. In a context in which it has so often been heard that the nation was on the verge of a "civil war," that "all are equally guilty," that the "authoritarian system was to blame," or in which supporters of Allende's Popular Unity coalition have been asked to apologize for their militancy or political beliefs, the panelists expressed their concern over the diffusion of responsibility and reminded the audience that evil is, first and foremost, the responsibility of individual perpetrators and specific institutions. As Jorge Arrate remarked, although one might argue that in some sense all Chileans were victims of state violence, "not all victims were victimizers." This was a way of reminding those present that the deaths of thousands of Chileans cannot simply be blamed on an amorphous, unagented "system." At the same time, full truth and full justice, he said, are necessary prerequisites for forgiveness and reconciliation.

One striking aspect of the Santiago forum was a general tendency to wonder about the symbolic relevance of a figure like Luz Arce for Chile today. For Patricia Espinosa, Luz Arce stands as a symbol of the ways in which betrayal and *entreguismo* (selling out) have become a natural part of the political landscape under the *Concertación*. Much in line with Diamela Eltit's and Nelly Richard's critiques of the early 1990s, Espinosa argued that Luz Arce—with her rhetoric of repentance and reconciliation—is a prime example of political transvestism and the accommodation of formerly "leftist" bodies to new, more conformist political paradigms. Like other "renovated" leftists, Luz Arce, Espinosa said, "lives in disguise" (*vive en el disfraz*). Gabriela Zúñiga and Jorge Arrate also expressed their concerns about Chile's consensus-driven and collaborationist democracy. According to Zúñiga, when authoritarianism is in play, collaborationism touches not only individuals but also a society's most sacred institutions: the government, the church, the media, the courts, political parties, academia, and so on. None of these entities have had their hands clean since the 1973 coup, and many have shared in the tacit or overt ratification of the dictatorship's neoliberal project.

The most intense moment of the forum was, by far, Gabriela Zúñiga's intervention. I met Gabriela just weeks earlier when she talked to my study abroad students about the Group of Families of the Disappeared organization's political activism. In the course of her talk, she mentioned that Luz Arce had caused the disappearance of her husband Álvaro and that uttering Arce's name, even after all these years, still filled her with anger and disdain. Of course, Gabriela did not yet know that I had written this book on Luz Arce nor that I had interviewed her on an ongoing basis for five years. I let the issue drop, thanked Gabriela politely for talking to my students, and went home. Later that week, I called her on the phone and asked if we could meet for a chat. After three hours of conversation I made the decision to tell her about my book and gave her a copy. The very next day, she called me and told me that she and a friend stayed up all night reading it and that for the first time she felt able to confront the figure of Luz Arce who, for her, had always been a "traitor beyond redemption." Not knowing how Gabriela would respond, I invited her to speak at the book launch forum and, to my surprise, she accepted. She said that she was ready to speak publicly about Luz Arce and, afterward, she told me that her speech had been an important, even therapeutic step in her personal journey toward coming to terms with the past. She filled Chile's National Library conference room with friends from the human rights organizations who came to "accompany" her (*acompañarla*) in her moment of vindication. Many of them weighed in at the forum, saturating the environment with negative, emotionally driven perspectives on Luz Arce.

When Gabriela Zúñiga exclaimed publicly her choice not to forgive Luz Arce, gasps were heard in the crowd. People lowered their heads. The scene was uncomfortable, to say the least. Despite the thought provoking comments that the panelists offered—including Gabriela—one got the feeling that any kind of real dialogue in Chile about collaboration was nearly impossible because lines in the sand were still so indelibly drawn. Many of the people gathered that evening at the National Library had—according to my perception—already made up their minds about Luz Arce and were unwilling to budge in their positions. Time had not assuaged their pain, nor had it made reconciliation any more possible. While some attendees truly seemed open to discussing the implications of Arce's experience, others clearly were not. I left wondering if an open and honest dialogue about complicity is really possible in Chile today.

***

Scene two. Just three days after the National Library forum, I was invited to an event at the University of Chile's Macul campus: a presentation of the Villa Grimaldi detention center's oral history archive, which will open to the public in late 2010 and contains over ninety lengthy video testimonies of survivors, family members, and other people linked to that site's history. As it was explained that day, the project seeks to talk about certain silenced topics (like collaboration) that have only been muttered about softly, in private, within the human rights community. The archive, as I see it, constitutes an amazing step forward in documenting memories of repression in Chile and will no doubt be a treasure trove of information for students and researchers. As I sat there and watched some video clips, I soon discovered that I was seated in a room of human rights activists—only a few of whom had been at my book launch earlier in the week, and all of whom had very different perspectives on collaboration under torture. Compared to the crowd assembled at the National Library forum, this group seemed much more willing to admit the "gray zones" of collaboration that the concentration camp paradigm produces. I was struck by the fact that the only Villa Grimaldi survivor chosen to speak at the event was Lautaro Videla, a leading MIR activist who was detained on February 10, 1975, and whose sister Lumi (killed in 1974) became one of the dictatorship's most emblematic victims because her body was thrown over the wall of the Italian Embassy to instill fear in the citizenry. Lautaro Videla was brutally tortured at Villa Grimaldi for six months and, like Luz Arce, after enduring unspeakable acts for quite some time, gave up some of his comrades. According to private conversations I've had with people in human rights groups, my sense is that reactions to Lautaro Videla are mixed. Some people winced when I mentioned his name and called him a traitor and a manipulator of memory. In his comments that day, Videla said that the "state of exception" within the concentration camp environment yielded two types of victims: "the strong" and "the weak." He spoke publicly in defense of those who were simply unable to be heroes or martyrs: "Not everyone was a superman," he said. "We have to recognize that!" "How are we to understand the torturer?" "How should we look at the weak man?" he asked. He complained that in Chile "feelings of hatred and animosity have taken precedence over love and understanding."

When Lautaro Videla finished speaking, Dagoberto Trincado, a survivor in the audience, asked an important question: "When are we going to be able to discuss these issues free from the baggage we carry from years ago? It wasn't a world of good and bad people. I wish we could talk about these things openly and without taboos."

Following the event, I attended lunch with a number of the survivors who Lautaro Videla called the "weak ones." Many of them knew Luz Arce personally and asked about her health; their attitudes were diametrically opposed to those I heard just a few days before at my book launch. I sat across the table from Samuel Fuenzalida Devia, a military conscript forced into service for DINA as a young man; he was later stationed as a guard at Villa Grimaldi. For ethical reasons, he fled military service in 1975, and went into exile in Germany. Upon returning, he has cooperated with the courts by providing key information, but has spent much energy, too, trying to avoid prosecution himself. As recently as June 2008, less than two months before our lunch, Fuenzalida had been a fugitive for ten days, ducking an order for his detention issued by Judge Víctor Montiglio for complicity with the Operation Colombo case. Fuenzalida eventually turned himself in, claiming his innocence. At lunch, he hardly spoke and gave only short answers to the questions I asked. The others at the table have protected and defended him, even praising him for his heroism and courage for telling the truth and distancing himself from DINA. Just weeks before, he was given a round of applause by many human rights activists at the launch of Mónica Echeverría Yañez's book (coincidentally, also about complicity) called *Krassnoff: Arrastrado por su destino* (Krassnoff: Beholden to his fate) (2008), whose main protagonist is the notorious DINA agent Miguel Krassnoff Martchenko. Fuenzalida, of course, is another figure of the gray zone.[13]

Yet, when we think of other contexts, and especially of Primo Levi's writings, we realize that the subject of collaboration is nothing new. Luz Arce is unfortunately *not* unique in the ethically murky and harrowing experiences she was forced to live. What is striking, though, is that Chile, as a *local* context, is only *beginning* to face this subject as part of its own national process of writing the past. When I wrote this book and took on the task of interviewing Luz Arce, I knew that the project would be controversial. But I wanted to hear Luz Arce tell her story again and give her an opportunity to respond to some of the harsh critiques that had been leveled against her over the years. I wanted to put her figure back into the public eye in order to detonate a conversation on collaboration that has yet to take place in the Chilean context. The book—admittedly—does not resolve the issues it raises, but hopefully points to some of the complexities of the detention center experience while signaling the need for a deeper reflection on complicity and on the ways in which dictatorial power operated on individual bodies and in society at large, even beyond 1990.

***

The writing of the past has its own rhythms and temporalities. Sometimes a person decides to speak publicly many years after a traumatic episode. (On July 7, 2003, for example, a retired air force subofficial divulged his complicity with Chile's "death flights"—dropping prisoners into the sea from military planes—on TVN's *Medianoche* news program. Curiously, the untimely death of his child several months earlier detonated pangs of remorse that led to his cathartic and dramatic confession.) In other cases, the subject continues to hide his past so as not to incriminate himself or compromise his hold on power. (Cristián Labbé, a former DINA agent, for example, is today mayor of Providencia, one of Santiago's most prominent and affluent neighborhoods.) These are the complicities and silences that need to be revealed and studied.

Luz Arce, then, is just one dramatic example of how the Pinochet regime sought to destroy revolutionary subjectivities, to quell revolutionary promise, and turn once insurrectional bodies into traitorous subjects forced to live with, accept, and even promote the neoliberal transformation of society that was its main end game. Arce's experience also reminds us that betrayal and complicity lie at the heart of the "new Chile" and, in many insidious ways, are among its constitutive elements.

Tamara Lea Spira

I approach the topic of Arce's text *The Inferno*—and Michael Lazzara's bold rewriting of it—from within the belly of the US imperial beast. I write from the vantage point of a transnational feminist critic, concerned with the dramatic world shifts that Arce's story reveals. Such shifts are, I contend, at once politico-economic and *psycho-affective*: shifts of both the *world* and the *soul* that have transpired in but one generation.

I read Arce's text and its various rewritings on a level that is at once *geopolitical* and *intimate*. How might we ethically and accountably struggle with the story of a woman, once imbued within a collective revolutionary dream, ripped apart by US-sponsored terror, and stitched back together according to the rhythms of "normative" neoliberal hegemony? How might we do so in a way that refuses to cede to the rules of neoliberal sociality, in a way that neither individualizes her story through ahistorical narratives of a bootstraps individual responsibility nor unmoors it from its location in the so-called Chilean "test case" of neoliberalism, from a decisive moment and site in political history?

While extreme, Arce's story is the product of a decidedly postdictatorial sensibility. Told in a moment in which the left and the right seem to have ceded to the narrative of revolution's demise, it cannot be decontextualized from programs of counterrevolutionary backlash that were formalized in 1973 but extend far beyond the bounds of the official space-time of "dictatorship."[14] It cannot be understood outside of what the Zapatistas refer to as the "fourth world war of neoliberalism"— that *normalized* war erected from the ashes of ongoing and multiple *golpes* (hits, coups): "scar[s] . . . bruise[s] . . . fracture[s] . . . mutilation[s] . . . surprise[s] . . . accident[s] . . . assault[s] . . . pain" whose lingering effects continue to constrain the reconstitution of radical dreams in Chile and beyond.[15]

Nor is the "case" of Luz Arce "out there" as an isolated question, even for the reader separated by the pretenses of geography, language, and power. Rather, it exposes the conditions of possibility for the contemporary world order as we know it. As such, it cannot be treated adequately through debates about culpability versus innocence or damage versus salvation, about one *individual* gazed upon from a comfortable distance.

Instead, I would like to ask: What can this story of a self proclaimed revolutionary-turned-collaborationist teach us about the normalized conditions of our present? What does it reveal about the tacit contours of neoliberal selfhood and about the life worlds and memories of revolutionary struggle that must be continually repressed and forgotten in the normative neoliberal present? How might a reckoning with this story inform a deeper meditation upon the logics of amnesia and unmourned loss that underwrite current formations of empire? And, what unresolved questions might Lazzara's text spark, creating a foothold from which we might imagine deepened forms of radical justice that continue to linger, even in this dramatic tale of revolutions defeated, hopes quashed?

***

It is crucial to situate Luz Arce geopolitically in a highly significant "transition" from revolution to neoliberalism and in the shift from affective intensities and politicized modes of subjectivity to flattened, managed lifescapes—at least within dominant narrations of social and political life. Indeed, Arce's "case" speaks worlds about an attempted dismantling of *el sueño*—of the dream of the *ancho camino* (broad avenue, a metaphor for revolutionary political possibilities) that loomed large in the Chilean context and that compelled a generation to wage struggles for justice across the hemisphere. While flawed, incomplete, and fraught with internal hierarchies, the moments culminating under the banner of Popular Unity were themselves the product of radical multiplicity and possibility. They emerged in concert with a spate of intersecting anticolonial, Third World, indigenous, Black Power, feminist, and socialist struggles that came to crescendo throughout the second half of the twentieth century.[16] Never singular or isolated, the dream of Popular Unity thus transgressed national borders and boundaries, inciting radical hopes that reverberated far and wide.

As Norbert Lechner and Pedro Güell suggest, in the period prior to Pinochet's installation, there was an affective and impassioned quality to politics that transcended political-ideological affiliation. There was, as they put it, no "ideological-political neutrality, nor affective indifference."[17] Whether one believed that, as Víctor Jara sang, the utopian *ancho camino* was opening up, or that Allende was the devil himself, "everyone felt at one time or another hatred and happiness, hope and fear."[18] One need only listen to the forms of dreaming evoked in Víctor Jara's passionate ballads or in footage of the impassioned *"momias"* (bourgeois, right-wing women who opposed Allende) to glean the deep seated energies unleashed in a world historical moment in which one's attachment to the political exceeded individual notions of agency or subjectivity.

Therefore, regardless of whether Arce can be redeemed or not, regardless of whether she was "truly" committed to struggle or an instrumental "chameleon"— terms around which the axis of debate often pivots—at stake in her un/remaking are the conditions of political, affective, and psychic possibilities for revolutionary selfhood.[19] Under attack in the torture chamber were not solely the "skin" and "soul" of Arce, as she puts it in *The Inferno,* but *hope, radical imagination,* and the possibility of inhabiting passionate dreams for justice.

Within Arce's consolidated space-time of terror, it was thus the audacity of measuring desire against calculated possibility that came under assault. At stake was not only Arce's future as an individual but "the form in which new generations of Chileans (would) live, think, study, work and rest ... [as well as] how they clothe themselves, the food they eat, how they distribute their free time."[20] The construction of the neoliberal "free world," for which Chile would serve as a blueprint, was to be erected on a terrain that was simultaneously political, economic, and *psycho-affective.* Change was to be harvested in the hearts, minds, and souls of *"el pueblo"*—within the Chilean "test case" for neoliberalism, and beyond.

***

In contrast to the affective intensities inhabited during the revolutionary era, Arce's plea for acceptance in *The Inferno* indexes a dawning era of deflated dreams, an era in which the dictates of the neoliberal market were coming to subsume *el sueño,* delimiting collective demands for radical freedom. *The Inferno* unwittingly reveals the implicit rules of the normative neoliberal "free world" taking form. As such, it serves as a barometer through which we can read a series of incommensurable conversions: from *justice* and *struggle* to *measurement, management,* and *constraint,* from the figure of *el Hombre Nuevo* (the New Man) to *homo economicus*—unstable conversions on which the fallacy of "transition" to a post-political world has been forged.

Enshrined within this ethos of the normative, Arce's *The Inferno* attempts to appeal to burgeoning scripts of postdictatorial neoliberal democracy, defined according to values of reconciliation, privatized individual responsibility, and forms of justice narrowly punctuated within the (im)possibilities of legal redress. Following the contours of Christian narratives of reconciliation, legalistic language, and the rationalized logic of capital, she relies on dominant scripts of a self resutured, drawn back together by the normative political structures and rhythms of neoliberal democracy. It is precisely on the tropes of reintegration and the hope for a normal life that her pleas for tenable subjecthood and ongoing survival rely. Narrating *The Inferno* through an aesthetic of incorporation—albeit fraught with moments of rupture—Arce thereby needs to exceptionalize the dictatorship, displacing its trauma to the temporal past; she does so from the perspective of an ostensibly peaceful present. Consequently, complex and ongoing contestation over the organization of society is reduced to one woman's plea for forgiveness and acceptance.

With the creation of *Luz Arce and Pinochet's Chile,* Lazzara presents Arce's story for reconsideration, hence dramatizing rather than submerging the forms of selfhood Arce has willed so hard to emulate. Combining legal deposition, interview, and testimony from different temporalities, Lazzara's text underscores the resutured quality of the story. As the Arce of the present becomes more and more entrenched in a "dictatorship of the market"—a regime cemented under nearly three decades of *post*dictatorial rule—rough edges harden, amnesias solidify. Revealed is the further consignment of *revolution* to the annals of oblivion and the displacement of struggle to the domain of the individual.

Revealed is also an ever deepening chasm between the bold dream of the *ancho camino* and the strained worlds of resignation and compromise that currently permeate mainstream political imaginations. If the Arce of *The Inferno* winces in the face of recent assault, in *Luz Arce and Pinochet's Chile* scabs harden. Questions of collective justice, healing, and reparation are further reduced to matters of legal technicality. In both texts, we witness the dangerous slide between *repentance for collaboration* to *repentance for revolutionary participation,* thus underscoring a disavowal of the "politics of antagonism" that continues to produce the present. If *The Inferno* holds glimpses and glimmers of a fleeting revolutionary dream, Lazzara's text reveals the historiographical slip of hand whereby such a dream was doomed from the start.

It is for these reasons, I would argue, that Lazzara's text performs a bold move, inciting passionate and widespread responses from those whose lives ostensibly bear little relation to it. The contrast of texts within the book raises the question of whether the norms of neoliberal sociality to which Arce aspires are indeed livable, and if they are not themselves fictions. This juxtaposition forces us to measure up the flattened, managed worlds celebrated under the banner of a normative postdictatorial sensibility, and ask what other dreams for justice must be submerged therein. Moreover, the book demands that we stare in the face of the injuries sustained and promises disappeared and ask: Can we really afford to proceed pretending that we are living in times "beyond" the need for revolution(s)?

***

As a "limit case," and an incredibly horrific narrative of torture, Arce's story thus forces the reader to contend with the (im)possibility for restitution, justice, and healing when trapped within the false closures, evasions of pain, and suffocation of history that compose the neoliberal imperative. In this sense, it is unique because it allows us to investigate the means through which a former revolutionary and torture survivor reemerges as a narrating subject, time and time again.

However, perhaps more critical here is the degree to which Arce's narration lends insight into the psycho-affective dynamics of neoliberal amnesia, *not in the torture chamber, but from her contemporary vantage point as a "free" subject within the "free world."*

Thus, rather than individualizing the story, I ask: What are the hopes, dreams, and revolutionary possibilities that Arce must belittle, forget, and consign to oblivion to operate as a normative and proper subject in the *post*dictatorship? What is it about the psycho-affective conditions of the neoliberal "free world" that demands that Arce psychically repress the revolutionary past? What would it look like to resist those conditions on the level of subject-making?

These questions, I would like to suggest, take on increasing importance for all of us, particularly in a moment in which not only the Chilean left but also other previously disenfranchised subjects are enjoined to serve as imperial gatekeepers and guardians of an order that has never served us. As discourses of racial and gender justice become increasingly coopted, and claims to bringing sexual freedom are heralded as a cry to war, do not all of our deferred and unfulfilled passions, hopes, and desires for radical justice become the affective grounding for unending violence, racism, and war? How do our losses themselves become affective resources for empire, even as the neoliberal promise of bootstraps ascendency and individual gain wears thin?

These questions also take us to the heart of the politics of trauma that lies at the center of neoliberal affect not only in Chile but on a transnational scale in our so-called postrevolutionary era—which is a moment marked by relentless conditions of empire, seemingly unconquerable global capitalism, and permanent global war. For Arce, suppressing the past becomes a precondition to normative claims that reconciliation equals justice or that neoliberalism could ever allow for true democracy. To believe in the promise of a neoliberal future, other more just possibilities and dreams of freedom must be completely blocked out. In her attempt to stitch herself back together, Arce must disavow revolutionary desires and psychically repress the revolutionary lifeworlds that once appeared possible.

In this sense, Arce might be read as an *emblematic* subject of neoliberal democracy. Rather than simply a "limit case" within the "test case" of Chile, her story creates a moment for the reader to ask questions about the multitude of revolutionary lives and histories whose pasts have been suffocated and whose futures—when trapped within the parameters of neoliberal selfhood—remain forever encased in stone.

With this English translation of Michael Lazzara's *Luz Arce: Después del infierno*, I invite readers to grapple with such provocations, redirecting the gaze away from questions of individual guilt or innocence, repentance or damnation. Arce's slips, blockages, and forms of oblivion speak worlds about what it takes for a subject to accept the conditions of a "failed" revolution without (re)committing to a rejuvenated project of contestatory politics. What, then, are the unanswered imperatives for collective liberation that we might be compelled to heed? What visions of justice lurk within our midst? How might we animate them toward more just and collective presents and futures?

Notes

Foreword

1. Cited by Greg Grandin, "The Instruction of Great Catastrophe: Truth Commissions, National History, and State Formation in Argentina, Chile, and Guatemala," *The American Historical Review*, February 2005, accessed June 18, 2010, http://www.historycooperative.org/journals/ahr/110.1/grandin.html.
2. Luz Arce, *El infierno* (Santiago: Planeta, 1993).
3. Marcia Alejandra Merino Vega, *Mi verdad. Más allá del horror. Yo acuso.* (Santiago: ATG, 1993).
4. See Luz Arce, *The Inferno: A Story of Terror and Survival in Chile,* trans. Stacey Alba D. Skar (Madison: University of Wisconsin Press, 2004), 74.
5. Orlando Letelier, Allende's defense minister, was killed in a 1976 car bomb assassination organized by Chile's secret police in Washington, DC. This well-known crime was part of Operation Condor, a term that refers to the coordinated intelligence efforts of various right-wing South American dictatorships in the 1970s and 1980s.
6. Nancy Guzmán, *Romo: confesiones de un torturador* (Santiago: Planeta, 2000), 172.
7. *La Flaca Alejandra: vidas y muertes de una mujer chilena,* videocassette, 57 min., INA, France, 1994.
8. Arce, *Inferno,* 163.
9. Hernán Vidal, *Política cultural de la memoria histórica: derechos humanos y discursos culturales en Chile* [The cultural politics of historical memory: Human rights and cultural discourse in Chile] (Santiago: Mosquito Comunicaciones, 1997).
10. Ibid., 74.
11. Arce, *Inferno,* 247.
12. Ibid.
13. Vidal, *Política cultural,* 65.
14. Arce, *Inferno,* 138.
15. This was suggested by Vidal, *Política cultural,* 82.
16. See Mónica González and Héctor Contreras Alday, *Los secretos del comando conjunto* (Santiago: Ornitorrinco, 1991).
17. Diamela Eltit, *"Vivir, ¿dónde?"* in *Emergencias: escritos sobre literatura, arte y política* (Santiago: Planeta, 2000), 59.
18. Ibid., 56.
19. Ibid., 50.
20. Ibid., 51.
21. Stacey Alba D. Skar suggests the difference between Marcia Alejandra Merino's emphasis on justice and reconciliation and Luz Arce's appeal to divine justice in her article *"Relecturas del testimonio contemporáneo en Chile: desde 'el infierno' a 'la verdad,'"* in *Ideologías y literatura: homenaje a Hernán Vidal* [Ideologies and literature: essays in

honor of Hernán Vidal], ed. Mabel Moraña and Javier Campos (Pittsburgh: Instituto Internacional de Literatura Iberoamericana, 2006), 281–98.

22. See Munú Actis, Cristina Aldini, Liliana Gardella, Miriam Lewin, and Elisa Tokar, *Ese infierno: conversaciones de cinco mujeres sobrevivientes de la ESMA* (Buenos Aires: Sudamericana, 2001). In English, see *That Inferno: Conversations of Five Women Survivors of an Argentine Torture Camp,* trans. Gretta Siebentritt with a foreword by Tina Rosenberg (Nashville: Vanderbilt University Press, 2006).

Introduction

1. For an excellent study of the traitor figure in the Argentine case, see Ana Longoni, *Traiciones: La figura del traidor en los relatos acerca de los sobrevivientes de la represión* [Betrayals: The traitor-figure in narratives about survivors of repression] (Buenos Aires: Norma, 2007). Pilar Calveiro also provides a nuanced discussion of the phenomenon of collaboration and its social effects on Argentine survivors; see *Política y/o violencia: Una aproximación a la guerrilla de los años 70* [Politics and/or violence: An approach to the guerrilla period of the 1970s] (Buenos Aires: Norma, 2005), 177–90. Little to no bibliography exists on this topic in Chile.

2. The quoted expressions paraphrase ideas found in Nelly Richard, *Cultural Residues: Chile in Transition,* trans. Alan West-Durán and Theodore Quester, foreword by Jean Franco (Minneapolis: University of Minnesota Press, 2004). The original Spanish version was published as *Residuos y metáforas: Ensayos de crítica cultural sobre el Chile de la Transición* [Residues and metaphors: Essays in cultural critique about transitional Chile] (Santiago: Cuarto Propio, 1998).

3. Diamela Eltit has been one of the major critical voices to analyze Arce's narrative and signal her chameleonic ideological shifts. Her three essays on Arce—*"Perder el sentido"* (To lose sense); *"Vivir ¿dónde?"* (To live, where?); and *"Cuerpos nómadas"* (Nomadic bodies)—are reproduced in her book *Emergencias: Escritos sobre literatura, arte y política* [Emergencies: Writings on literature, art, and politics] (Santiago: Planeta/ Ariel, 2000), 48–77. Nelly Richard offers a similarly acerbic reading in *Cultural Residues,* 31–46. Another "canonical" reading of Arce, slightly more generous, is Hernán Vidal, *Política cultural de la memoria histórica: Derechos humanos y discursos culturales en Chile* [The cultural politics of historical memory: Human rights and cultural discourse in Chile] (Santiago: Mosquito Comunicaciones, 1997), 65–111. Vidal observes, "Passing value judgments is not the best way to learn from a testimonial voice. It seems better to try to understand the contradictory forces that converged in Luz Arce's life to make her figure so strangely exemplary" (88).

4. Throughout this book, I use the annotation "DINA/CNI" to indicate Luz Arce's affiliation with both of these secret police organizations. The reader should always bear in mind that these were separate entities. DINA began to function in June 1974. It was replaced by CNI in August 1977 largely due to the bad reputation DINA had acquired for human rights violations. Torture and disappearance continued as official policy under CNI, but to a lesser degree than under DINA.

5. I formulated my interview questions based on extensive archival research at the offices of the Vicariate of Solidarity and the Ministry of the Interior's "Human Rights Program." I would also like to thank a Chilean journalist, who prefers to remain anonymous, for allowing me access to copies of Arce's legal testimonies and of depositions by people—victims and victimizers—who mention her. According to that journalist, a Chilean judge gave the documents to her because he was interested in preserving them

for posterity. The judge claimed that testimonies about the Pinochet dictatorship have a strange tendency to "disappear" from the archives. He said that only certain "valiant" judges like himself have been truly committed to "safeguarding history for future generations."

6. I base this sketch of Luz Arce's experience on my interviews with her, on her legal testimonies, and on my reading of *The Inferno*. In certain instances, I elliptically cite material from those documents.

7. Luz Arce stated in our conversations that she only trained for clandestine missions abroad; they never actually came to fruition.

8. The citations are from a February 17, 1995, legal testimony by Luz Arce. Today Arce prefers the phrase "analyst of public, open-access information" instead of the phrase "political analyst." This is because, in her words, "they're not the same thing."

9. In the original Spanish version of this book, I chose to use the pronoun *usted* uniformly because it most captured the tenor of our exchanges.

10. The term *onces* refers to the daily Chilean ritual of a six o'clock tea time.

11. The Rettig Commission prepared the summary of the declaration, not Luz Arce.

12. I am grateful to Tamara Spira for her friendship and intellectual generosity. Our hours of conversations about Arce have informed my vision. For an illuminating expansion of the points I raise here, see Spira's contribution to Part III of this book.

13. Primo Levi, *The Drowned and the Saved* (New York: Vintage, 1989), 53.

Part I

1. Editor's note: The text of this declaration, which is a summary of a longer declaration to the National Truth and Reconciliation Commission, first appeared in a March 18–31, 1991, special issue of *Página Abierta* magazine, a publication favorable to human rights matters. The magazine's cover highlighted the newsworthiness of the testimony contained therein: "LUZ ARCE TESTIFIES TO THE RETTIG COMMISSION: CONFESSIONS OF A DINA/CNI AGENT . . . A former Socialist Party militant who collaborated with security services for more than ten years . . . reveals the secrets of DINA/CNI: who they were, how they worked, and what they did." Since that original publication, this monumental register of the dictatorships' cast of repression has been relegated to the archives. Here, the summary is reproduced in its entirety, with corrections of punctuation and spelling errors and editorial comments to clarify certain terminology for English-speaking readers. This is an open public access document. The Chilean Ministry of the Interior's Human Rights Program, as it was configured during the presidency of Michelle Bachelet, generously provided this document for my research. I am grateful for their support.

2. Translator's note: An *intendente* is an administrative functionary who is in charge of a certain territory and is a commonly used term in the countries of the Southern Cone of Latin America (Chile, Argentina, and Uruguay). The word's etymology comes from the French and was introduced into Spanish and Spanish America by the Bourbon kings.

Chapter 1

1. The original members of GAP were from MIR (*Movimiento de Izquierda Revolucionaria*, Leftist Revolutionary Movement). However, when tensions developed between

Allende and MIR regarding the need for armed struggle to carry out the revolution, the members of GAP were replaced by socialists. Hence, Arce refers to GAP's "Socialist Party phase."

2. "Payita" was the nickname of Miria Contreras Bell, Salvador Allende's personal secretary and mistress during the Popular Unity government.

3. The term *Tancazo* (tank putsch) refers to an initial foiled coup attempt that took place on June 29, 1973. Led by army lieutenant coronel Roberto Souper, the mobilization against La Moneda palace was averted by General Carlos Prats and other constitutionalist military personnel loyal to Allende. The *Tancazo* served as a harbinger of the September 11, 1973, coup.

4. When the 1990 transition to democracy came, President Patricio Aylwin told the Chilean people that he and his government would strive to attain "truth and justice insofar as they are possible" (*verdad y justicia en la medida de lo posible*).

5. Carlos Altamirano was the secretary general of the Chilean Socialist Party from 1971–79. During the Popular Unity period, he distinguished himself as one of the most intransigent supporters of armed revolution, in opposition to Allende's dream of achieving a "peaceful road to socialism."

Chapter 2

1. In a judicial testimony dated October 28, 2004, Luz Arce provided the following details: "My collaboration was limited to turning in no more than eight or twelve people of whom, as I pointed out before, only four disappeared. Among the people I turned in were Carmen Sabai; Raúl Navarrete Hancke, who was freed, which let me know that he was a collaborator; and León Gómez Araneda, nicknamed 'Leo.' Wagner Salinas was executed in October 1973; he was a member of GAP. I also turned in a married couple. The woman was named Adriana; she was a sociologist who lived on Juárez Street. I also turned in a young man named Julio Cañas, a boy named Carlos Rammsy, and a party comrade whose alias was 'Guillermo'; they are all alive. I turned in those who had sought asylum first, then the dead and those who were already prisoners. I was trying to cause the least harm possible. I don't think that anyone was a total collaborator. One always holds back someone or something."

2. Luz Arce told me that she preferred not to reiterate here the names of the people for whose disappearances she was directly responsible. Thanks to documents I obtained from the "Human Rights Program" of the Chilean government's Ministry of the Interior, I have been able to verify that she is referring to the following individuals, who, to date, remain "detained and disappeared": Álvaro Barrios Duque (detained on August 15, 1974); Sergio Alberto Riveros Villavicencio (detained on August 15, 1974); Rodolfo Alejandro Espejo Gómez (detained on August 15, 1974); and Óscar Manuel Castro Videla (detained on August 16, 1974). These names are also documented in *The Inferno.*

3. The reference is to Miguel Krassnoff Martchenko, a DINA officer and leader of the groups *Halcón 1* and *Halcón 2* (Falcon 1 and Falcon 2). Krassnoff's groups were part of the Caupolicán Group, which, in turn, reported to the Metropolitan Intelligence Brigade (*Brigada de Inteligencia Metropolitana*, BIM).

4. Ricardo Lawrence Mires was a police lieutenant for *Carabineros de Chile* in 1974. He was the leader of *Brigada Águila* (Eagle Brigade) within DINA.

5. Rodolfo Valentín González Pérez was an air force recruit in 1973. Luz Arce dedicates a section to him in *The Inferno* in which she notes his altruistic qualities, describing him

as "more human" than the others. He treated prisoners with kindness and smuggled letters to their families, among other good deeds. He was killed by DINA as a traitor to the military. In her narrative, he symbolizes a capacity for good that continues to exist even in a context of extreme degradation.

6. Diamela Eltit's perspectives on Luz Arce can be found in her essays *"Perder el sentido"* (To lose sense); *"Vivir ¿dónde?"* (To live, where?); and *"Cuerpos nómadas"* (Nomadic bodies). All three essays appear in *Emergencias: Escritos sobre literatura, arte y política* [Emergencies: Writings on literature, art, and politics] (Santiago: Planeta/Ariel, 2000). See also Alejandro Montesino's interview with Eltit in the July 15, 2000, issue of the online newspaper *El Mostrador*: http://www.letras.s5.com/de221204.htm.

7. Rolf Gonzalo Wenderoth Pozo is an army officer who belonged to DINA's *Brigada Mulchén* (Mulchén Brigade). According to Arce's testimony, Wenderoth was her protector at Villa Grimaldi and later established an affective-sexual relationship with her. An article, *"Detienen en Osorno al coronel (r) Rolf Wenderoth"* (Retired army coronel Rolf Wenderoth detained in Osorno), published in *El Mercurio* on Friday, June 29, 2007, reported the following: "Retired army coronel Rolf Wenderoth, convicted in the 1975 kidnapping of MIR militant Manuel Cortéz Joo, was detained this Friday in Osorno by representatives of the Human Rights and Special Matters Brigade [*Brigada de Asuntos Especiales y Derechos Humanos,* BRIAES]. According to sources, the ex-officer will be transferred to Santiago and placed in the Cordillera prison . . . Judge Alejandro Solís ordered [Wenderoth's] immediate imprisonment so that he can begin serving his first sentence. Aside from this case, Wenderoth had been sentenced by the lower court to ten years and one day for the kidnapping of MIR militant Julio Flores Pérez. He has also been indicted in the Villa Grimaldi case, the Colonia Dignidad case, the kidnapping of MAPU militant Juan Maino Canales, and [the kidnapping] of the married couple Elizabeth Rekas and Antonio Elizondo."

8. In February 1975, DINA organized a press conference in which four MIR prisoners were forced to declare publicly on Chile's national television network that MIR had been defeated and that, consequently, any resistance against the dictatorship would be futile.

9. *Milicos* is a pejorative term for referring to the military.

10. Luz Arce refers to this priest as "Father Gerardo" in *The Inferno* because, at that time (1993), he preferred not to have his real name revealed. For purposes of this publication, Luz Arce told me that the priest authorized her to use his real name, Father Cristián.

11. *"Lo que no vio Luz Arce"* [What Luz Arce didn't see] *Apsi,* March 25–April 7, 1991, 381. In this article, Lautaro Videla, a Villa Grimaldi survivor and brother of Lumi Videla, who was killed by DINA in 1974 and whose body was flung over the wall of Santiago's Italian Embassy to instill fear in the those who had sought asylum on the inside, stated the following: "I met Luz Arce on the first day I fell into DINA's clutches. She gave me the impression of being a cold and sinister woman, distant, inaccessible. She gave the appearance that she was more committed to collaboration than most. Her testimony made me realize that I was wrong, that collaborators are products of torture and impunity, pain and desperation. Everything that she describes is a faithful reflection of what so many of us lived. Luz Arce caused irreparable damage to many families, but it's false to think that she did it voluntarily; she has had the courage to tell the truth. I'll never be able to forget the woman who turned my sister in, but I also can't ignore the fact that collaborators fell while fighting and suffering, and for a long time after that they suffered the unspeakable . . . I pity them."

12. Lumi Videla Moya was a MIR leader who, along with her husband, was detained by DINA in September 1974. After being savagely tortured, Lumi was killed two months later. Her body was flung over the wall of the Italian Embassy in Santiago as a strategy for cowing the citizenry. Her case has become emblematic of the sometimes overt, "public face" of the Pinochet regime's violence.

13. The List of 119 refers to a false media campaign waged by DINA to convince the Chilean people that 119 leftist militants had killed themselves—in the newspaper's words they had been "exterminated like rats"—in Curitiba, Brazil, and Buenos Aires, Argentina, in 1975. This psychological warfare and extermination campaign became known as "Operation Colombo" and should be understood in the context of "Operation Condor," a term that refers to the coordination of efforts by several South American dictatorships (Chile, Argentina, Uruguay, Paraguay, Bolivia, and Brazil) to wage counterrevolutionary warfare internationally. In this instance, the Chilean media cover-up was supported by Brazil and Argentina. For more information on Operation Colombo and the details of this case, see Lucía Sepúlveda Ruíz, *119 de nosotros* (119 of us) (Santiago: LOM, 2009).

14. Carlos Marighella (1911–69) was a Brazilian politician, guerrilla fighter, and protagonist in the struggle to bring communism to Brazil. He is the author of the *Mini-manual do Guerrilheiro Urbano* [Mini-manual of the urban guerrilla] (1969). An English translation was published in St. Petersburg, Florida, by Red and Black Publishers in 2008.

Chapter 3

1. Luz Arce is referring to a former militant whose alias was "Leo." His real name is published in *The Inferno*. She asked me not to reproduce it here to protect him from criticism in Chile. I respect her wishes. Arce said to me, "You can't fight for human rights by attacking people who have already gotten what was coming to them."

2. "The Tower" (*La Torre*) was one of the most notorious torture sites within the Villa Grimaldi camp. In his "Visitor's Guide" to Villa Grimaldi (Santiago: Productora Gráfica Andros Limitada, 2000), Pedro Alejandro Matta, a survivor of that detention center, describes "The Tower" as follows: "The 48-foot tower of oak wood that was built here in about 1900 to provide the Villa with water later served other uses. Agents occasionally tortured prisoners on the ground level. Isolation cells were built on the second and third levels and an observation post at the fourth and around the water tank for the armed guards who kept watch day and night. The isolation cells in 'The Tower' were smaller than the punishment cells at the other side of the Villa.... To enter a tower cell, the sliding wooden door was raised and the prisoner crawled in on hands and knees. Once inside and with the door shut, the prisoner could not stand upright or stretch out to rest on the floor. The cell was too small and the ceiling too low. Prisoners were forced to sleep in the fetal position. In the old cistern beneath 'The Tower,' prisoners were sometimes held for long periods in total darkness and isolation. Most of those brought to 'The Tower' disappeared. Their rate of survival was significantly lower than that of the prisoners never isolated there."

3. These events are narrated in the third chapter of part 3 of *The Inferno*. In the English version, see chapter 33.

4. On June 8, 2000, the Santiago Appellate Court took an interest in clarifying and probing a long list of details that Arce includes in *The Inferno*. Early in her deposition, Arce explains to the court her reasons for writing the book: "Regarding why I wrote

The Inferno, I should point out that from the time I resigned from CNI, in 1979, until 1988, I went through a period of extreme depression. At first I sought therapy from a psychologist friend of mine, and later treatment from a neurologist. When I started to get better, without yet having become a Christian, I asked them to take me to a priest, at random; I recounted to the priest, day by day, the many bitter experiences I had lived. After some months, the priest, whose name was Father José Luis de Miguel, told me that he thought that even though it might be painful, I should remember all the life experiences that for nine years I had tried to forget. He recommended that I write them down because, in his opinion, that would help me accept my past. The idea wasn't to publish what I wrote, but rather for it to be a kind of personal therapy. Because the military government was still in power, I was scared to write and keep my writings in my apartment. Father José Luis gave me access to the Dominicans' library so that I could write there and store the originals. After the government changed in 1990, I made the decision to testify to the Rettig Commission. As a result of that testimony, the human rights lawyers Carlos Fresno, Gastón Gómez, and Jorge Correa Sutil recommended, for my personal security, that I take up residence abroad. That's how in 1991 I came to live in Vienna, Austria. While I was in that city, a German publishing house from Hamburg contacted me and proposed that I publish a book about my experiences in the military government's security organizations. When they suggested it, I told them that a manuscript already existed in Chile, which turned out to be a good thing because I got a contract faster and was able to finance my stay in Europe. I asked Father José Luis to send me the manuscript, and he did. When I received the manuscript, I worked on the computer, first to write a timeline and then to give titles to all the chapters. According to the contract, the German publishing house would have exclusive rights to the German version, but I was authorized to publish the Spanish version wherever I wished. I returned to Chile in January 1992 and spent most of my time testifying in different courts. Toward the end of that year, I approached Planeta publishing house with a bound copy and proposed that they publish my book. I told them that based on commentaries by people who had access to my manuscript, especially Father José Luis, my experiences 'had been an inferno.' [Father José Luis] thought that *The Inferno* was an excellent title and, what's more, there was no other book of its kind by same name. The first edition appeared in 1993. In 1994, it was published in German, and pretty soon it will be published in English." Luz Arce, *The Inferno: A Story of Terror and Survival in Chile* (Madison: University of Wisconsin Press 2004).

5. Gonzalo Contreras is a novelist who belongs to the scene of "New Chilean Narrative." He is best known for his 1991 novel *La ciudad anterior* [The former city]. (Santiago: Planeta, 1991).

6. Fernando Lauriani Maturana, a retired army officer, led the "Vampire Group" (*Agrupación Vampiro*) within DINA's Caupolicán Brigade. He was known as *"teniente Pablito"* (Lieutenant Pablito).

7. Retired army coronel Marcelo Moren Brito was commander of the Villa Grimaldi detention center and of the Caupolicán Brigade within DINA. To date, he has been mentioned or indicted in more than 90 human rights cases.

Chapter 5

1. Romo was exiled to Brazil in 1975, where he was financially supported by DINA. He was extradited to Santiago, Chile, in 1992 and, after that, was jailed in Punta Peuco

prison, where he served time for human rights violations. He died a prisoner on July 4, 2007, at age 69. No one attended his funeral.

Chapter 6

1. Retired brigadier Pedro Octavio Espinoza Bravo was a leader in DINA during the dictatorship's early years. His name is linked to the notorious "Caravan of Death" case and to the internationally organized assassinations of Orlando Letleier, Allende's former defense minister, and General Carlos Prats, a "constitutionalist" general who was loyal to Allende and opposed to the coup plotters. Espinoza is currently in prison.
2. Juan Emilio Cheyre, "*Ejército de Chile: El fin de una visión,*" *La Tercera,* November 4, 2004. Cheyre was commander-in-chief of the Chilean army from March 10, 2002, until March 10, 2006.
3. Tomás Moulián, "*La liturgia de la reconciliación,*" in *Políticas y estéticas de la memoria,* ed. Nelly Richard (Santiago: Cuarto Propio, 2000), 23–25.
4. *La Teletón* (The Telethon) is a major event held every November or December in Chile to benefit those with childhood diseases, particularly muscular dystrophy. All the Chilean media outlets participate in this truly nationwide event. The 27-hour telethon began in 1978. Its host is famous television personality Don Francisco.
5. The *Valech Report* (*Informe Valech*), the final report of the National Commission on Political Imprisonment and Torture, was published on November 28, 2004, during Ricardo Lagos's presidency. The report synthesized more than thirty thousand testimonies of torture victims and explored the psychological, political, and social effects of political violence.
6. The 1978 Amnesty Law, a notorious legacy of the Pinochet regime, has been one of the greatest impediments to justice during the transition. At the time of this writing, the law still hasn't been overturned. It covers many human rights violations committed during the period 1973–78, in which most of the crimes occurred.

Chapter 7

1. Stacey Alba D. Skar, "*Relecturas del testimonio contemporáneo en Chile: Desde 'el infierno' a 'la verdad,*'" in *Ideologías y literatura: Homenaje a Hernán Vidal* [Ideologies and literature: Essays in honor of Hernán Vidal], ed. Mabel Moraña and Javier Campos (Pittsburgh: Instituto Internacional de Literatura Iberoamericana, 2006), 281–97.
2. Paula Chapín, "*La conversión de Luz Arce*" (Luz Arce's conversion), *Apsi,* March 25–April 7, 1991, 381. In this article Chapín wrote, "It seems that different people and institutions linked to the Church—without explicit intentions to do so—gave [Luz Arce] the final push she needed to break with her recent past and finally tell the truth. With her characteristically smooth voice, almost sweet and calm in tone, while chain-smoking one unfiltered cigarette after another, she started to unleash her liberating narrative last October. 'This was a decision that she made over a long period of time. It was very personal and not without difficulties. She felt that she had to contribute to truth, justice, and reconciliation. She especially put a lot of emphasis on reconciliation,' Father José Luis de Miguel affirmed. The Dominican priest had been her professor at the Catholic University of Chile's theology department, where Luz Arce studied for two semesters before leaving for Germany in December. 'She is a layperson who is committed to her faith; her desire to receive academic training in the Bible and

theology stems from there. In addition, she's a very studious and intelligent woman.... She is delicate and gives the impression of being quite sweet. When she has to make a decision, she does so wholeheartedly. She is a normal woman, sensitive to pain, to those in need, and to people in general. This is her biggest obsession, a concern she shares with Jesus Christ,' the priest added."

3. Patricio Quiroga Z, *Compañeros: El GAP, la escolta de Allende* (Santiago: Aguilar, 2001), 242–43.

4. In a legal declaration before the Santiago Appellate Court (June 9, 2000), Luz Arce testified, "Regarding what *'Operación Celeste'* [Operation Sky Blue] was about, I have to say that because of the 1978 [Beagle Channel] conflict with Argentina, CNI decided to send spies to that country. [The operation was] called *'Celeste'* because, in its different stages, it would involve both Uruguay and Argentina, [whose flags contain the color light blue]. Uruguay was chosen as the headquarters for the first stage because, in that country, the sociopolitical conditions were ripe for developing the infrastructure that would help me in the future. We also talked about the possibility of my becoming Uruguayan, of my adopting that country's accent and customs. I even had to learn the names of the soccer players from that time. Because I quit before the second stage began, I'm unaware of the details of the mission. But before leaving Chile in February 1979, General Mena [leader of CNI] held a meeting at Cuartel Borgoña, which was also attended by Captain Manuel Provis, in which I was told in general terms that I should capture military information, particularly from the navy. The objective was Emilio Massera." Massera was the infamous leader of Argentina's Naval School of Mechanics (ESMA), one of the most notorious detention and torture centers of that country's military dictatorship. He was also an original member of the Argentine junta.

5. Bachelet's father, air force general Alberto Bachelet, was killed by the dictatorship.

6. Carlos Sánchez also tells the following anecdote in his *Plan B* article: "From those afternoons of conversation with [Luz Arce], I got the idea to do a radio program. So we got in touch with María Pía Matta, director of *Radio Tierra,* and we created a show dealing with human rights. Luz Arce revealed the security agents' résumés and told about life inside the detention camps.... The show was a success, until someone called on the phone to complain: 'Hello, Mr. Carlos Sánchez? Good afternoon. This is a listener speaking. The woman sitting next to you detained my husband in our home, and ever since, he has been detained-and-disappeared. Luz Arce, how can you talk about human rights?' the voice said wrathfully. 'Who's calling?' replied Luz Arce. 'You know very well who's calling. I have known you for years. We lived in the same neighborhood, and you were the one who took my husband away. Don't tell me they were forcing you, because you were the one who was the most enthusiastic during the raid. Remember how you walked in with a machine gun, blowing to bits anything that crossed your path?' the listener insisted. Luz never lost her cool. She remained silent. Then she said, 'In those extreme cases, I was taught that I should give up the peons, never the king.' 'That's what I did,' [Luz Arce] concluded. That episode on the radio, coupled with the fact that Gladys Marín, [an important Communist Party leader], refused to participate [in the programs] if Luz Arce was present, spelled the end of our project, which never received financial support. 'Look at my foot. There's the hole from the bullet that Marcelo Moren Brito shot at me. Damn him! Of course I'll never forget that,' [Luz Arce] said while complaining about the pain she experienced while walking. 'Sometimes I understand La Flaca Alejandra and her addiction. She prefers to sleep rather than remember what happened to us.' That's how Luz justified the actions

of Marcia Alejandra Merino, alias La Flaca Alejandra, a member of MIR who also became a collaborator and a drug addict."

Part III

1. Pilar Calveiro, *Poder y desaparición* (Buenos Aires: Ediciones Colihue, 1997), 147.
2. The term "repressive experience" is used here to mean kidnapping and torture followed by imprisonment or murder and disappearance, all carried out by state agents against Chilean leftist social and political organizations.
3. This is the standard definition of "victim" as set forth by *La Real Academia Española.*
4. Ana Longoni, *Traiciones: La figura del traidor en los relatos acerca de los sobrevivientes de la represión* [Betrayals: The traitor-figure in narratives about survivors of repression] (Buenos Aires: Norma, 2007), 27.
5. Steve J. Stern, *Remembering Pinochet's Chile: On the Eve of London 1998* (Durham, NC: Duke University Press, 2004), 31.
6. The reference is to a television program, *Grandes chilenos* (Great Chileans), produced and aired in 2008 on Chile's National Television Network (TVN). A public voting format was used to determine the ten most significant Chileans in history. The winners were Pablo Neruda, Gabriela Mistral, Violeta Parra, Saint Alberto Hurtado, Manuel Rodríguez, Arturo Prat, Lautaro, Víctor Jara, José Miguel Carrera, and Salvador Allende.
7. Ricardo Piglia, *Artificial Respiration,* trans. Daniel Balderston (Durham, NC: Duke University Press, 1994), 77.
8. Diamela Eltit, *Emergencias: Escritos sobre literatura, arte y política* (Santiago: Ariel/ Planeta, 2000) and Nelly Richard, *Residuos y metáforas: Ensayos de crítica cultural sobre el Chile de la Transición* [*Cultural Residues: Chile in Transition*] (Santiago: Cuarto Propio, 1998).
9. The case of Argentina comes to mind. Proposed by the administration of President Raúl Alfonsín and ratified in 1986, the "full stop" law (*Ley de Punto Final*) prohibited both the investigation and prosecution of crimes committed during Argentina's "Dirty War" (1976–83). The law was repealed and deemed unconstitutional in 2005.
10. The 1980 Constitution was penned by the Pinochet dictatorship and included many assurances for the continuation of the dictatorship's economic and political legacy. The binomial electoral system favors coalitional politics insofar as it requires a two-thirds majority for electing representatives to congress. Because of this system, throughout the transition to democracy, the opposition, until 2010 the political right, had disproportionate representation in congress, thus making it difficult for the *Concertación* to pursue its agenda. Many critics have called the binomial system one of the biggest impediments to democracy in Chile.
11. Gonzalo Vial Correa (1930–2009), voted the most influential Chilean intellectual in 2005, was a historian notorious for his complicity with the Pinochet regime. He is well known as the author of the *Libro blanco del cambio de gobierno en Chile* (White book of government change in Chile) (Santiago: Secretaría General de Gobierno, 1973). Written shortly after the 1973 coup, the *White Book* denounced "Plan Z," a theory fabricated by the military regime whereby sectors of the Chilean left supposedly planned to kill members of the opposition, the armed forces, and even Allende. Plan Z was used as a justification for the coup's violence.
12. I am grateful to Idelber Avelar for first suggesting the existence of a "first wave" and a "second wave" in postdictatorship reflection. I follow his lead in my use of these terms.

For more on this, see his article "History, Neurosis, and Subjectivity: Gustavo Fer-reyra's Rewriting of Neoliberal Ruins," in *Telling Ruins in Latin America,* eds. Michael J. Lazzara and Vicky Unruh (New York: Palgrave Macmillan, 2009), 183–93.

13. See Mónica Echeverría Yáñez, *Krassnoff: Arrastrado por su destino* (Santiago: Catalonia, 2008).

14. Analysts are beginning to question the ways in which the left has conceded to the narrative of revolution's demise. For example, see John Beverley, "Rethinking the Armed Struggle in Latin America," *Boundary 2* 36, no. 1 (2009): 47–59. See also Neferti Tadiar, *Things Fall Away: Philippine Historical Experience and the Makings of Globalization* (Durham, NC: Duke University Press, 2009).

15. Diamela Eltit, *"Las dos caras de la moneda,"* in *Emergencias: Escritos sobre literatura, arte y política* (Santiago: Planeta/Ariel, 2000), 17.

16. Such struggles were built on other unfinished revolutions, such as struggles against slavery and anticolonial formations, and have themselves yet to be completed.

17. Norbert Lechner and Pedro Güell, *"Construcción social de las memorias en la transición chilena,"* in *Subjetividad y figuras de la memoria,* ed. Elizabeth Jelin and Susana G. Kaufman (Madrid: Siglo XXI Editores, 2006), 31.

18. Ibid.

19. Diamela Eltit, *"Cuerpos nómadas,"* in *Emergencias: Escritos sobre literatura, arte y política* (Santiago: Planeta/Ariel, 2000), 61–77.

20. Joaquín Lavín, *Chile: Revolución silenciosa* (Santiago: Zig-Zag, 1987), 1.

Contributors

Jorge Arrate (M.A., Economics, Harvard University) is a Chilean lawyer, economist, and socialist politician. The author of many books, including *Memoria de la izquierda chilena* (2003), he has been a faculty member at the University of Chile, the University of Santiago, the Catholic University of Chile, and at the University of California, Berkeley. He was a minister during the Allende, Aylwin, and Frei administrations and Chilean ambassador to Argentina during the Lagos government. He ran for president during the 2009 election season.

Gloria Elgueta Pinto (M.A., Philosophy, University of Chile) has worked as a journalist, and since 1998, as coordinator of publications and cultural activities for the Chilean Consortium of Libraries, Archives, and Museums. Her articles and essays have appeared in Chilean and international media, and in edited collections. She has participated actively in the process of recovering the former detention and torture center at 38 Londres Street and in transforming it into a memory site.

Patricia Espinosa Hernández (Ph.D., Literature, University of Chile) teaches at the Institute of Aesthetics at the Catholic University of Chile, where she also coordinates the Diploma in Journalism and Cultural Critique and directs the prestigious journal *Aisthesis*. Among her many publications is the edited volume *Territorios en fuga: Estudios en torno a la obra de Roberto Bolaño* (2003).

Carl Fischer (cotranslator) is a doctoral candidate in the Department of Spanish and Portuguese at Princeton University. He holds a master's degree in Spanish from Stanford University and bachelor's degrees in American Studies and Spanish from Occidental College. He has worked as a translator for a number of years, both freelancing and also for the Chilean government. He is currently working on a dissertation about economics and sexuality in contemporary Chilean literature.

Jean Franco (foreword, Ph.D., Literature, King's College, University of London) is widely known for her pioneering work on Latin American literature, particularly on women's writing. She is currently professor emeritus at Columbia University in the Department of English and Comparative Literature. The recipient of many prestigious international awards and distinctions, she is the author of nearly ninety articles and nine books, including *Plotting Women: Gender and Representation in Mexico* (1989) and *The Decline and Fall of the Lettered City: Latin America and the Cold War* (2001).

Victoria Langland (Ph.D., History, Yale University) is assistant professor of History at the University of California, Davis. Her research focuses on twentieth-century Latin American social, cultural, political, and gender history; history and memory; and transnational American history. Her publications include the coedited volume *Monumentos, memoriales y marcas territoriales* (2003, with Elizabeth Jelin) and numerous articles. Her book manuscript, "Speaking of Flowers: Student Movements and Memories of 1968 in Military Brazil," is under contract with Duke University Press.

Michael J. Lazzara (Ph.D., Spanish, Princeton University) is associate professor of Latin American Literature and Culture at the University of California, Davis. He is the author of *Chile in Transition: The Poetics and Politics of Memory* (2006); *Diamela Eltit: Conversación en Princeton* (2002); *Los años de silencio: Conversaciones con narradores chilenos que escribieron bajo dictadura* (2002), and numerous articles on Latin American literature and culture. He is also coeditor of *Telling Ruins in Latin America* (2009), with Vicky Unruh.

Pedro Alejandro Matta was a student leader at the University of Chile Law School and a member of the youth branch of the Chilean Socialist Party when the September 11, 1973, coup occurred. Without being charged with any crime, he was arrested by DINA in May 1975, and spent more than 13 months imprisoned at Villa Grimaldi. After 15 years in exile in the United States, he returned to Chile in 1991 and since then has dedicated himself to meticulously documenting the history of various torture centers and to advocating for human rights. In addition to being an invited speaker in prestigious international venues, Matta currently works closely with several foreign study program in Santiago.

Tamara Lea Spira (Ph.D., History of Consciousness and Feminist Studies, University of California, Santa Cruz) is a UC President's Postdoctoral Fellow at the University of California, Davis. She has published widely in the fields of feminist, postcolonial, queer, and ethnic studies. She is currently completing a manuscript entitled "Movements of Feeling: Affect, Neoliberalism and (Post)Revolutionary Memory in the Americas."

Gabriela Zúñiga Figueroa is a former socialist militant. She was married to Álvaro Barrios Duque, who disappeared in 1974, when Luz Arce knocked on his door and turned him over to Pinochet's secret police. Zúñiga is a prominent member of the Group of Families of the Disappeared and, at present, is in charge of public relations for the organization. She is a fervent human rights activist.

Index

CPSIA information can be obtained
at www.ICGtesting.com
Printed in the USA
LVHW08s1505100918
589569LV00006BA/13/P

9 780230 622760